# THE CHICAGO SCHOOLHOUSE

# THE
# CHICAGO
# SCHOOLHOUSE

## DALE ALLEN GYURE

*Center Books on Chicago and Environs*
Center for American Places at Columbia College Chicago

The Center for American Places at Columbia College Chicago
600 South Michigan Avenue
Chicago, Illinois 60605-1996, U.S.A.
www.americanplaces.org

Distributed by the University of Chicago Press
www.press.uchicago.edu

ISBN: 978-1-935195-19-1
18 17 16 15 14 13 12 11 10    1 2 3 4 5

Library of Congress Cataloging-in-Publication Data

Gyure, Dale Allen.
  The Chicago schoolhouse : high school architecture and educational reform, 1856-
2006 / by Dale Allen Gyure. — 1st ed.
      p. cm. — (Center books on Chicago and environs ; 15)
   ISBN 978-1-935195-19-1 (alk. paper)
   1. High school buildings—Illinois—Chicago—Design and construction—History.
2. High schools—Illinois—Chicago—History. 3. Chicago (Ill—Buildings, structures, etc. 4. Educational change—Illinois—Chicago. I. Title. II. Series.

   LB3218.13G98 2010
   727'.20977311—dc22

                                    2010026039

# CONTENTS

# LIST OF FIGURES

The *Chicago Schoolhouse* could never have been completed without the generosity of the following people and organizations and I thank you all: Richard Seidel of the Chicago Board of Education Archives, the staffs of the Regenstein Library at the University of Chicago, the Chicago History Museum, the Chicago Public Library, the Art Institute of Chicago, and the Lawrence Technological University library for research assistance; Eula Davis and Bobbi Bogan of Chicago School Associates and Elizabeth Simmons and Steven Rajewski of Lawrence Tech for help with images; Richard Guy Wilson, Kevin Murphy, Eric Bredo, John Maciuika, Bob Hampel, and an anonymous reviewer for reading and commenting on various drafts; John Sheoris for lending his wonderful collection of EFL publications; David Chasco, Edward Orlowski, Maria Vaz, and Lewis Walker of Lawrence Tech for easing my teaching schedule so I could spend more time on the book; Dan and Jayne Gyure for providing room, board, and loving support during many research trips; and Jan, Matthew, and Jeffrey for being patient and understanding.

This study was supported by grants from the Graham Foundation for Advanced Studies in the Fine Arts, the Spencer Foundation, and the University of Virginia Graduate School of Arts and Sciences and College of Architecture.

# INTRODUCTION

School buildings are vitally important in American lives yet largely invisible in the landscape of architectural studies. Between the ages of five and eighteen, the average American child probably spends more time in a school building than any other single place outside the home. The schoolhouse's significance cannot be overestimated in a country where education is not only compulsory, but is also an integral part of our national self-image. Freedom, democracy, and education have been linked for centuries in the United States, from the founding fathers' belief in the necessity of an educated electorate, to the 1960s Civil Rights movement, to the current "No Child Left Behind" program.

Given education's salient position in American culture, one might assume school buildings—the physical structures where formal education actually happens—would be the objects of historical curiosity and scholarly analysis. Unfortunately, this has not been the case. In the field of educational history, although a rich body of literature has increased our understanding of administrative and curricular issues, scholars have made few attempts to connect educational reform with school architecture. Although some progress has been made in charting changes in school buildings as a result of increasing emphases on student health and educational necessity, none of these studies have confronted the issue of school architecture's relationship with societal, cultural, and institutional reforms.[1] Architectural historians have also largely ignored school buildings as an area of study. This is traceable in previous decades to a modernist bias against historicist architecture, which rejected any school building designed before 1940 or in a conservative manner as being inadequate and outdated, and also to the fact that few of the famous post-World War II architects designed schools. Even today, however, school buildings are passed over in survey texts and left out of most architectural guidebooks.[2]

*The Chicago Schoolhouse* redresses this neglect and creates a narrative for one specific city, at the high school level, that seeks to illuminate nationwide developments. It explains how we arrived at the current state of school architecture, using Chicago's high school buildings as examples. Architecturally, school buildings have been mostly conventional; until recently, school buildings were rarely considered avant-garde, and few were created by "star" architects. But they should not be discounted for their lack of marquee value. The value of school buildings is not so much in the architectural details of their creation and construction as in their relationship to the social context from which they arise. Buildings such as those examined in this book record social and cultural attitudes toward education and youth in ways other buildings cannot. School buildings as a type have been works in progress since the 1850s, consistently evolving, through the interaction of educators and architects, in an effort to make structures that not only enclose but also enhance the educational processes occurring in the spaces between their walls.

This book relies on two premises. The first is that high school buildings are valuable objects which can help us to understand the aspirations and attitudes of our predecessors. As inheritors of their built and institutional legacies, it behooves us to comprehend the foundations upon which our educational systems rest. The second premise is that educational and social reforms created the modern high school building by the 1920s. Since then, while the parade of educational reforms marches on, only minor adjustments to school buildings have been made, usually involving stylistic elements or construction materials and techniques. Thus, our current high schools have a pedigree over a century old.

## Methodology

I began this study with a simple question: What is the relationship between educational reforms and school buildings? *The Chicago Schoolhouse* attempts to answer that question by examining nationwide trends as they were manifested in one particular city. I take a broad look at secondary school architecture, addressing such issues as how the buildings were designed, who created them, what factors influenced their design, how they were used, and what their function was in the educational system and American life.

My goal in this work is to account for the differences between a high school built in 1880 and one built in 1960 or 2000 by looking not only at the buildings themselves, but also at the educational system that utilized the buildings and the society that gave rise to and supported the educational system. These buildings provide a way to engage multiple facets of American history during a one-and-a-half-century period. Throughout this investigation I was mindful that the creation of architecture is always a social act–by and for people. To determine the true nature of such acts, and in order to understand the architecture of a given time, we need to know what the general public felt was meaningful or relevant. In this case, such an analysis involves examining cultural attitudes toward children, their well being, and their place in society as well as the purpose of education as a whole.

*The Chicago Schoolhouse* belongs to a growing body of work that employs an intermediate approach between traditional architectural history and vernacular studies to understand particular building types.[3] While this book shares with those studies an interest in transgressing the boundaries of architectural history's traditional focus on "high art" and individual creation to achieve a broader understanding of buildings as determined by social and cultural processes, it differs somewhat in its greater emphasis on chronology and development. The story of high school architecture lends itself to this approach, because there was visible progress in these school buildings, in the sense that they became more enmeshed with pedagogical and curricular advances over time, in contrast to the histories of hospitals or libraries in which the stories of architectural evolution may not have been as straightforward.

One of the goals of this book then is to break new ground by providing a chronology of high schools as a building type. The lack of a historical narrative of school buildings shaped my methodology. I chose an inductive method, letting the historical material mold the story. What the evidence told me was that school architecture responded to a shifting group of concerns over the course of 150 years. For much of the 1800s, high school buildings were little more than simple containers for a highly disciplined pedagogical process that emphasized memorization and recitation. Toward the nineteenth century's end, the high school's societal role grew, and educational reforms in administration, curriculum, and pedagogy required adaptations in school buildings. High school architecture then entered a period of stasis, changing very little in cities such as Chicago between the 1920s and the late 1940s.

After World War II a new set of influences affected school architecture, the most significant being skyrocketing enrollments, limited budgets, pedagogical experiments, and the cultural adoption of modernist architecture. At the beginning of the twenty-first century, high school architecture and American education are demonstrating a return to the principles of 100 years earlier, seen in an emphasis on traditional academic subjects and a rebirth of architectural features like monumentality, striking visual appearance, and simple floor plans.

For numerous reasons I use the specific story of Chicago's public high schools to engage the history of high school architecture. I wanted to focus on urban schools, because my research revealed, as one might expect, that until the post-World War II era larger cities were the point of origin for most educational and architectural innovations.[4] In architecture, such innovations usually began at the secondary level; high school buildings set the standard that grade schools followed. The high school's functional transformation in the late nineteenth century also was much greater than any similar adjustments to the elementary schools. Whether a child went to elementary school in the 1880s or the 1980s, the school's mission was to teach him or her basic fundamentals of core subjects. The same could not be said for the high school, however, for the institution changed dramatically in that time in terms of courses offered and overall purpose.

Chicago proved to be a wonderful setting for tracing the interactions of architectural and educational reform. I selected it as the location for this story partially for selfish reasons—I grew up in the Chicago area, knew the city, and it was not far from my current home. But beyond those advantages the city had much to offer. I was fortunate to be able to draw from a rich secondary literature on the broad history of Chicago's educational events and issues.[5] As one of the nation's largest cities, there was a substantial collection of existing buildings to investigate, and those buildings nicely demonstrated the trajectory of high school architecture over the last 150 years. Nothing about high school architecture was invented in Chicago nor first developed there–it was a mainstream city that almost always followed the latest trends, which made it a perfect subject for this study.

The reader may wonder why two potentially significant educational topics are introduced but not developed in detail in this book. The first concerns the stories of the people who actually used the high school buildings–the students, teachers, and administrators. What impressions did the physical environment of the school buildings leave on these individuals? How did the school's spaces shape their behavior? Knowing how these people experienced schools and how they felt about them would certainly enhance the architectural story. Unfortunately, while there are many recorded memoirs of student days, scarcely any discuss the school buildings in which they transpired. There are equally few teacher narratives, and they likewise fail to provide useful descriptions or analyses of school spaces.[6] Users' experiences in high school buildings is a topic worthy of further scholarship, and hopefully more information will be uncovered in the future to augment our understanding of these important sites.

A second area of nominal attention concerns race. It appears in small segments in the fourth and sixth chapters to give some indication of the substantial racial tensions in Chicago. But because this book outlines the architectural development of public high schools, and because race had little effect on architectural progress, I have minimized race in my discussion. This is not to say there have not been racial aspects to school architecture in cities such as Chicago. There certainly have been multiple experiences–such as I describe with Chicago's DuSable High School in Chapter Five–in which non-white schools were denied the same level of funding for design and/or maintenance as their white counterparts, or where de facto segregation occurred. And Southern cities, in addition to border cities such as St. Louis and Washington, D.C., maintained legally separate schools for blacks for much of the time period covered in this book. Overall, however, the same architectural evolution occurred in high schools regardless of students' race were black, white, or any other ethnicity, or whether there were adequate funds and talented designers or not, although the pace of change may have differed drastically under certain circumstances.

One of the goals of this book is to help the reader understand that high school buildings in Chicago, as well as across the country, have not merely reflected educational reforms and innovations, but rather acted as partners in the educational endeavor. Architects have been actively allied with educators since the last quarter of the nineteenth century through architectural and educational organizations, governmental committees (at the federal and state levels), publishing ventures such as the *American School Board Journal* and *American School and University,* and the position of board of education architect. The increasing teamwork involved in designing a high school has insured that, as much as possible, the relationship among the curriculum, teaching methods, and physical spaces of education have been cooperative rather than conflicting.

## Outline

*The Chicago Schoolhouse* utilizes a three-part structure to tell the story of Chicago's high schools, corresponding to three distinct chronological periods in the history of high school architecture. One of this book's theses—that the modern high school was developed between 1880 and 1920—is reflected in the content of the book's parts, with the section covering this crucial time period examined in more detail.

In Part 1, I follow the American high school from its establishment in the 1820s to the beginning of a widespread transition in public education in the 1880s. I discuss the early high school's purpose–to strengthen students' minds and firm up their moral character–and its curriculum. Students in this era studied "classical" subjects such as Greek, Latin, history, and literature. The recitation method forced them to memorize large amounts of factual information and recite it upon command; educators viewed this "mental discipline" approach as ideal for training the mind muscle, which was more important than training students for any particular career. This section also introduces the Chicago's school system's formation and early years, including the creation of the city's first high school in 1856 and the Division high schools of the 1880s. It also discusses the nineteenth-century schoolhouse, which tended to be a simple two- or three-story cube of identical rooms and identical floors. The classical curriculum and recitation method made few demands on school architects. Large, well-lighted rooms with seats bolted to the floor facing the teacher were typically the only requirements.

In Part II, I examine the nineteenth-century schoolhouse's transformation into the modern twentieth-century school building in Chicago. The story spends considerable time in the period between 1880 and 1920, when the modern school building truly was created. Chapter Two begins in the last few decades of the nineteenth century, as high school buildings began to be constructed with new types of rooms, including laboratories, libraries, and gymnasiums. Aesthetically, the high school buildings evolved from unassuming structures, usually mimicking commercial buildings or wealthy houses, to more elaborately ornamented monuments, as the high school became an integral part of American society. The chapter describes this process in its early stages as evidenced by the second generation of Chicago's Division high schools. Also, since educators and reformers came to realize that the schoolhouse's physical environment could either facilitate or hinder students' health, two topics that really rose to the forefront of design concerns—schoolhouse lighting and ventilation—are discussed.

Chapter Three locates the high school's transformation at the turn of the century within the larger societal context. The chapter begins by looking at changing conceptions of childhood and adolescence, child labor and compulsory attendance laws, and the high school's evolving role as an "adolescent-raising institution." Progressive Era Americans placed a greater emphasis on education than at any previous time in the nation's history as the public education system swelled from urban migration, foreign immigration, and compulsory attendance laws. The high school was the capstone of this system. From its beginnings as a sparsely attended and rather elite institution for the children of mostly middle-class workers, the high school grew to become the locus for the social training of massive numbers of youth of all social classes. High school buildings became civic monuments that expressed a significant societal investment in children and their education. Their larger size and enhanced historical decoration reflected this new status.

Chapter Three begins to uncover educational reforms that had a more direct effect on the schoolhouse's architectural transformation. Educators revised high school curricula during the Progressive Era to make them less humanities-oriented and more applicable to the exigencies of everyday urban life. Manual training and vocational education programs multiplied as high school administrators strove to deal with masses of students who often had no inclination or ability to proceed to college. Classes in machine- and metalwork, carpentry, cooking, and household maintenance took their place beside traditional subjects such as geometry and history. Architects responded to expanded curriculum requirements by transforming the simple nineteenth-century schoolhouse into a complex structure of differentiated architectural spaces that could facilitate the instruction of diverse subjects. School planners adapted these buildings to changed circumstances in a manner applauded by efficiency-minded educators. Progressive political ideas and "efficiency-mindedness" also led to the centralization of educational systems across the country; this was accomplished by altering the size and composition of school boards to make them more efficient (and more like corporate Boards of Directors) and reorganizing the schools' administrative structure.

Chapter Four completes the story of architectural transformation by looking at Chicago's Progressive Era high school buildings and the men who designed them. The chapter highlights the work of three Chicago board of education architects: William B. Mundie (1898–1904), Dwight Heald Perkins (1905–1910), and A. F. Hussander (1910–1922). During the span of approximately twenty years, Chicago high schools grew from moderately scaled and decorated structures into monumental palaces designed to hold thousands of students, to allow large numbers of assorted courses, and to proclaim boldly the institution's newly important status to the public. In the course of telling that story, the chapter covers the search for an appropriate architectural style and the rise of "open" floor plans, as well as the city's growing racial and educational polarization. It also outlines the tribulations of board architects working within a highly politicized school system.

The high school building's evolution during this period was remarkable—from closed floor plans and plain, Romanesque Revival, or "Queen Anne" facades to open plans and muted classical, medieval, or colonial styles. And there was a corresponding increase in size. A large high school building in the 1880s typically contained ten-to-sixteen identical or nearly identical classrooms, an assembly room, and perhaps one or two science laboratories and a recitation room/study hall. A 1919 survey of high school floor plans found 109 different room types in use, including gymnasiums, swimming pools, specialized rooms for all types of manual training and domestic science, laboratories for physics, chemistry, biology, geology, and horticulture, commercial rooms, large and small auditoriums, drawing, drafting and art rooms, teachers' lounges, lunchrooms, locker rooms, libraries, and music rooms. These varied spaces were necessary to support the revised secondary school curricula created by educators in an effort to provide useful vocational or academic training to accommodate the broad social backgrounds and differing academic goals of the nation's youth. The differentiation of spaces inside the modern high school thus mirrored the differentiation of courses.

In Part III, I observe the Chicago high school's development after its formative years, with the premise that the constituent parts were largely determined and in place by 1920 and thereafter the only modifications to school architecture involved the arrangement of those parts or the classroom's basic layout. Chapter Five begins the section, covering the period from 1920 to 1945, when high school architecture in cities such as Chicago continued the massive size and historical styles adopted earlier in the century, while scandals, economic depression, and war affected the school system. Chapter Six introduces the postwar era, when circumstances forced school officials to deal with a new set of issues. Soaring student enrollments and inadequate resources characterized this period. Chicago responded with a series of ambitious building campaigns to create a system of neighborhood schools in the new modernist manner; the previous generation's grand monuments were now viewed as hopelessly old-fashioned. The newer high schools, designed by private architectural firms rather than the school board's architecture department, rejected historical ornament or references, utilized much steel and glass, and strove to project a different, almost casual image through flat roofs, horizontal rather than vertical emphasis, smaller scale, and campus plans with multiple buildings connected by walkways (sometimes called "California schools"). But the basic elements of these 1950s high schools were the same as the 1910s high school—specialized rooms for specialized spaces laid out according to some form of "zoning" (floor plans grouping like activities together). Inside these structures the "differentiated curriculum," emphasizing personal growth over traditional academic learning, remained the norm. Some of these newer high schools became sites for the racial unrest that racked the Chicago Public Schools during this time, as Superintendent Benjamin Willis fought to preserve his neighborhood school policy against mounting pressure to reduce racial inequality in a city known for its vast divide between blacks and whites.

The furious pace of high school construction slowed in Chicago in the 1960s but resumed in the seventies with a new, extensive building campaign. The board of education began to team with the Chicago Public Building Commission and the Chicago Park District to locate high schools in city parks and toyed with the "educational park" fad–massive clusters of elementary and high schools centrally located to draw students from across the city. As this was happening, the school buildings were going through stylistic changes, and unique pedagogical experiments affected some of the interior spaces. Concepts such as magnet schools and "house plans" also modified buildings as administrators strove to find alternatives to traditional secondary education.

The last chapter brings the story into the twenty-first century, beginning in the 1980s when shifting demographics, decreasing enrollments, poor student performance, financial problems, and administrative mismanagement brought the Chicago Public Schools to its nadir. Within a few years, the schools began to rebound after Mayor Richard M. Daley took control of the system and initiated a series of programs to raise the quality of education and improve the students' physical environment. Chicago was also swept up in a nationwide "back to basics" movement that began as an effort to overturn the differentiated curriculum's life skills-orientation and then spread to school architecture. At the 150th anniversary of secondary education in Chicago, pedagogy, curriculum, and architecture seemed to be returning to nineteenth-century roots.

# THE
# CHICAGO
# SCHOOLHOUSE

# PART I

# BEGINNINGS

Although public high schools were introduced to America in the 1820s, their supporters faced many challenges throughout the nineteenth century. In the beginning these institutions tended to be poorly defined, and not often needed, as the proportion of students who where willing and able to extend their education beyond the grammar school level was extremely small. Early high schools served mainly as college preparatory academies or finishing schools for young ladies and gentlemen. Educators considered training the students to think more important than preparing them for any particular career. Reflecting this emphasis, the curriculum of the American public high school was limited to traditional "classical" subjects such as Greek, Latin, history, and literature. Consequently, the buildings that housed these early public high schools were simple, consisting mainly of standard classrooms with orderly rows of desks facing the teacher where the preferred pedagogical technique—the recitation method—could take place. After the Civil War, as enrollments began to increase and curricula expanded to include more nontraditional subjects, high school buildings were built with more ornamented exteriors and more specialized rooms inside. Chicago's high schools, beginning with the Central High School of 1856 and extending through the Division high schools of the 1880s, followed these national trends.

# Chapter One

# EDUCATION AND ARCHITECTURE IN EARLY CHICAGO

On an October day in 1856, the young city of Chicago opened its first public high school. Students in the entering class began their advanced studies in a handsome, three-story bluestone building just west of the city's downtown area. Many of them would be working side-by-side with other children of the same age and educational level for the first time in their academic careers. High schools were rare at that time, and specially-made high school facilities were even more unusual, so the students should have felt privileged to be able to continue their education in such a fine building.

Chicago High School was an investment in the city's future. In addition to embodying Chicagoans' belief in the efficacy of training their talented youth for future success, prosperity, and citizenship, the school also signified educators' faith in the eventual triumph of free public education over extensive criticism and financial instability, as well as their assuredness that this specific building could accommodate the educational activities taking place inside. All of these aspects of the city's endeavor were speculative at a time when many Americans regarded high schools as unnecessary, when public schools competed for students—especially at the secondary level—with private academies and parochial schools, and when educational architecture was far from an exact science, or even a recognized specialty. Public high schools were still a relatively new concept. The Chicago High School, then, was a symbol of hope for the city. The building, and its counterparts in larger cities across the country, also exemplified a type of architecture that serviced specific educational ideas. Within a generation, those ideas would be challenged, new theories would begin to take their place, and the architecture that served them would begin a radical transformation, eventually leading to the development of the modern high school building.

## The Birth of the American High School

The country's first public high school, the English Classical School, opened in Boston, Massachusetts, in 1821, but the public high school's role remained nebulous for more than fifty years. From the beginning, reformers and critics engaged in a spirited debate over the necessity and nature of secondary education. That debate would help to shape the institution into its present form by the early twentieth century.[1]

American public high schools originated as part of a largely middle-class movement to organize and standardize the nation's fledgling educational system. The reformers envisioned a massive public investment in the country's future through an extensive organization of tax-supported schools intended to impart republican values like "ambition, hard work, delayed gratification, and earnestness" in young students.[2] The ultimate aim of the system was no less than to preserve social order and, in the process, the new republic. In many ways, education formed the bedrock of American political thought. The motto "Educatio Populi Salus Reipublicae" ("the education of the people is the safety of the republic") served as a rallying cry for some school reformers.[3] In 1836, the editor of a Midwestern newspaper made a more bombastic argument:

> If our union is still to continue . . . if your fields are to be untrod by the hirelings of despotism; if long days of blessedness are to attend our country in her career of glory; if you would have the sun continue to shed his unclouded rays upon the face of freemen, then EDUCATE ALL THE CHILDREN OF THE LAND. This alone startles the tyrant in his dreams of power, and rouses the slumbering energies of an oppressed people.[4]

Before the end of the Revolutionary War, educators began to lay the foundations for a free public schooling system in New England. At the time the district school was the cornerstone of American rural education. Neighboring localities formed district schools by pooling resources and students to create an independent school administration, and funded them through a combination of taxes and tuition. Not limited to rural regions, district schools also appeared in urban areas, where they competed with private academies, church schools, and free charity schools. Educational reformers condemned these latter types of schools for their lack of uniformity, their freedom from state controls, and their dearth of students from lower social classes. The reformers' preferred alternative was the "common school," named for their desire to have students across the country educated using common materials and methods. By 1860, concerned citizens had succeeded in establishing public-supported common schools throughout the northern states and parts of the South.[5] A core conception of the common school movement was that there were appropriate levels of education for each child. Its supporters thought that while everyone should receive elementary schooling, the ideal educational system should be constructed as a pyramid with the uppermost level reserved for the most talented children. At the system's summit would be the high school—the "people's college."

The first American high school that truly may be called "public" was the Boston English Classical School. It opened in 1821 as an alternative to the city's venerable Latin Grammar School. Boston Latin, which dated back to 1636 and boasted such illustrious alumnae as Rev. Cotton Mather and Samuel Adams, was shaped around a "classical" curriculum with Latin and Greek as the main subjects. The English Classical School, by contrast, was more practically oriented. Boys over twelve years of age who passed a rigorous entrance examination were eligible to undertake a three-year course offering advanced work in English literature, ancient and American history, mathematics, and science. Boston educators hoped this curriculum might appeal to a wider population base while providing the same quality training as Boston Latin. The Classical School's founder, Samuel A. Wells, boasted that the school "would raise the literary and scientific character of the Town, would incite our Youth to a laudable ambition of distinguishing themselves in the pursuit and acquisition of knowledge, and would give strength and stability to the civil and religious institutions of our Country."[6] Such aspirations were typical of the middle-class Americans who established public secondary schools in the country's larger urban areas.

Establishing the public high school was not an easy task, however. The nineteenth-century populace tended to consider secondary education a luxury for three important reasons. First, many considered the high school to be wholly unnecessary. Children received appropriate moral education and the basics of "the three Rs" at the elementary school level; beyond that, there seemed to be few persuasive reasons to continue one's education. Job training was certainly not a consideration because the fledgling high schools did not teach practical skills; apprenticeships and on-the-job-training were the time-tested methods of learning either craft or profession.

The second, and often more significant, opposition to the high school involved child labor. A child in school was a child not working. Most families could not afford to keep their children out of the labor market, whether that meant the family farm or the local factory. Before the "invention" of childhood and the "discovery" of adolescence in the early 1900s sharpened the divisions between children and adults, children were valuable wage earners, farmhands, or caregivers for all but the wealthiest families.[7] Children's vital economic support often superseded any personal benefit they might receive from education. Nineteenth century Americans recognized this by allowing—and even encouraging—children to work. Child labor was prevalent among immigrant families, especially in urban areas. The first U.S. Census to investigate child labor in 1870 found (and surely underestimated) more than 13 percent of all ten- to fifteen-year-olds employed.[8] Compulsory attendance laws, designed in part to get children out of the workplace and into the schoolhouse, were uncommon before the 1870s; when enacted they tended to be lightly enforced. For these and other reasons, high school enrollment in the post-Civil War era was extremely small. As a consequence, before the free public high school gained popularity late in the nineteenth century, secondary schools were mostly populated by middle- and upper-class children preparing for college or a profession.

Finally, public school opponents perceived high schools as inequitable and elitist institutions with no appeal for the general population. Critics attacked everything from the institution's name (implying that the word "high" was too exclusive), to the possible "moral contamination" of middle- and upper-class children from mixing with their poorer counterparts, to the unfairness of using public tax revenue to create a "palace of privilege" for the wealthy.[9] Popular opinion in some cities viewed high schools not just as superfluous but possibly undemocratic—the very antithesis of the institution that educational reformers saw themselves creating. The *Chicago Tribune*, for example, argued for a greater investment in the lower grades rather than the high school by asking its readers "whether it is more important that a large number of persons should learn to read, write, and cipher, or that a smaller number should learn the differential calculus and the catalogue of the ships."[10] There was some measure of truth to these criticisms. Despite educators' best intentions and efforts, public high schools throughout the nineteenth century catered to children with business-class or professional fathers who could afford to let their offspring spend three or four years preparing for the future rather than working (although upper-class parents also were more likely to send their children to private academies).[11]

Urban enrollments revealed the public high school's limited appeal. Throughout the 1870s, no more than 3 percent of all Chicago children ages fourteen-to-seventeen were enrolled in public high schools; nationally, approximately 6 percent of children in that age group attended public high schools by 1890.[12] As late as 1893, a National Education Association committee report on secondary schooling recognized the high school's restrictive nature by describing its function as "to prepare for the duties of life *that small proportion* of all the children in the country—a proportion small in number, but very important to the welfare of the nation—who show themselves able to profit by an education prolonged to the eighteenth year, and whose parents are able to support them while they remain so long at school. . . ." (emphasis added).[13]

School reformers worked tirelessly to expand the narrow socio-economic range of secondary education students and improve public perceptions. For example, before widespread tax-supported public schools, some communities provided free education to indigent children, a remnant of the early national period when the only free schools in the country were charity schools. Despite good intentions, such charitable actions actually provided more fuel for critics who opposed the use of public money for high schools. While some Americans complained of elitism and perceived secondary education as inequitably catering to the upper classes because of its similarity to the private academy, others associated free public schooling with charity and resisted it on an ideological basis because of a widespread belief that poverty was the result of moral failure rather than outside circumstances.

Opponents further attempted to block high schools by challenging the legality of their tax-supported status, complaining that money from the many should not be used to benefit the few. Even after the high school became an established public institution in the early twentieth century, elitist perceptions persisted, and critics continued to raise questions about its usefulness.

## Public Education in Chicago

Chicago's public school system developed quickly in the early nineteenth century. The area had been settled by whites of European origin following the 1795 Treaty of Greenville, in which a group of Ohio Valley Indian tribes relinquished certain midwestern lands to the United States government for forts and portages. The land included "one piece of land six miles square at the mouth of the Chikago river, emptying into the south-west end of Lake Michigan," where Jean Baptiste Point DuSable had established a trading post some twenty-six years earlier. The U.S. Army erected Fort Dearborn on the site in 1803 to protect the area. Settlers shortly began to appear in this rather inhospitable but strategically valuable location where lake, swamp, and prairie converged. In 1833, twenty-eight residents voted to incorporate as the city of Chicago. A year before, the first local schools had opened in primitive conditions; two were housed in churches and one in a log stable. By 1837, when the city drafted its first charter, there were 325 students in five schools, the result of a growing population that then numbered over 4,000. This dramatic increase was propelled by the construction of the Illinois and Michigan Canal, which connected Lake Michigan to the Mississippi River and opened the interior to commercial traffic.

During a financial panic in 1837, all of Chicago's schools closed, in part because of the Illinois Bank failure. Ironically, as the schools disappeared the first official framework for a public school system was established. The city charter of the same year gave the city council, made up of aldermen representing each of the city's wards, ultimate control over the public schools. These councilmen would appoint a group of unsalaried school inspectors, who were responsible for examining prospective teachers, selecting textbooks, providing school buildings, visiting schools, and dividing and distributing income from the school fund.[14] The charter further called for each of the city's separate school districts to elect three trustees to hire teachers and oversee attendance issues. When the city charter was amended just two years later, the council gained even more power. New regulations allowed the council to control all school lands and funds, appoint trustees, choose textbooks, prescribe courses of study, and oversee all school contracts.[15]

Chicago fought back from the financial depression with vigor. During the 1840s, the city's population grew to almost 30,000; total school enrollment over the same period increased from 317 to 1,919 students.[16] The Illinois and Michigan Canal had turned Chicago into a major nexus for water and stagecoach transportation, and the city was becoming the nation's leading lumber, grain, and meat distributor. By mid-century, Chicago would be the world's largest railway center. The schools rebounded from the depression-era depths and the shape of Chicago education changed through a series of legislative and administrative actions. In 1853, the city council created the position of superintendent of public schools to help run the school system. Four years later another amendment to the city charter established a fifteen-member school board to serve as the Chicago public schools' chief administrative arm. The board replaced the inefficient organization that relied on school inspectors, but the board had limited powers, exerting no control over the superintendent, teachers, courses of study, buildings, or finances. Not until an 1872 state law was passed did the board of education gain the right to dismiss or appoint the superintendent and its own president. The board's makeup changed as well. According to the city charter, the mayor was given the authority to appoint fifteen school board members for a three-year term (subject to city council approval). This procedure insured that political partisanship would dominate Chicago's educational administration in the future. The board gained additional duties with the new legislation, such as the ability to levy taxes, employ teachers, rent buildings, select textbooks, and fix salary schedules. In the end, however, the city council retained the ability to manage the schools' finances. Combined with mayoral control over its composition, this meant the Chicago Board of Education would not be an autonomous organization.

The early days of Chicago education, like elsewhere in America's larger cities, were characterized by turmoil. The school system expanded at an alarming rate, continually straining the city's resources. In 1850 there were only twenty-one teachers for almost 2,000 students in Chicago's schools.

The average class size by the decade's end was eighty-one in the primary schools.[17] Teachers routinely taught seventy to 100 students of all ages and abilities in one classroom, which meant that a thirteen-year-old with years of reading experience might be seated next to an illiterate six-year-old. In 1840, recognizing the dangers inherent in such an atmosphere, the school inspectors recommended the creation of a secondary school to remove the older students from multi-graded classes, but the suggestion was ignored. The schools faced a shortage of available space so drastic that classes met wherever they could—in private houses, rented stores, churches, etc. Chicago's first permanent school building, constructed in 1845 on the north side of Madison Street between State and Dearborn, was an early attempt to improve the enrollment crisis. The Dearborn School was a two-story brick building of Greek Revival style that cost $7,500, a sum viewed as outrageous by critics who believed the school unnecessary. The press dubbed it "Miltimore's Folly," after Ira Miltimore, city councilman and school inspector who adamantly fought for the school's creation. Mayor August Garrett even joined in the criticism, saying that the building was too large and might better be used as "a factory or an insane asylum for those responsible for its erection."[18] Miltimore and his followers were validated when the school enrolled 543 students in the first year and 843 in 1846.

Other school buildings followed, but nothing seemed to stem the tide of students. By 1854, Chicago's seven schools were so full that approximately 1,000 students were turned away.[19] Meanwhile, the situation remained bleak for the city's older students. School inspectors had repeated their request for a high school in 1847, and again were rebuffed. They raised their request for a third time five years later. In an impassioned report arguing for "schools of a higher character, into which the more deserving and promising pupils should be introduced," a committee of school inspectors listed the many benefits of public high schools, including an egalitarian plea that secondary education:

> opens the door to a general, not to say a good education for the poor as well
> as the rich . . . it is politically unfair that any class should attain a promi-
> nence of position, imparting political advantages which cannot be reached
> by any other portion of the community . . . the rich can have access to the

best academies and colleges in the country, while the poor, for want of the requisite means, are excluded. Let education then, be freely imparted to all.[20]

This time the city council's school committee agreed with the inspectors, but it took the full council two years to officially authorize the establishment of a high school. Finally, in 1856, construction was completed on a new building on Monroe Street between Des Plaines and Halsted streets near the western edge of the city's center. Grammar school graduates over the age of twelve who passed rigorous entrance examinations in reading, writing, spelling, grammar, geography, arithmetic, and United States history were eligible for admission to the new school with a choice of studies in three departments—Classical, English, and Normal (teacher training). The Chicago High School was open to both girls and boys, making it a pioneer in coeducational secondary education.[21]

## The Chicago High School

As a freestanding structure devoted solely to the high school, the Chicago building was unique for its time. Public high schools were rare and separate buildings for them were even more uncommon. In larger cities before the Civil War, and in rural areas throughout the nineteenth century, teachers often taught high school classes alongside primary classes in the same building, or wherever space was available.[22] Cleveland, Ohio, for example, opened the first public high school west of the Allegheny Mountains in 1846 in a church basement, and St. Louis's first high school held classes in a primary school room for two years before a separate building was constructed.[23] Both cities built their first detached high school buildings between 1855 and 1856. These schoolhouses, and many others across the country, shared similarities in room types and uses, and in overall arrangement. Sparse enrollments and narrow curricular and pedagogical requirements lessened the need for specialized spaces. Teachers typically taught all subjects in the same classroom. They required students to memorize large quantities of information and recite it upon command (some schools included small recitation rooms for this purpose to avoid interfering with the other students' studying). Children sat on benches or at desks bolted to the floor in neat, orderly rows facing the teacher's desk that was often raised on a platform. Class sizes varied, but in bigger cities they ranged from thirty to seventy students.

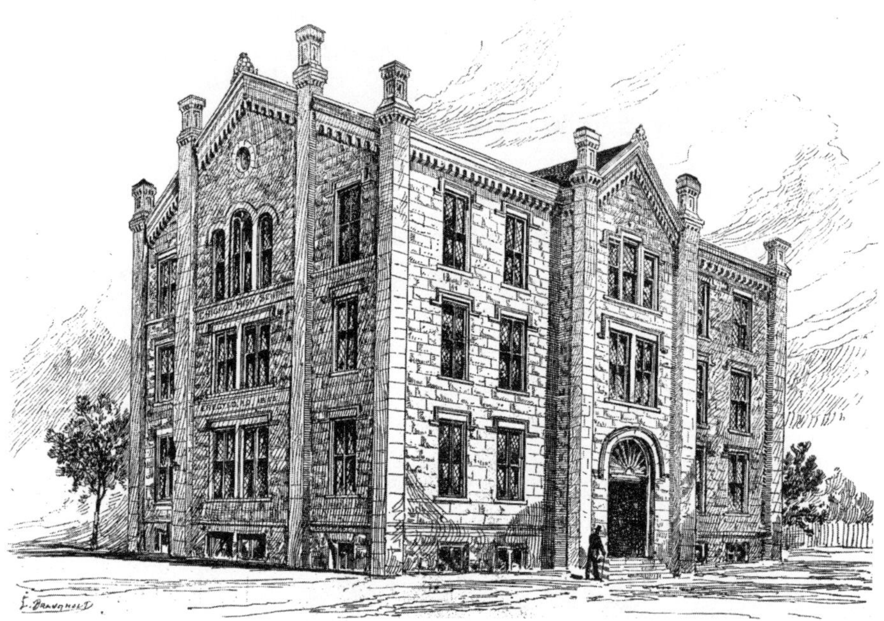

Fig. 1.1. Van Osdel and Baumann, Chicago Central High School, 1856.

Chicago's first high school building was a three-story, rectangular stone and brick structure measuring 88' x 52' (Fig. 1.1). Vertical buttress-like elements dominated the exterior, giving it a Gothic appearance, much like a castle or medieval church, although there were none of the rooftop pinnacles or lancet windows that characterized the early high schools in St. Louis, Cincinnati, and Cleveland. Despite impressive facades, such buildings were arranged simply inside. The Chicago schoolhouse's three floors were almost identical, with four 23' x 35' rooms grouped around a central stairwell on each level (Fig. 1.2). On the top floor the partition wall between two rooms was omitted to form one large area that served as a combination assembly hall/lecture room/study hall. Classrooms were multipurpose in the sense that all subjects were taught in them, from history to science to music. The only specialized spaces in the building were cloakrooms, a tiny library, and a small principal's office. Despite these rather austere accommodations, the high school was expensive; the building and its furniture cost the city approximately $50,000, with another $20,000 spent on the land.[24]

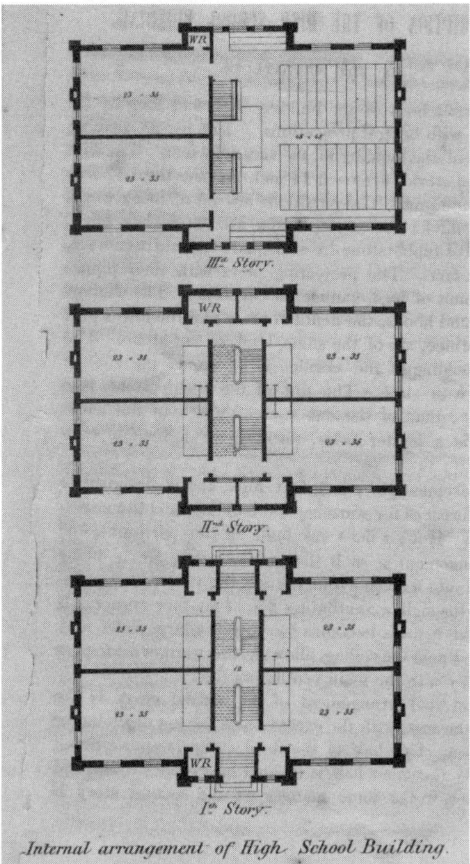



Fig. 1.2. Floor plans, Chicago Central High School. Typically, the first generation of American high schools had simple, symmetrical floor plans with no specialized spaces.

Chicago High School welcomed its first class of 114 students on October 8, 1856. Enrollment rose to 151 the following spring. With each subsequent year the schoolhouse's originally comfortable accommodations grew more cramped as the high school became more popular than its creators imagined and Chicago's incredible growth fueled an already significant enrollment problem. Between 1850 and 1870, the city's population jumped nearly 1,000 percent, from just under 30,000 to almost 300,000.[25] The high school building, intended to hold approximately 400 students, was filled to capacity within a decade.[26]

The city council refused to allocate funds to expand the school, however, so the school board implemented a series of branch high schools in the city's three geographical districts (the north, west, and south divisions, determined by the Chicago River's branches).[27] In 1869, the board established two-year high school courses for students in these divisions inside preexisting grammar schools. Upon the successful completion of a branch high school course, the student would transfer to Chicago High School for the last two years of his or her studies. Shortly thereafter, a two-story wooden frame building was constructed next to the high school to handle overflow students.[28]

The catastrophic 1871 fire changed the complexion of secondary education in the city. The fire destroyed one-third of all city schools, along with all school records. The Chicago High School escaped undamaged, but for the next year it was used as emergency quarters for the county court and recorder of deeds. Upon reopening with a new name—Central High School—the school's enrollment dropped sharply as many students who had relocated to division schools after the fire failed to return. Recognizing this trend, the school board began to review the city's secondary school organization. In 1880 it granted division schools full high school status with four-year programs. Central High School merged with North Division High School and the original building became school board property.

## The First Generation of Division Schools

Rising enrollments at the branch high schools eventually led the board to construct a series of new buildings. After the branch schools were converted to full-time, independent status, the city's 1,236 high school students increased to 3,527 by 1890.[29] To meet this demand, the board built four secondary schoolhouses during the 1880s. The first three appeared in a concerted building campaign, beginning with West Division High School (Augustus Bauer, 1880) at the intersection of Morgan and Monroe Streets on the city's West Side. It was followed by North Division High School (Julius Ender, 1883), at Wendell and Wells Streets, and South Division High School (James R. Willett, 1884) on the corner of Wabash Avenue and 26th Street. All three buildings shared the same vertical organization, with utilities in the basement and classrooms above. Basements housed separate bathrooms for teachers and male and female students, separate boys' and girls' "playrooms" (there were grammar school classes taught in each of

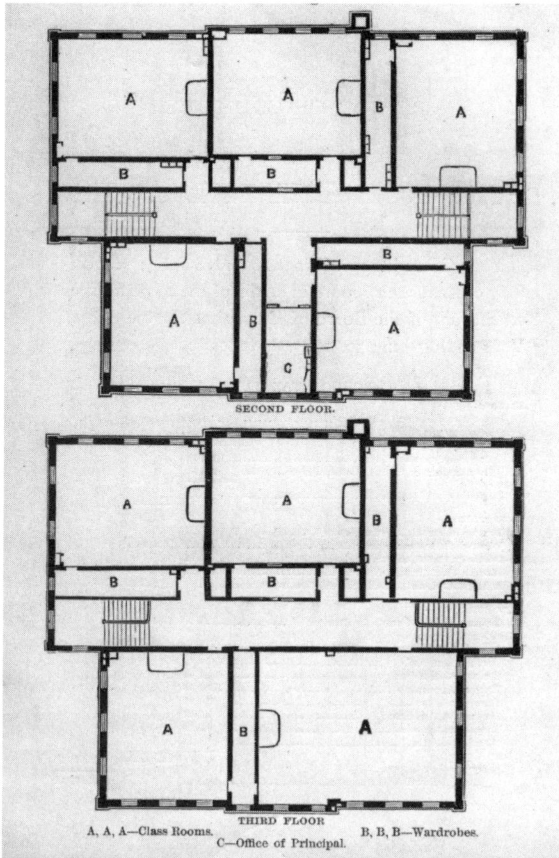



Fig. 1.3. Second- and third-floor plans, West Division High School. A typical 1880s school plan of nearly identical rooms stacked into nearly identical floors.

these high schools), and equipment for the mechanical ventilation system. The West Division schoolhouse contained fifteen multipurpose classrooms on three floors (Fig. 1.3). Crammed between the classrooms were fourteen small wardrobes or closets. The only other room in West Division was a principal's office on the second floor above the entrance. The North Division High School held twelve classrooms, eighteen wardrobes, and a principal's office, but also three "Teacher's Dressing Rooms" and a recitation room on the first floor, a recitation room and "Cabinet" on the second floor, and a small library, an "Apparatus" room, a laboratory, and an assembly hall on the

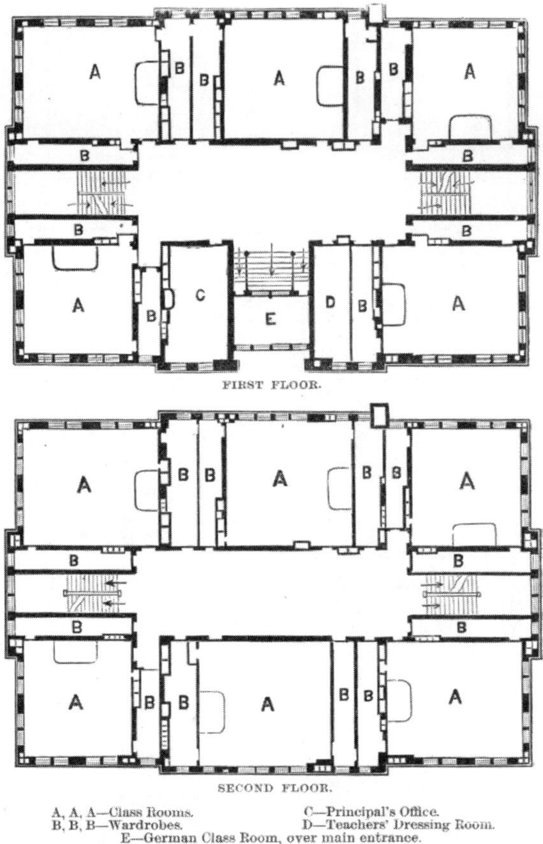



Fig. 1.4. First- and second-floor plans, South Division High School. The allocation of space is slightly more complex than in the two previously built division schools but remains relatively simple.

top floor. South Division, completed a year later, had eighteen classrooms, thirty-seven wardrobes, a principal's office, a teacher's room, a laboratory, and a fourth floor devoted entirely to an assembly hall capable of seating 500 students (Fig. 1.4). With each successive building there had been a subtle expansion of facilities.

In addition to their increasing interior amenities, the exterior of each new division school noticeably changed. West Division had the simplest facade, characterized by an overall plainness (Fig. 1.5). Its architect, Augustus Bauer, was one of a small team of experienced builders who had re-

Fig. 1.5. Augustus Bauer, West Division High School, 1880.

constructed downtown Chicago after the 1871 fire, a group of men who, it has been noted, "had as many commissions as they could handle, and for two years . . . they kept track of their designs in terms of miles of building fronts constructed."[30] This may account for West Division's similarities to the city's post-fire commercial buildings. A brick building over a stone basement, West Division's modest architectural embellishments included a small pediment projecting slightly from the central portion's flat roof, a bracketed cornice, attached columns at the building's corners, and a slight emphasis of the three entries.

North Division was somewhat more elaborate. The building's form was a rectangular brick and stone box like West Division. But North Division featured a few aesthetic flourishes (Fig. 1.6). An ornamental group centered above the main door punctuated its flat roof. The facade's middle section projected slightly, marked by applied columns in the corners; the main entry, within this central portion, was announced by a triple archway. The facade projected a little on each side of the entry midway to the corner, converting a flat wall into a multi-planed surface. Architect Julius Ender also varied the shapes of the stone lintels above the windows. Those on the first story were rectangular, while on the second and third floors they were peaked;

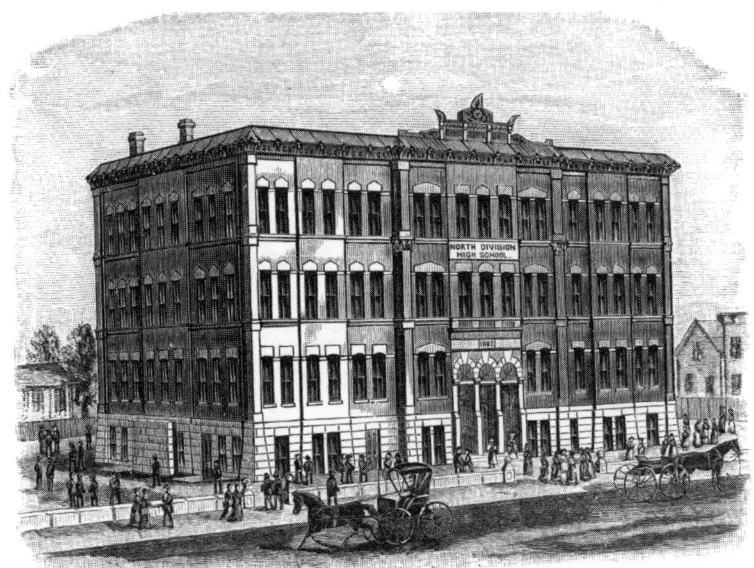

Fig. 1.6. Julius Ender, North Division High School, 1883.

within the central portion, two windows shared one lintel on either side of the entrance. These were all minor details, but they imparted visual interest nonetheless, and taken together they made the North Division schoolhouse more visually sophisticated than West Division.

That trend continued with South Division High School. Architect James R. Willett discarded the flat roof, opting for steeply pitched gables and a multitude of chimneys and ventilating shafts (Fig. 1.7). The energetic roofline was the most significant change from the previous division schools. Its design reveals an architectural movement toward school buildings that were domestic than commercial in appearance. Whereas West Division resembled downtown business buildings, South Division appeared to be visually similar to the period's more expensive homes. In keeping with this trend, Willett avoided classical features like columns and pediments. His lone concession to classicism was a large arch over the main door. The South Division building also included varied window sizes and groupings, and stone basement walls.

In the span of four short years, the three successive Division high school buildings evolved into more complex architectural creations, both inside and out. The increasingly elaborate accommodations were not justified by neces-

Fig. 1.7. James R. Willett, South Division High School, 1884.

sity, since the city's high school enrollment rose by only 300 students between 1881 and 1884. Instead, it seems that Chicago's educators sought to use architecture to project a certain status for the schools. Superintendent George Howland expressed this attitude when he wrote, "The High School is the crown of our Public School System. It is the Citizen's College."[31] Howland's comment captured two of the new high schools' salient aspects. The first was the drive to promote the high school as an especially important component of the educational hierarchy—the capstone of the public education system. Students were now able to receive an education beyond the basic "three Rs" that might help them achieve something better in their lives. But this had to be balanced against public perceptions of elitism. So the high school was further identified as "the Citizen's College," a place belonging to and oriented toward the common folk. School board president Martin A. DeLaney elaborated this point a few years earlier when he wrote: "These [high] schools are firmly established as part of our school system, and should be liberally maintained, as, without them, higher education would be confined to the wealthier classes, producing a more clearly defined class distinction than is desirable in a country governed by Republican principles."[32]

## Educational Theory and Practice

The growth of secondary education in Chicago was typical of northern cities in the late nineteenth century, but this enrollment surge belied a nation-wide problem. Public high schools of the 1880s remained ill-defined institutions with multiple problems. High school enrollments continued to comprise only a small portion of the nation's total student population. A mere 4 percent of America's public school students in 1873 were in high schools.[33] In 1880, only 2.5 percent of Chicagoans ages fourteen to seventeen were enrolled in high school, while the national figure for that age group was only 3.7 percent (see Table 1B).[34] A survey conducted in 1890 found that the average high school student attended just eighty-six days and the graduation rate was a paltry 10.7 percent.[35] High school teachers, including many recent high school graduates, were barely competent and facilities were inadequate. But the most pressing problem concerned the curriculum. Urban educators in the late nineteenth century were not prepared for the types of students the high schools were responsible for educating. A mass exodus from country to city, rising foreign immigration, and increasing child labor and compulsory attendance legislation brought more students to America's high schools, but these schools were not set up to accommodate the newcomers' wide-ranging interests and abilities.

## Curriculum and Pedagogy

Nineteenth-century high schoolers, who constituted a very small proportion of all public school students, generally were a privileged group of middle- to upper-class youth whose parents could afford to keep them out of the workplace. The small high school enrollment was partially due to the fact that few of America's public school students in the nineteenth century had a family income that allowed them to consider attending college.[36] High school students tended to be disproportionately the children of clerks, merchants, craftsmen, and businessmen. These fortunate scholars tended to take academically oriented courses that leaned heavily toward classical fields of study such as Latin and Greek, algebra and geometry, history, and sciences like geography and botany. Curricula across the country showed a high degree of similarity. In Chicago, however, the board of education could not seem to make up its collective mind about the proper high school curriculum. It vacillated over the years between a uniform, classically-inspired course and a set of multiple courses that catered to the needs of non-college-bound students.

The original Chicago High School offered four courses of study: Classical (three years), English (three years), "Normal" or teacher-training (two years), and a combined Classical & English course (four years). In 1861, the Classical and English courses were each extended to four years, and the board required all students, no matter which option they chose, to take Latin or German throughout the first two years. The board of education reduced the Classical course to three years in 1865 following sharp criticism; in 1869 it made the Classical course four years again, with an option to complete it in three years if the student decided to eschew elective classes.

The establishment of the branch high schools led the board to create a new two-year curriculum for them with a more practical orientation for those students who would not pursue their education beyond the branch school. Students in this program took mathematics, English or German, and natural science classes every day, supplemented by such offerings as algebra, physiology, rhetoric, and civil government. When Central High School closed and all students were routed to the three Division schools, the board again restructured the high school curriculum into three courses: English (two years), College Preparatory (three years), and a complete high school course of four years. Then in 1884 the school board took the drastic step of abolishing Greek from the high schools, which limited the schools' ability to prepare students for college.[37]

Despite this confusing series of changes, educators' two ultimate goals for the Chicago high school curriculum remained constant through the 1880s: to train students to think and to bolster their moral character.[38] Training the mind was accomplished through "mental discipline." Advocates claimed mental discipline provided the properly-instructed mind with the ability to easily adapt itself to any future endeavor. Two prevalent theories of knowledge and its attainment formed the basis for this outlook. The faculty theory of psychology held that a number of distinct parts or "faculties" (reason, memory, emotion, etc.) made up the human mind, and each of these faculties could be strengthened—like a muscle—through exercise. Also, many scientists and academics "regarded knowledge as objective systems of facts and laws," and "portrayed knowing as a relatively passive process, in which the mind learned from the habitual association of data impressed upon it by the external world."[39] These two beliefs combined to have a profound affect on the educational process. More important than preparation for any specific vocation was the broad knowledge and reasoning ability that any cultured person was expected to possess. Chicago Public Schools Superintendent William H. Wells expressed support for this approach in 1860, when he wrote, "The highest and most important object of intellectual education is mental discipline, or the power of using the mind to the best advantage. . . . It is this alone that can strengthen and envigorate [sic] the noble faculties with which we are endowed."[40] Two decades later Superintendent George Howland, in a nine-and-a-half-page section on "Memory in Instruction" in the *Annual Report*, wrote that "The memory of course must play an important part during the years of school life, for by its aid alone all reason and intelligence are made possible."[41]

Chicago schools followed traditional methods of instruction associated with the mental discipline approach—methods that remained virtually unchanged for centuries despite the best efforts of educational reformers.[42] In schools throughout the city and across the country, students sat in precisely arranged rows of desks facing the teacher (Fig. 1.8). They raised their hands to answer questions and stood when speaking. Historian David Macleod summarized primary school instructional methods: "By the late nineteenth century, teachers had settled into a routine of marching students through textbooks. Some teachers . . . merely prescribed assignments and checked their completion, commonly by catechizing students. Others . . . organized exercises, unison recitations, and competitions. A third group . . . actually 'clarified and elaborated' materials for students. Yet all three teaching styles settled for rote reproduction of skills or knowledge."[43] These same techniques would have been used in the high schools. Students in each grade studied the same texts at the same speed; they either learned or were left behind. In this strict environment the main vehicle of instruction, as it had been for centuries, was the recitation method. Recitation was designed to develop the "mind muscle" through memorization. Students memorized long poems, multiplication tables, historic events, and geographical locations from textbooks, then recited them to the rest of the class. Even science education depended on textbooks and recitations rather than laboratory work.

Fig. 1.8. Classroom, Carlisle Indian Industrial School, 1901.

Teachers controlled the recitation process with a steady stream of questions. A study of New York City teachers found, for example, that they asked an average of two-to-three questions each minute. In a forty-five-minute period, teachers could ask from twenty-five to 200 questions. The study's author concluded that teachers were "drillmasters instead of educators."[44] Educational critic Dr. Joseph M. Rice reached a similar conclusion. Rice visited elementary schools in thirty-six cities during a five-month period in 1892 to observe American education first-hand. His investigation provided the first comprehensive evaluation of American teaching. Overall, Rice found both good and bad teaching in the nation's schools, but his judgments tended to be caustic and critical and his final evaluation was that there was much "ludicrous teaching" in these schools due to "unscientific management."[45] In too many "mechanical" schools (including those in Chicago), Rice discerned, "the aim of instruction is limited mainly to drilling facts into the minds of the children, and to hearing them recite lessons that they have learned by heart from text-books."[46] While Rice examined only elementary schools, we can assume his findings were applicable to secondary education as well.

The ubiquitous formal recitation classroom was shaped by larger social and cultural beliefs. Historian Larry Cuban perceived this when he noted that this method of teaching was laden with "assumptions about the social and economic role of schools, knowledge, children, and learning consistent with the profound changes occurring at the turn-of-the-century in the larger society."[47] A widely-held assumption was that public education should include moral training. Good character served a vital, two-fold purpose: individual morality was the main vehicle for preserving freedom and democracy, and it would anchor American society as it faced the unsettling tides of modernization, industrialization, and immigration. "In the minds of nineteenth-century Americans," wrote historian B. Edward McClellan, "the price of liberty was rigorous self-discipline and upright personal conduct."[48] The public education system created in the nineteenth century emphasized moral character in the form of discipline and order from the lowest grades up through the high school.

The main source for character education was the Christian religion. A dominant Protestant ideology led educators to see nothing incompatible about including Christianity in public education. For example, the National Teachers Association passed a resolution in 1869 declaring that the Bible should be "devotionally read, and its precepts inculcated in all the common schools of the land."[49] In public high schools across the country, students began their day with Bible readings, hymns, and prayers. Christianity was enlisted to teach morality in less overt ways as well. Prior to reaching high school, students would have advanced through an educational system that continually emphasized such Protestant values as "industry, piety, righteous living, thrift, self-reliance, and individualism."[50] *McGuffey Readers*, the most popular grammar school textbooks, reinforced these values in countless stories. Students also encountered desirable character traits in high school science and mathematics textbooks.[51] Almost every subject presented textbook writers with the opportunity to teach students qualities like "love of country, love of God, duty to parents, the necessity to develop habits of thrift, honesty, and hard work in order to accumulate property, the certainty of progress [and] the perfection of the United States."[52]

Moral development was not limited to the curriculum. Some educators, such as Rhode Island Commissioner of Public Schools (and later the first

U.S. Commissioner of Education) Henry Barnard, believed the schoolhouse itself could teach valuable lessons about order, organization, and beauty. "Every school-house should be a temple," wrote Barnard, "consecrated in prayer to the physical, intellectual, and moral culture of every child in the community."[53] This was actually a common conviction in the antebellum period: many saw the value of architecture as a material means of reinforcing Protestant-republican virtues. Architect Oliver P. Smith spoke for them when we wrote, "nothing has more to do with the morals, the civilization, and refinement of a nation, than its prevailing Architecture."[54]

## Schoolhouses

Character education and the mental discipline approach went hand-in-hand. Both were designed to instill the types of values and abilities that educators and parents felt were necessary to maintain order in a rapidly changing society. However, the educational system utilizing this method placed few demands on school architecture. As a result, architects created a generation of schoolhouses that were spatially organized and controlled but not very complicated. Since teachers taught almost all subjects in the same manner, the requirements of schoolhouse rooms rarely varied.

For most of the nineteenth century, creating a school building was a rather straightforward task. Room and window sizes were relatively standardized. Architects merely applied agreed-upon formulas for determining these elements to calculate the number of rooms necessary for the projected enrollment, and added some stairways and small corridors for interior circulation, a small assembly hall, and some type of ventilation/heating system to complete the schoolhouse.

The 1880s Division high schools in Chicago displayed a number of characteristic features of mid- to late-nineteenth century high school architecture. Schoolhouses across the country tended to be square or rectangular and one- to four-stories high. If the building had an assembly hall—none could legitimately be called an auditorium—it was almost always on the uppermost floor, reflecting not only its insignificance, but also the old schoolhouse's structural limitations. Technology was not sufficiently advanced to allow a large open space anywhere other than immediately below the roof. Basements held heating and ventilating apparatus, storage rooms, wardrobes, washrooms, and occasionally playrooms for younger children. Above were nearly identical floors, divided into equal-sized classrooms. Classrooms came in a variety of dimensions, but most were rectangular or square with windows in all exterior walls. Jamming students into these spaces without adequate ventilation could have disastrous results.[55] In recognition of this potential health problem, some of the earliest attention paid to any aspect of school architecture was directed toward ventilation systems.[56] Some school buildings also contained offices for the principal and/or superintendent, small recitation rooms, or a "special" room for science experiments. Occasionally a classroom was altered by introducing scientific equipment, or removing walls to increase its size, but as a whole there were few specially-designed rooms in the schoolhouse.

A growing number of educators became interested in using school buildings to communicate a message to the community—beyond the domestic symbolism visible in buildings such as South Division High School—through their mere presence. An expensive, attractive schoolhouse could advertise the high school at a time when secondary schooling had yet to prove its worth to a large portion of society. The elaborate St. Louis High School (1855), for example, proved a successful part of the school board's effort to attract new students. Enrollment from the city's wealthiest sections increased immediately after the building was opened.[57] Superintendent John Tice saw this as justification for this "model school edifice." He felt a high school building should be more than four walls and a roof; instead, "A splendid edifice is not without its uses to the community in which it stands. It is an expression of the refinement, public spirit, and taste of that community."[58]

Almost a decade prior to John Tice's comments, Henry Barnard wrote that schoolhouses should "be calculated to inspire children and the community generally with respect for the object to which it is devoted," and be comparable in "attractiveness, convenience and durability with other public edifices."[59] Barnard's comments on school buildings are notable given his prominence in American education. He founded the nation's most important early educational journal—the *American Journal of Education*—in 1855 to promote the intelligent discussion of educational issues and to spread his personal pedagogical views. Those views included a significant place for school architecture. Barnard was also the author of a groundbreaking book on the subject, *School Architecture, or Contributions to the Improvement of School-Houses in the United States* (1848). This book was the first comprehensive guide to designing American schoolhouses. Barnard was interested in all aspects of school architecture. He wrote on topics ranging from proper room arrangements and ventilation systems to the school's symbolic and pedagogical aspects. In a typical passage, Barnard wrote, "No public edifice more deserves, or will better repay, the skill, labor, and expense, which may be necessary to attain this object, for here the health, tastes, manners, minds, and morals of each successive generation of children will be, in a great measure, determined for time and eternity."[60] These strong sentiments were further manifested in the *American Journal of Education* through drawings and articles on prominent schools around the country. During its twenty-six year run, the *Journal* published more than 800 woodcuts of school buildings.[61]

By the late 1870s some of the high school buildings in larger American cities were highly visible public monuments capable of vying for attention with civic landmarks like courthouses and city halls. School architecture, according to noted historian William Reese, "became one of the clearest expressions of bourgeois social values throughout the nineteenth century. The size, shape, and cost of public facilities revealed dominant attitudes about cultural authority, centralized power, and the special role of high schools in the common system."[62] Cleveland Central High School (1878) was a prominent example of this emerging trend. Architecturally, the building blended nineteenth-century Victorian exuberance with what one writer called "the South-German Gothic of the thirteenth and fourteenth centuries" (Fig. 1.9)[63] A church-like tower and spire at the entry, rising to twice the height of the main body, dominated the building. The facade included visual highlights like multi-colored stonework, a main door ornamented like a Gothic cathedral porch with paired columns and a gabled pediment, and a roofline dominated by steep gables, smokestacks disguised as pinnacles, "roof crestings . . . ornamental crockets, finials," and crosses.[64] Inside, the floor plan superimposed a Greek cross onto a rectangle, with an open shaft of space rising vertically through the building's hollow center. The structure's three stories were divided into twenty-five rooms—most of them for recitation—with a top-floor assembly hall capable of seating 1,000 people. On the day of the dedication ceremony, officials kept the building open until 7 p.m. to accommodate public curiosity.

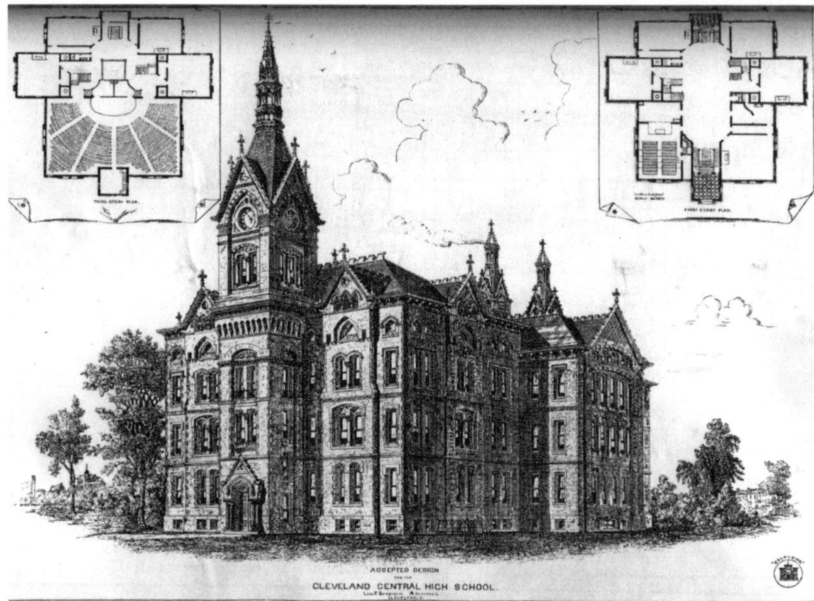

Fig. 1.9. Levi T. Scofield, Cleveland Central High School, Cleveland, Ohio, 1878, Some second generation high school buildings were larger and more visually striking than their predecessors, partly to advertise secondary education to middle-class parents.

Although ornate schoolhouses became objects of civic pride for many, others criticized such architectural muscle-flexing as extravagant and unwarranted. "While we devote all our available means to the erection of beautiful buildings, and make no provision, or almost none, for the great intellectual wants of the school," asked a writer in the *Massachusetts Teacher*, "shall we wonder at the complaint that the girls of our schools care more for dress than learning? [sic] and that our boys like any other place quite as well as the school?"[65] An anonymous writer for the *New England Journal of Education* slighted the Cleveland High School for sacrificing "unity and centrality to general ornament."[66] A few years later the president of the St. Louis Board of Education invoked Cleveland's high school as an example of the kind of school building his city did not need: "The objection to the new buildings recently erected in Boston, Cleveland, Hartford and other cities is that, apart from being unsuited to our needs, they seem to be built rather more to affect the passer-by than to serve the immediate purpose of school buildings. It is sincerely to be hoped that the committee will protect the community against what is becoming known as 'legislative architecture.'"[67]

These statements reveal friction in educational circles concerning the schoolhouse's appearance. Some favored the type of attention-grabbing public school architecture promoted by John Tice thirty years earlier. For others, showy architectural statements were contrary to the spirit (and resources) of public education. These critics seemed to be the minority, however, as educators began to construct elaborate high school buildings in larger northern cities, perhaps to bolster the high school's still tenuous position in American society. And the general public seemed to accept them, for as the *New England Journal of Education* writer stated, high schools like Cleveland Central "show the strength of public sentiment in the unanimity of the people in erecting so durable and costly structures."[68]

Chicago high school buildings illustrated many aspects of the schoolhouse's early transformation up to 1890. Like its counterparts in other American cities, the Chicago public school system erected a simple, pseudo-Gothic building to house its first high school in the mid-1850s, then added schoolhouses through the 1880s that became successively larger, safer, healthier, more complex, more aesthetically prominent, and contained a wider variety of differentiated spaces than their predecessors. These changes to the Chicago buildings, as well as others across the nation, were the result of a number of social, cultural, and architectural factors influencing architects and educators. Within the next two decades, the early schoolhouses would evolve into modern high school buildings.

PART II

# TRANSFORMATION

The modern twentieth-century school building developed between 1880 and 1920. The high school building's transformation during this period, both inside and out, was extraordinary. During that time, high schools evolved from rather plain structures bearing a visual resemblance to commercial buildings or houses to ornate civic monuments. Inside, all of the specialized spaces that we associate with contemporary schools—such as gymnasiums, auditoriums, libraries, woodshops, etc.—became standard. There were a number of reasons for these changes, most arising from the simple fact that high schools became more important. The Progressive Era saw a greater emphasis on public education than at any previous time in America's history, partly due to pressures from increasing student populations. Educational reformers revised high school curricula from their reliance on traditional humanities-oriented courses to more practical studies by adding manual training and vocational education programs to appeal to the broad social backgrounds and differing academic goals of the nation's youth. Architects, working with educators, incorporated expanded curriculum requirements by transforming the simple nineteenth-century schoolhouse into large, complex structures filled with divergent architectural spaces. In Chicago, public school architecture achieved national renown as these advanced ideas were introduced to Chicago schools by school board architects William B. Mundie, Dwight Heald Perkins, and A. F. Hussander.

Chapter Two

# THE TRANSFORMATION
# OF THE SCHOOLHOUSE

In the late nineteenth century, educators and architects across the country began to reshape the schoolhouse into its modern form. Curricula expanded beyond narrow academic limits to encompass new courses as the public high school evolved from its traditional origins. In response, high school buildings, like Chicago's second generation division schools, would need to include unprecedented spaces to accommodate these new demands. At the same time, the educational world focused its attention on issues of children's health to a greater degree than ever before. These forces ushered in a period of rapid change and drastic architectural transformation.

## A New Type of School

Chicago high school buildings in the 1890s were the product of an architectural evolution that began much earlier. In the period just after the Civil War, neither educational nor social circumstances required a sophisticated high school building outside of a few rare examples in the nation's largest cities. By the late 1880s, however, high schools were increasingly the subject of architectural and educational interest as a result of social, educational, and technological developments. Even before Chicagoans built the first generation of Division high schools, the roots of architectural change had been

Fig. 2.1. George A. Clough, Latin and English High School, Boston, Massachusetts, 1877–80.

established in Boston. In an 1881 letter to the *American Journal of Education*, John D. Philbrick, former Boston school superintendent, described the newly opened Boston Latin and English High School as "by far the best specimen of school architecture in the country,—the first conspicuous example of a new type. . . ."[1] Philbrick's boast was not without merit since the building contained many architectural aspects previously unknown in American schools, such as interior courtyards, a military drill hall, and toilets on every floor, as well as infrequently used features like a gymnasium and an assembly hall large enough to hold the entire student body.[2] The Boston Latin and English High School represented a significant step toward the transformation of the high school building in America (Fig. 2.1).

Boston Latin and English was the capstone of John Philbrick's illustrious educational career.[3] Decades earlier he had been involved with the development of the "graded school" concept, whereby children were separated into classes according to their age and expected to follow a graduated curriculum. This contradicted the previous practice of lumping students into the same classroom regardless of their age or ability. The so-called "Quincy Plan," named after a Boston-area school, affected school architecture, since the age-graded system required teachers to have separate rooms for their particular classes. One-room schoolhouses could not adequately support such a program.[4]

Fig. 2.2. Akademische Gymnasium, Vienna, Austria.

Philbrick's interest in educational environments continued during two terms as Boston's superintendent (1857-1874 and 1876-1878). He toured Europe and became intrigued by German and Austrian school architecture. As Philbrick wrote in a letter to Henry Barnard (printed in the *American Journal of Education*), he was deeply impressed by the Akademische Gymnasium (1867) in Vienna (Fig. 2.2).[5] That school was also included in a highly-regarded book on school architecture by English architect E. R. Robson.[6] The Akademische Gymnasium building was a four-story hollow square with classrooms arranged along the building's exterior walls and corridors ringing an interior court open to the sky. Like many German and Austrian schools, it included a gymnasium for physical activities and a grand examination hall for large group instruction, in addition to regular classrooms for forty to sixty students. There was nothing comparable, in terms of size, layout, and special rooms, anywhere in America.

The Akademische Gymnasium's plan would influence the Boston Latin and English High School. Boston's city architect George A. Clough designed the school in 1877, possibly with help from Philbrick. Boston Latin and English's building was unique in many ways. For example, it held a wide variety

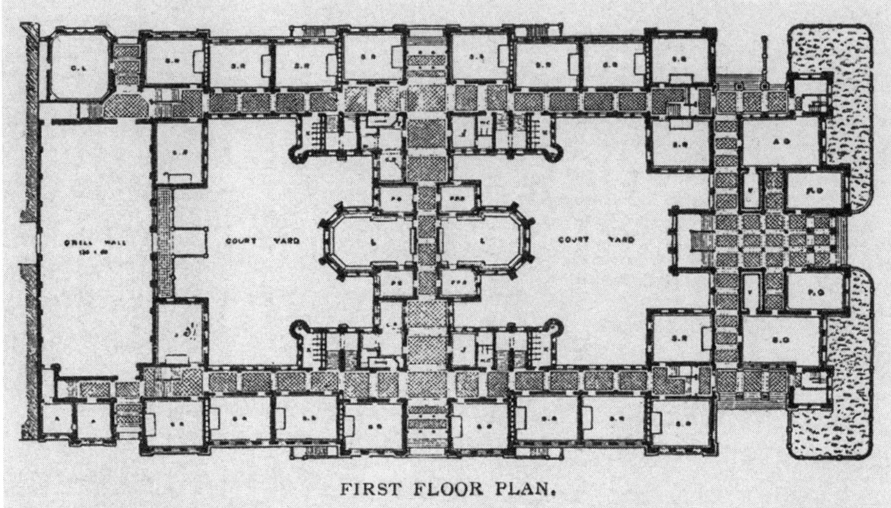



Fig. 2.3. First-floor plan, Boston Latin and English High School. Compare with Chicago's contemporary Division schools (Figs. 1.6-1.7).

of specialized rooms beyond classrooms: science lecture rooms, a chemistry laboratory, a military drill hall, a gymnasium, and administrative offices. Other high schools from the period contained some of these rooms, but rarely all of them. Boston Latin and English's salient characteristic, adapted from the Akademische Gymnasium, was the open interior courtyard (Fig. 2.3). This may have been the first instance of such a plan in an American school.[7] Clough arranged rooms around the courtyards along one side (the outside) of a corridor, just as in the German and Austrian schools Philbrick admired. As Philbrick pointed out in the article, "The superiority of this court plan over what may be called the solid plan, which has hitherto prevailed, is found more especially in the advantages it affords for light and air."[8] These open courtyards allowed light and air to enter the classrooms from windows in both the exterior facade and the interior corridor. Light therefore penetrated deep into the rooms, while air circulated freely through the building. The plan also facilitated students' movement through the school's various spaces through wide hallways and strategically placed stairs.

Besides these innovations, other factors helped shape the building's design. Health concerns inspired administrators to include the gymnasium. Safety concerns were evident in the state-of-the-art fireproof construction.

Care was taken to furnish the corridors with sculptures to enhance the students' aesthetic appreciation. Overall, Philbrick believed there were sixteen characteristics that truly set the school apart from its contemporaries, the most significant being the courtyard plan.[9] Some aspects of the design, however, were firmly within nineteenth-century tradition. Room sizes were standardized at 32' x by 24', with no spatial differentiation for the subjects taught within them. The auditorium was located on the top floor, indicating that it was predominately for student use and not generally accessible to the public. The Boston Latin and English High School's facade reflected common stylistic tastes with its large, hipped roofs and prominent chimneys.

The Boston Latin and English High School was an early milestone in school architecture reform. Boston educators thought so highly of the project that they sent the plans to the Paris Exposition of 1878, where an "international jury on secondary education" awarded the design a gold medal.[10] Decades after opening, the building still drew praise from educators and architects as the first well-designed American high school building. The dean of American school architecture in the late nineteenth century, Edmund M. Wheelwright of Boston, wrote in 1898 that "in the Latin and English High School of Boston . . . is found the first important application of sound principles of architectural planning to the school buildings of this country."[11] Similarly, noted Kansas City high school principal Gilbert B. Morrison identified it as "the first high school building which marked distinctively an epoch in school house architecture in this country."[12]

Despite the success of Boston Latin and English High School, the advice of early reformers concerning the schoolhouse's contribution to students' health and safety, as well as its didactic and inspirational value, seems to have been largely unheeded by a significant number of school architects into the 1880s. Urban schoolhouses like Chicago's high schools continued to be built in "egg-crate" fashion, with identical floors of square or rectangular boxes cut into equal size rooms stacked one above the other.[13] These buildings would be unable to accommodate the radical changes in enrollment and curriculum that were forthcoming in the next decades. A new type of school building would be needed that integrated educational, architectural, and social developments.

In the mid-nineteenth-century schoolhouse, as described previously, the connection between architecture and education was tenuous—except for rare cases, social, technological, and educational forces did not yet impact school architecture. Specially-designed school buildings were unnecessary given the limitations of a classroom method that emphasized memorization and recitation and the late nineteenth-century high school's constricted curriculum. But a few visionaries like John Philbrick realized that American schools were severely lacking when compared to their European counterparts. "Vienna knows how to build," wrote Philbrick in 1873. "The reason of this is, that in Vienna, when a school-house is planned, it is done by the combined science and wisdom of the most accomplished architects, and the most accomplished pedagogists. No mere whim of a schoolmaster, and no mere whim of an inexperienced and uneducated architect, is allowed to control the design."[14] English architect E. R. Robson made a similar point in 1874, writing that American school architecture had not yet been "reduced to a science."[15] Robson evaluated the state of school buildings here: "As in England, there is much critical investigation and discussion of education itself, but no trace that some of the vital points affecting the buildings (and, therefore, indirectly the education), such as the proper amount, distribution, and kind of light, the necessity of 'through'—or summer—ventilation, the most wholesome, efficient, and economical kind of artificial ventilation, and others, have, as yet, been sufficiently tackled at close quarters or in the careful manner common to Germany."[16] American school architecture in general, and Chicago schools in particular, would indeed be "reduced to a science" by the early 1900s, as designers developed standard architectural solutions to problems of health and safety, organization and arrangement, and aesthetics.

## The Last Division High Schools

Writers in Chicago journals and newspapers during the late nineteenth century did not discuss such issues of school architecture. Instead, both school officials and the public seemed to realize the urgency of simply getting schools built. Chicago's population doubled between 1880 and 1890 as the city established itself as the economic capital of the Midwest. People flocked to Chicago from surrounding rural communities and immigrants poured in from central and northern Europe. By 1880, more than 10 percent of the city's population had been born outside the United States, and that figure would climb close to

Fig. 2.4. John J. Flanders, West Division High School, 1886. Flanders' buildings were the first in the city to architecturally express the high school's growing importance to society.

40 percent in the subsequent decades.[17] And an 1889 annexation brought the nearby townships and villages of Jefferson, Lake View, Lake, and Hyde Park into Chicago's city limits, adding 120 square miles and over 300,000 citizens to the city, as well as six high schools. The first generation of Division high schools, created amid a flurry of construction in the early 1880s, had been an initial effort to surmount a critical high school enrollment crisis resulting from the population explosion. As the decade wore on, the city council authorized a second pair of division schools that notably deviated from their rather heterogeneous predecessors. The last two division schools would introduce the most contemporary ideas on educational architecture to the city.

## West Division II

The first Chicago high school to be consciously designed according to the same late-century interest in aesthetics that spawned buildings like Cleveland Central High School was the second incarnation of West Division High School (John J. Flanders, 1886) (Fig. 2.4). Rising high school enrollments in Chicago's central section necessitated an additional building. The North and South Division schoolhouses had been built with an eye toward future expansion, and were larger than necessary when opened.[18] North Division, designed to hold 624 students, enrolled approximately 300 in its first year, while South Division's initial enrollment was 391 in a similar 624-seat building. The situation at West Division, however, was much different. Intended to accommodate 735 students, the first-year enrollment reached over 600.[19] Only six years after opening, West Division was so overcrowded that a new four-story, twenty-four-room building for 1,000 students was erected about 2.5 miles west of downtown at the intersection of Ogden Avenue and Congress Street.

This second West Division High School (West Division II) diverged from its predecessors in size and appearance—it was much larger and deliberately intended to be an eye-catching work of architecture. Chicago Board of Education Architect John J. Flanders introduced a new kind of architectural embellishment to the city's schools. Flanders, who was not an educational specialist before becoming board architect, liked to use red brick walls above a light-colored stone base; combined with stone entablatures and window lintels, the ensemble created lively interactions of color. He increased his schools' visual complexity with multi-gabled roofs and octagonal or rounded bays running the full height of the building and topped with octagonal towers. The prominent rooflines added a third distinguishable color to the polychrome buildings.

For West Division II, Flanders employed all of these elements and added some new details: a tall clock tower, ventilation shafts disguised as belfries, and elaborate stepped gables on the roof, and oriels and closely-spaced banks of windows on the facade. With its strong picturesque profile and many visual highlights, the building's ebullient facade advertised secondary education's increasing prominence in Chicago. His work at West Division II and other schools was praised by the *Inland Architect and News Record*, an influential Midwestern professional magazine: "The buildings erected from [Flanders'] plans have cost less, are better adapted to the purpose, are more sightly than any the city could boast of, and they compare favorably with any in the country."[20]

West Division II's floor plan also departed from the previous division schools. It was considerably larger, and rectangular in form, with long corridors traversing the building. Besides its twenty-four classrooms, West Division included small recitation rooms on each of the first through third floors and a lecture room and science laboratory on the third floor. An assembly hall occupied the entire fourth floor. These amenities came at a price: West Division II cost the city $132,000, considerably higher than the $37,000 price tag of its predecessor or the $90,500 expenditure for South Division.[21] This aroused the ire of quite a few Chicagoans, including an editor for the *Chicago Tribune*, who argued that the first West Division School, "a plain and substantial building," was adequate and did not need replacement, especially "at the immense cost of $140,000." The writer further criticized the board of education for indulging in "useless ornamentation at the expense of the public" and being "too generous in its dealings with the contractors."[22]

Part of the higher cost may be attributable to the building's advanced heating and ventilation systems. A year before West Division II opened, school board president James R. Doolittle, Jr., listed in the *Annual Report* four major reasons why the Chicago public schools had abandoned hot air furnaces: the classroom atmosphere was "vitiated and de-vitalized" by being subjected to great heat; deleterious gases escaped through the overheated iron and poisoned the air; it was too difficult to secure the equal distribution of warm air in different parts of the building; and furnaces were fire hazards because of accumulated combustible dust in the flues.[23] To control these problems, West Division II was equipped with the most modern steam heating/ventilating system available. This was an important aspect of contemporary school architecture, for schoolrooms were designed with an eye toward proper ventilation. Educators and architects targeted the dark, dusty, poorly ventilated schoolhouse as a leading threat to the health and well being of young Americans, enlisting science as an ally to combat this threat. Psychologist G. Stanley Hall spoke for many when he declared that "the schoolhouse, which has been called more important for the development of the average child than the home itself, ought to be a *palace of health* (emphasis added)."[24]

Heating and ventilation issues were among the most vital aspects of school architecture to architects and educators alike. They were influenced by reports from leading medical and educational figures and organizations. For example, health investigators found extremely high levels of "carbonic acid" in the air in New York City classrooms; an article in the *Journal of the American*

*Medical Association* described the American classroom as "a propaganda of contagion;" a United States Bureau of Education pamphlet condemned the ventilation systems of the nation's schoolhouses; and engineer John S. Billings complained that "of all classes of municipal buildings in the United States, public or private, there are probably none which have until recently, been in such an unsatisfactory condition, as regards their ventilation, as the public schools."[25] Chicagoans recognized these issues as well. As early as 1874, the *Chicago Tribune* attacked poor schoolhouse ventilation. "It is a notorious fact that very few of the public-school-buildings are constructed with reference to scientific or thorough ventilation," claimed the author. "In cold weather, the children are compelled to breathe bad air, which is all the worse from being heated. In hot weather, the only way of ventilation is by opening windows and letting a strong draft of air upon the heads of children, the results of which is that the more delicate pupils invariably take cold."[26]

The classroom's form, height, and window size had important consequences for the manner in which air could be circulated. Many schoolrooms in cities around the country, including some in Chicago, had no provisions for air flow other than open windows, and were overcrowded with students. Before the 1870s there was little in the way of technical guidance for architects designing school buildings.

A growing interest in student health led late-century architects to think about improving schoolhouse heating and ventilation. Two major considerations, prompted by a desire to avoid the debilitating effects of vitiated air in the classroom, shaped their activities: the amount of cubic feet of air space needed for each student and the amount of cubic feet of fresh air-per-minute-per-student. Architect Charles Dwyer had previously recognized these problems in an 1856 book, in which he exclaimed, "Want of pure air is the certain agent of destruction to our youth; and of all places its terrible effects are more potent and more certain in the school-room than in any other, because of the mass of exhalation from so many lungs, some already diseased and pouring forth their noxious vapors to be inhaled by the victims around."[27]

A concern for healthy student bodies influenced architects and educators to implement improved ventilating systems. Ventilation standards seemed to be set fairly early although they were subject to variations among authorities. School designer James Johonnot addressed the first major issue—the amount of air space needed by each pupil—as early as 1871. Proceeding from the premise that "every child has a right to his own personality and his own share of uncontaminated air, and whatever deprives him of these becomes an outrage," Johonnot recommended 250 cubic feet of air space for each pupil.[28] He did not, however, relate how this would be worked out in designing the room or the ventilation system. Johonnot's advice was either amazingly prescient or represented an already-established standard—during the next fifty years architects hardly deviated from his recommendations. Almost all published authorities prescribed between 200 and 300 cubic feet of air space per pupil as a minimum.[29]

The air space-per-student requirement of a typical classroom was a determining factor in the size and shape of educational spaces. It related to the second major issue in heating and ventilation—the amount of air provided to each student per minute. Like the standards for cubic feet of air space, the cubic feet-per-minute regulations varied. Between the 1880s and 1920s, experts and amateurs recommended anywhere between twenty and forty cubic feet of air-per-minute for each pupil, with thirty being the most popular figure.[30]

School architects searched for ways to address these air space-per-pupil and fresh air-per-minute concerns. To add to the complexity, circulation mechanisms were inextricable from heating systems. Late nineteenth-century schoolhouses were heated either directly and indirectly. Direct radiation was the oldest form of heating. It consisted of a stove or a set of radiators in the room. The stove held a fire that radiated heat out into the room; radiators accomplished the same result using hot water or steam. Direct heating systems were notoriously inadequate, and their failures led to the widespread installation of indirect systems in urban schools by the 1870s. Indirect systems introduced air to the classroom that had been heated somewhere else, usually in the basement. Ventilation played a different role in these two heating systems. In direct radiation buildings there tended to be little or no ventilation, prompting teachers to open windows for fresh air. Indirect heating systems included air circulation mechanisms to provide fresh air as well as heat.

The heating and ventilating apparatus in most large urban high school buildings prior to the 1890s used heated flues to induce airflow and control temperature. The most common method of doing this was with a gravity system, used in Chicago schools before the 1880s. Hot air, hot water, or steam from the furnace heated the ducts that traveled to individual rooms. Air circulated through the building because the air outside the structure was colder and heavier than the air inside; the temperature differential caused outside air to be drawn into the building through vents and up through the system. Hot air systems, which forced heated air directly from the furnace to the classroom, proved difficult to regulate and produced additional problems.

The intricate nature of ventilation systems inevitably led to problems. Gravity systems never worked as well as planned. They were at their best in very cold weather. Most often, though, rooms were stiflingly hot—which prompted teachers to open windows, thereby defeating the entire system—or extremely cold. The accumulation of discharged air from fifty or more bodies in a classroom was difficult to expel through temperature regulation. Windy days adversely affected the building by pushing cold outside air through the schoolhouse's many cracks and openings. And gasses and dust from the fuel (usually coal) used to heat the air managed to find its way through the flues and into the classrooms. As a result of these problems, some school architects and engineers began to experiment with circulating air through the school building by mechanical means. By the end of the nineteenth century, mechanical ventilation (using fans to circulate the air rather than temperature differentials) had become the method of choice. Englishman J. D. Sutcliffe reported that on an 1891 tour of American school buildings on the East Coast, approximately 90 percent of the ventilation systems he inspected used the "Smead System" hot-air furnace.[31] When Sutcliffe returned to the States in 1905, the Smead System was nonexistent, and all the schools he visited combined steam or hot-water heating with a fan system. These "plenum systems," like the one installed in West Division II, were an improvement over the complicated gravity systems of the earlier generation. Plenum systems used mechanical power to drive large basement fans that circulated heated air through the building. A less-popular relative was the exhaust system, which placed the fans in the attic and pulled rather than pushed air through the ventilation circuit.[32]

Plenum systems became widely used in the early twentieth century. Electricity eventually allowed for such systems to become centrally controlled. The advantage (or disadvantage, depending on one's position) was that the central air system did not require the teacher to control room temperature. Unfortunately, the advanced designs often worked as poorly as their nineteenth-century precursors. Despite improved ventilation technology, the classroom situation was not always ideal, even into the 1920s. A teacher at the 1921 National Education Association convention complained about inadequate ventilation, uncomfortable temperature ranges, and unclean floors.[33] A 1924 study of New York City schools found that only 2 percent of the city's classrooms had functioning ventilation systems.[34] These conditions often led to conflicts between teachers and administration when the teachers opened windows to make their classrooms more comfortable and principals blamed them for creating ventilation problems.

Schoolhouse ventilation improved by the 1910s, mainly due to the application of the new mechanical systems. While the changes in heating and ventilation did not affect the school building as visibly as the changes in lighting, there were, nonetheless, repercussions for the entire school building. Modern high schools were intricate machines with huge mechanical instruments and miles of hidden ducts, flues, and pipes. The complexities of the improved air delivery machinery forced school architects to gain important knowledge about the mechanics of heating and ventilation, or to associate themselves with experts in the field. Some cities employed full-time engineers to design and implement ventilation systems. Chicago had an engineering specialist by the mid-1880s; when Englishman J. D. Sutcliffe visited in 1905, he found that the school board's heating, ventilation, and sanitation expert, Thomas J. Waters, co-designed school buildings with William Mundie, the school board architect.[35]

## North-West Division

West Division II was a notable step toward change and modernization in Chicago high school architecture. The last division school to be built carried that beginning boldly forward. Flanders' North-West Division High School (1892) was constructed at the corner of Claremont Street and Potomac Avenue (Fig. 2.5). The building's exterior was the antithesis of West Division II—instead of being highly decorated and visually stimulating, it was rather stark and utilitarian compared to Flanders' other works. Inside, however, Flanders made use of some of the most current developments in American school architecture. He supplemented North-West Division's basic classrooms with improved lighting features, a large lecture room, a drawing room, an assembly room, and a gymnasium—the first ever in a Chicago school (Fig. 2.6). There were even specialized rooms such as boys' and girls' dressing rooms, and

Fig. 2.5. John J. Flanders, North-West Division High School, 1892.

biological, physical, and chemical laboratories. Such room diversity reflected changes in the high school curriculum. Teachers were using more experimentation and less recitation in science classes; lectures were becoming more common; and administrators promoted physical education as a necessary part of secondary education (Fig. 2.7). Flanders also arranged the rooms so that standard classrooms comprised the base of the U-shaped plan and labs and other atypical spaces occupied the arms—an early Chicago example of the growing practice of "zoning" high school interiors by use. Curriculum and architecture evolved together as the American high school began to enter a new phase of existence.

One of the more advanced features of Chicago's North-West Division High School was the "unilateral lighting" found in its classrooms. The building had fifteen classrooms, and in every one of them light entered the room through windows in only one wall. This 100 percent ratio far exceeded the previous division schools: the first Division school—West Division—had unilateral lighting in only 20 percent of its classrooms, while the North Division building contained a mere 8 percent. Unilateral lighting represented the most progressive thinking of the day on an extremely important topic. Shortly after North-West Division opened, architect Warren Richard Briggs wrote, "Probably more has been written concerning the amount of light re-

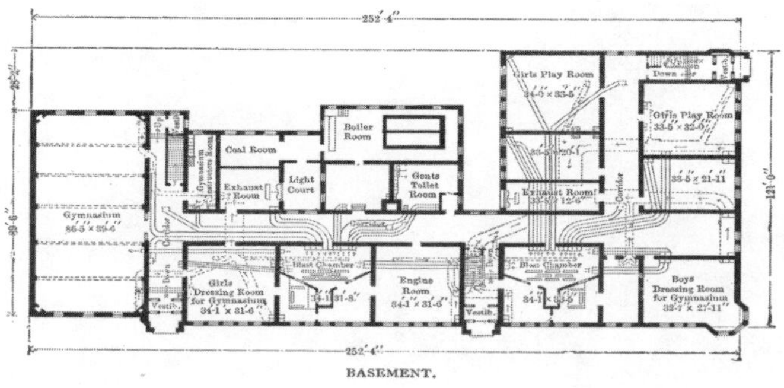

Fig. 2.6. First- and second-floor plans, North-West Division High School. The number and variety of non-traditional classroom spaces inside the high school increased as the curriculum expanded.

quired, and the way it should be introduced into the schoolroom, than about any other feature of school construction."[36] This claim was hardly an exaggeration; beginning in the 1870s, the schoolroom's adequate lighting became a vital aspect of school design.

Light was considered essential for protecting students' eyesight. Efforts to control light's proper distribution were warranted because of decades' worth of "evidence" that poor lighting had damaged students' eyes. A later book on schoolhouse lighting, for example, began with three "indisputable" statements based on decades of data collection: "1. A large percentage of the children in our schools have defective eyesight. 2. This percentage increases as the children advance from one school year to the next. 3. The cause has been traced in part to the school."[37] Writers quoted scientific studies that revealed American students' poor vision. A test of 1,000 Rhode Island school children found one-third of students had "defective vision" in one or both eyes;

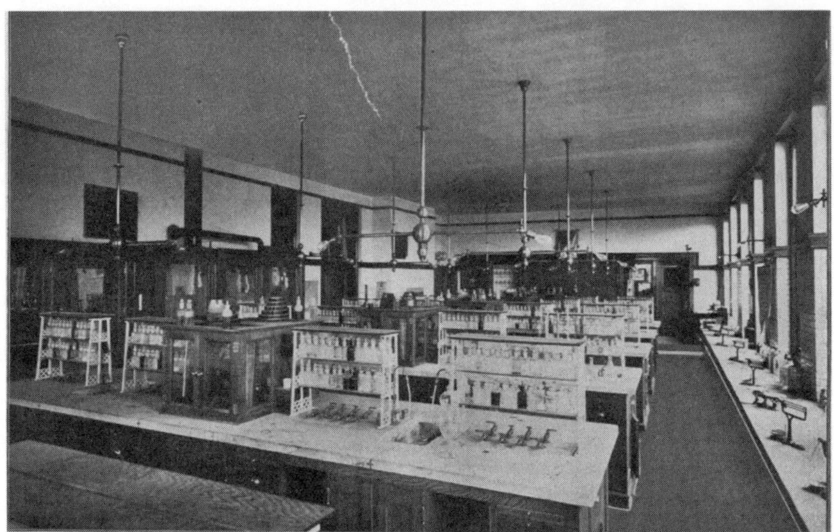

Fig. 2.7. Chemistry laboratory, Waller High School. Classes such as these required specific equipment and could not be properly conducted in the older school buildings.

a similar study of over 4,000 Chicago students uncovered 35 percent with problems.[38] In response to this study, the *Chicago Tribune* reported that the director of the Chicago Board of Education's Department of Child Study demanded, "something must be done at once, at almost any cost, to save school children's eyes."[39] Studies like these influenced the rapid evolution of lighting standards during this period. These standards would affect educational architecture by changing the typical classroom's size and shape and the school building's overall layout.

The earliest writers on school architecture had addressed the issue of adequate lighting in very general terms. Henry Barnard's *School Architecture* (1848) suggested "arrangements for light should be such as to admit an abundance to every part of the room, and prevent the inconvenience and danger of any excess, glare, or reflection, or of cross-light."[40] Allowing light from only two sides of the classroom, through windows located three to four feet from the floor and not behind the teacher or facing the students, would accomplish this goal. In *School-Houses* (1871), James Johonnot recognized that "too little attention is given to admitting light into school-rooms. . . ."[41] He suggested that pupils neither sit facing windows nor be attacked by "cross-lights" (light from windows in two walls at right angles to each other). According to Johonnot, these guidelines were not just common sense observations—they were supported by research.

Architects were not alone in recognizing the dangers of inadequate lighting. As early as 1875, Chicago Public Schools superintendent Josiah L. Pickard alerted his colleagues to the need for proper lighting, suggesting that all school buildings be constructed to allow light into their classrooms only over the students' left shoulders (because of the assumption that all children would be writing with their right hand). "The tendency to assume such awkward and unhealthy positions [of the head]," wrote Pickard, "arises from the lack of sufficient light, in still many more from the admission of the light in the wrong direction."[42] Chicago Board of Education President Norman Bridge included a section on "Increase of Light" in the 1882–83 *Annual Report*, where he commented on scientific standards for window area and lighting amounts "essential for the preservation of the eyesight of our pupils."[43] Later, in the 1910s, "hygiene experts" with an imprecise understanding of ophthalmology warned of inadequate lighting's disastrous effects on students' eyesight in passages like this: "the results of careful examinations made in all progressive countries prove conclusively that school conditions are responsible for a large part of the nearsightedness prevalent among the children of the higher grades."[44]

Educators and architects clearly believed the way school buildings allowed light to enter classrooms and corridors played an important role in protecting students' vision. By the 1890s, the idea that pupils should receive natural light from a single row of windows behind their left shoulder (the "uniform source rule") would become well established.[45] The desire for unilateral lighting altered schoolhouse design, as classrooms were rotated in various directions in an effort to comply with the uniform source rule. Plans of all types during this period—like North-West Division's—depict classrooms turned in divergent directions to allow unilateral lighting. Blank, windowless walls—an attempt to avoid "cross lights"—became widespread in schools after 1900 though they would have appalled architects of the previous generation (see, for example, Fig. 4.8). Often the blank wall appears as an awkward space on the building's exterior that interrupts the window rhythm. Photographs of buildings from this time period show many with blank walls, obviously a consequence of following the unilateral lighting rule. There were, however, other ways to reconcile function and aesthetics. Many architects placed laboratories or other non-classroom rooms—where students participated in more active learning than sitting and reading—in a building's corners, and lined the classrooms along the sides; this allowed all classrooms to have only single exposures while maintaining the rhythm of the windows and avoiding blank walls. The maxim that students should only receive light over their left shoulder remained virtually unchallenged until the widespread introduction of artificial illumination in the 1920s rendered it obsolete.

The increased attention to light's effects on student eyesight modified the individual classroom's form. Architects calculated the schoolroom's proper dimensions based in part on the amount and source of light. According to renowned Boston school architect Edmund Wheelwright, American classrooms were too large and could be reduced—to 24' x 32' for primary schools and 28' x 32' for grammar schools. This would allow light to properly penetrate all parts of the room from a bank of windows along the left-hand wall as students faced the teacher's desk. Ideally, such windows would begin at a height three feet above the floor and extend to within six feet of the ceiling. Chicago architects followed these decrees: classrooms in the second West Division High School were 25' x 32' while those in North-West Division were only slightly larger at 27' x 32'. These dimensions would hold steady in later years; most classrooms in the 1919 Robert Lindblom High School, for example, were 24' x 29'.

Even after electrical illumination became prevalent, the typical classroom's size and shape and its location in the plan remained unchanged. The windows' importance also influenced the schoolhouse's exterior, as the banks of regularly spaced windows required to light the individual classrooms created a distinguishable rhythm across the facade. Consequently, fenestration patterns became a prominent aesthetic aspect of schoolhouse facades in the early twentieth century.

Proper lighting eliminated the possibility of excessive glare and strong contrasts, both of which were thought to damage students' vision. Reformers believed the dark, cramped mid-nineteenth century schoolhouse was a dangerous place where "the eye is dazzled, irritated, and often permanently injured by working on objects that are directly illuminated by the sun."[46] Architects, educators, and hygiene experts expounded on the proper color for blackboards (gray or green), classroom walls (buff, cream, or light green), ceilings (light but not white), dados (the bottom portion of a divided wall—dull but harmonizing with the rest of the room) and window shades (light or cream), as well as acceptable materials for walls and floors.[47] The *Chicago Tribune* even joined in the discussion, suggesting "an improved system of lighting schoolhouses, especially the banishment of blackboards and frequent whitewashing of the walls, might save some eyes."[48] The *Tribune* writer was repeating the popularly-held belief that white was to be avoided in the classroom, for, as Walter J. Kenyon explained in 1906, "It is the common testimony of physicians that the glaring whitewash intensifies nervous afflictions and injures the eyes."[49] Later writers were even more scientific on the subject of color and illumination, often citing appropriate figures for "candlepower per square inch" or "Lumens per square foot."[50] The combination of rational planning and improved technology did not, however, eliminate students' vision problems, which led some experts to blame teachers. In 1904, educator Stuart H. Rowe found teachers "indirectly responsible for the majority of defective eyes found among pupils enjoying the advantages of well-lighted modern buildings;" their greatest sins were the "careless and ignorant manipulation of the shades," failure to correct bad reading posture, and inattentiveness to students with poor vision.[51]


## The End of the Century

As health concerns were reshaping Chicago's public high school buildings toward the end of the century, the city leaped into national prominence through a series of both flattering and infamous events. The World's Columbian Exposition of 1893 brought millions of visitors to the city from around the world, while the Pullman Railroad Strike the following year brought violence and the U.S. Army. Chicago had grown into the commercial and economic powerhouse of the Midwest. It was the nation's second largest city behind New York, and its schools were becoming more overcrowded than ever. Between 1890 and 1900, the number of pupils in Chicago's public schools almost doubled, from 135,541 to 255,718 (see Table 1A).[52] The high school growth rate was even more rapid, rising over 300 percent.[53]

Chicago's schools were the focus of an intense debate in 1893 over the proper curriculum and, by extension, the fate of working-class children. A "fads and frills" controversy erupted with roots in a nationwide economic depression that left the city's schools in a precarious financial position. Although the school system owned some of the most expensive real estate in the city, dating back to the original platting of Chicago in 1837, the city council, which controlled those lands, rented them far below market value to businesses like the *Chicago Tribune*.[54] Coupled with a lack of interest income from the school fund and insufficient tax revenues, this dearth of resources greatly affected the board of education's ability to provide enough classroom space for the city's youth.[55] In the midst of a weakened economy, conservative elements concerned about overcrowding attacked what they thought were frivolous and costly courses; in particular, the conservatives lashed out against physical education, foreign languages (especially German), singing, drawing, nature study, and clay modeling. The *Chicago Record-Herald* estimated that teaching these unnecessary subjects cost $1 million per year.[56] Rival *Chicago Tribune* published thirty editorials in 1893 against "fads and frills," depicting the expenditure for such subjects as a crime when children were being turned away from the public schools for lack of space.[57]

Organized labor aligned itself against these conservative interests. Labor representatives felt that eliminating special topics would deprive working-class students of the same rich educational experience enjoyed by their wealthier counterparts. The *Tribune* countered by ridiculing the suggestion that all students should receive an equal education. Heralding a bitter debate over vocational training that would shake the school system twenty years later, the *Tribune* warned that allowing children to study needless subjects would eventually lead to the undesirable and untenable policy of "sending to college all the children of working men."[58]

The fads and frills controversy mainly affected the city's primary schools. Chicago's high schools, on the other hand, flourished. A new era of high school building began in the 1890s in Chicago and other cities across the country. Architects created these buildings with more attention to students' health and safety and the school's curriculum than ever before. Curriculum expansion created more varied courses of study, which in turn necessitated unprecedented spaces within the schoolhouse. And the buildings simply needed to be larger than those of previous generations. Chicago's high school

Fig. 2.8. John J. Flanders, Hyde Park High School, 1894.

student population swelled from just under 3,000 in 1890 to over 36,000 in 1920—a phenomenal growth rate of 1,280 percent during a period when the total school population grew by 290 percent and the city's population rose by 240 percent (see Appendix).[59] High schools also acquired a more visually prominent appearance as their creators and overseers attempted to materially represent the institution's increasingly important role in everyday life.

There were ten public high schools in Chicago in 1890. Six had been brought within the public schools' jurisdiction after the 1889 annexation. One annexed community, Hyde Park, already had a three-story, thirteen-room brick high school building that needed replacement, especially in light of the city's decision to transfer students to Hyde Park from the overcrowded South Division building. Board architect John Flanders' designed the new Hyde Park High School (1894) (Fig. 2.8). The building was larger than the division schools, with eighteen classrooms, multiple science laboratories, a gymnasium, and an assembly hall. Almost 1,000 students could be accommodated under its broad roof. For Hyde Park's scenic exterior, Flanders returned to the visual complexity of West Division II. The building featured color and material contrasts, octagonal towers, and an active roofline of gables and chimneys. From the outside an observer could see that Hyde Park had far more window area than any previous

Chicago high school, to the extent that the building's facade was comprised almost as much of glass as stone. This feature promised a well-illuminated set of rooms inside. The board of education, proud of its new secondary school, boasted that "in architectural beauty [it] will compare favorably with any other public-school building in the country. It is supplied with the most perfect system of steam heating, sanitary ventilation, and electric service. It is the largest High School building in the city, and in the finish and furnishing throughout is considered to be the most complete and suitably adapted for the purpose of its erection."[60] Architecturally, Hyde Park High School exhibited the early stages of a transition wherein high school buildings required different types of spaces on the inside and architects struggled to find an appropriately monumental exterior expression to highlight the building's importance.

The architectural transformation of Chicago's public high schools began in earnest in the 1890s, precipitated by mixture of social, educational, and technological factors. The most important influences on this transition can generally be grouped into two main categories—the high school's evolving role in American society, and administrative and curricular reforms. The next chapter examines these forces in detail as they interacted to create the modern high school building.

## Chapter Three

# EDUCATIONAL AND SOCIETAL REFORMS

## High School and Society

The high school's function began to change in the late nineteenth century. Societal demands and governmental legislation combined to transform the secondary education system from a rather limited institution for imparting mental discipline and moral virtue to a mass public institution focused on managing the behavior of large groups of adolescents and preparing them for life as citizens in a modern industrial democracy. High school enrollments across the country multiplied at incredible rates due to stiffer child labor and compulsory education laws, foreign immigration and rural migration, the recognition of adolescence as a distinct period of life, and a new public attitude toward secondary education. This rich mixture of myriad forces reshaped schoolhouses in Chicago and other cities in ways that would make them much different from their nineteenth-century predecessors.

## Child Saving

A substantial shift in Americans' perspective on childhood occurred in the nineteenth century. In the 1700s, people tended to view childhood as an inconvenience—something to get through as quickly as possible on the road to adulthood. Adults thought of childhood as "a vulnerable, frustrating period of human inadequacy."[1] Children were often dressed and treated like miniature adults, and expected to participate in adult activities to supplement family incomes. Large numbers of children worked at part-time or full-time jobs, whether on farms, in shops, or in the increasingly common manufacturing plants. Financially stable families also encouraged (or forced) their children to work, simply because many adults considered education a waste of time. In the early nineteenth century, however, a new attitude toward childhood began to develop. Manufacturers started producing more child-specific goods like infant clothes, toys, and small furniture, targeting middle- and upper-class parents. Adults began to take more interest in children's play, and a more sentimental opinion of childhood arose. By the century's end, evolutionary theory's substantial inroads into American culture contributed to revised ideas about children. Most significant was the concept that children are biologically and mentally different from adults. The public began to view childhood as a special stage of life, to be protected, if possible, to allow for proper moral and cognitive development. This emerging model has been described as "sheltered childhood."[2]

Unfortunately, for many families the sheltered childhood was an unrealistic middle-class dream. The harsh reality was that countless Americans were introduced to working life at a very young age. The United States Census Bureau reported 765,000 children ages ten to fifteen were "gainfully employed" in 1870 (13 percent of the population for that age group), 1,750,000 in 1900 (18 percent), 1,990,000 in 1910, and 1,061,000 in 1920, though these numbers are estimates and probably underrepresented the actual figures.[3] An Illinois Bureau of Labor Statistics investigation found over 5,000 children working ten- to fifteen-hour days in Chicago in 1880. A subsequent study two years later calculated that 5 percent of all Chicago children ages eight to fifteen had never attended school.[4]

Such statistics appalled progressive reformers, whose beliefs were molded by the ideal of the sheltered childhood where children were unsophisticated and largely helpless beings who needed to be nurtured by adults in a sympathetic environment. Child labor was the antithesis of this ideal. Activists considered the long hours and sometimes brutal conditions under which children often labored a source of mental and moral degeneration, which in turn resulted in higher levels of juvenile delinquency and antisocial behavior.[5] The reformers therefore directed a sustained attack on child labor to get more children out of the workplace and into school. Focusing mainly on crowded urban environments, the child labor movement was another link in a lengthening chain of nineteenth century "child saving" initiatives promoted by social reform groups. Chicago's famous settlement houses, like Jane Addams' Hull House and Graham Taylor's Chicago Commons, also became substantially involved in anti-child labor activities.

Chicago's educators were keenly aware of child labor's dangers. As early as 1865, Superintendent Josiah L. Pickard lamented that "many a child has been sacrificed mentally and morally as well as physically to the pecuniary interest of the parent."[6] But the "evil" of child labor was not easily combated due to the combined effects of parental necessity or neglect and opposition from American business. Some parents saw no need to educate their children or simply could not afford to lose the child's income, while businesses objected to efforts to constrain their pool of inexpensive workers. The most common reform approach to dealing with these obstacles was to regulate, rather than eliminate, child labor. Beginning in the late nineteenth century, lawmakers restricted the hours children could work and the age at which they could begin working.[7] Illinois' first child labor law, adopted in 1893, prohibited employment of any child under thirteen without a special certificate (with liberally granted exceptions). A tougher 1903 law barred all children under fourteen from working at "remunerative labor" and allowed fourteen- to sixteen-year-olds to work only if they had received an "age and school certificate" approved by the superintendent.[8] These restrictions certainly reduced child employment levels throughout the state. The Illinois Chief Factory Inspector was proud to report that the number of children employed in the state had decreased from 8 percent in 1893 to 1.5 percent in 1907 (9 percent in Chicago).[9] Nonetheless, there were still thousands of children working, especially in the Chicago area.

Child labor legislation often went hand-in-hand with compulsory attendance laws requiring children to spend a certain portion of each year in school. By 1918, every state had mandated school attendance to some degree. These laws generally obligated children between the ages of five and fourteen to spend most of their days in school. The Illinois General Assembly passed its first compulsory education legislation in 1883. The law required all eight- to fourteen-year-old children to attend school at least twelve weeks per year. Illinois was neither early nor late in its commitment to required attendance. Massachusetts had instituted the nation's first compulsory attendance law in 1852, but by 1886 only fifteen states, or 39 percent of the country, had enacted similar laws.[10] The Illinois statute faced strong opposition and was never widely enforced. In the early years, public opinion on the issue seemed to be split. The *Chicago Inter-Ocean* newspaper expressed the sentiments of many when it proclaimed, "Compulsory education is preposterous. Education is not necessary for everyone."[11] The fact that the Chicago Board of Education felt the law was unenforceable, and freely granted "good cause" exemptions, did not help the reformers' cause.

As the years passed, however, public support for compulsory attendance grew. The *Chicago Tribune* chastised the school board in an extended series of editorials in 1888-89 for its lackadaisical enforcement of the state compulsory education law, and the Chicago Woman's Club presented the board with a petition urging stricter application of the law to battle "the appalling increase of crime among youth, the large number of vagrant children, and the employment of child labor in the City of Chicago."[12] Noncompliance with the child labor law was so widespread, and criticism so virulent, that the school board formed a special committee to explore the problem and suggest solutions. The committee concluded that overcrowded schools—not children's employment or disinterest—were the main problem, and it recommended better implementation of the state rules, free textbooks for poor children, and the creation of a department of compulsory education.[13] The board responded by calling a public meeting of interested civic organizations and announcing a new commitment to compulsory education.

The Illinois General Assembly amended the state compulsory attendance law in 1889 to boost mandatory school time from twelve to sixteen weeks per year, with at least eight of those weeks to be consecutive. Chicago thereafter instituted a campaign to identify the number of children working in the city. Weak compulsory education laws and ineffective enforcement remained a sticking point with many critics, however, including the *Chicago Tribune*, which dedicated thirty editorials to compulsory attendance issues in a ten-month period during 1890.[14] The Illinois compulsory education law "does not yet work thoroughly," wrote Chicago's school superintendent in 1899. "As a consequence . . . the average school life of the Chicago child is but five years."[15]

Although every state had passed some form of compulsory education legislation by 1918, these laws tended to be less successful for high school-age youths, since most provisions either stopped at fourteen or leniently granted excuses or work permits for those over that age. Yet there was an incredible rise in the number of high school students. Nationwide high school enrollment grew from 202,963 in 1890 to 1,851,965 in 1920, representing an increase of over 900 percent in three decades, while the general population rose by 245 percent (see Table 1B).[16] Only 3.7 percent of the nation's fourteen- to seventeen-year olds attended high school in 1880 compared to 31.2 percent in 1920.[17] During that same period the number of public high schools in America swelled from 2,526 to 14,326.[18]

Compulsory attendance and child labor laws cannot wholly explain the enrollment explosion, although those forms of legislation did act to rescue thousands of adolescents from the working world. Immigration was another major contributor. Over twenty-three million immigrants arrived in America between 1880 and 1920, many flooding the northern industrial cities. In Chicago, for example, between 1890 and 1920 some 30-40 percent of the population was comprised of foreign-born whites; in 1880, that figure had been only 12 percent.[19] In 1908, the U.S. Senate Immigration Committee studied nearly forty cities across the country and found that 58 percent of all public school students in those cities had fathers who were born abroad. Chicago had the second highest ratio (behind New York) with almost seven out of ten students with foreign-born parents.[20] These numbers are particularly compelling when considered in light of the decreasing population of native-born Americans during the same period.

Rural-to-urban migration patterns also brought more students into the nation's high school classrooms. America officially became an urban nation during this period. The percentage of the national population living in urban areas (defined as those with over 2,500 people) grew from 35 percent in 1890 to 51 percent by 1920.[21] The "Great Migration" of blacks from the rural South to the industrial North beginning in the late 1910s affected such figures. Significantly, however, this exodus had little impact on high school enrollment. Despite Chicago's reputation as a magnet for rural blacks seeking employment, and the fact that the city's black population more than tripled between 1890 and 1920, the number of black students in the Chicago schools rose by less than 200 percent.[22] Nationwide, blacks accounted for less than 2 percent of all high school students by 1920.[23]

## Adolescence

An evolving public attitude toward childhood and a concern for working youngsters were not the only new influences on American secondary education. In the early twentieth century, the stage of life that we now know as "adolescence" was first recognized as a result of psychological studies of the differences between younger and older children. The "invention" of adolescence had a permanent effect on American society.[24] Historian Joseph Kett has pointed out that in the decades after 1900, "a biological process of maturation became the basis of the social definition of an entire age group," which resulted in "the massive reclassification of young people as adolescents and the creation of institutions to segregate them from casual contacts with adults."[25]

Educators, psychologists, journalists, jurists, and social workers were largely responsible for distinguishing this age group. A major catalyst for such interest was the seminal book, *Adolescence*, by psychologist G. Stanley Hall, leader of the "child study movement" in the late nineteenth century.[26] Like much work in developmental studies at this time, Hall's approach was informed by evolutionary theory and its emphasis on change over time. Hall described the teenage years as "a stormy period of great agitation, when the very worst and best impulses in the human soul struggle against each other for its possession," and recommended that young adults be provided opportunities to participate in athletics, group activities, and special organizations to shelter them from the pressures of the adult world while they negotiated their way through this often-confusing stage of life.[27]

A salient characteristic of the adolescent stage was a powerful desire to form peer associations. Hall therefore suggested that rather than lose boys to wanton street gangs, their natural impulse to congregate could be accommodated through boys' clubs and playground organizations, which would provide them with productive outlets for their energies.[28] Chicagoans embraced these ideas with particular fervor. The city became a center of the developing "playground movement" in the early 1900s.[29] Progressive Era playgrounds were not simply urban parks with teeter-totters and sandboxes; they also provided the opportunity for adults to properly direct children's behavior in ways that would promote moral and cognitive development. Between 1899 and 1909, Chicago spent nearly $15 million on playgrounds and recreation centers.[30] Nationally, city governments spent over $100 million on playgrounds during this the same period.[31]

Other factors in addition to shifting conceptions of childhood and adolescence have been advanced to explain the prolonging of childhood dependency in the nineteenth century, including the shrinking ratio of children to adults (making children scarcer and more precious) and the increasing complexity of the "production-oriented society."[32] There was a Darwinian argument as well; according to a Chicago school superintendent, evolution favored extended childhood. "We are realizing and striving to obey the biologic law," wrote E. Benjamin Andrews, "that the species, race or nation that longest protects and trains its young is the most powerful in the struggle for life."[33] Whatever the sources, the consequence of this revised perception of American youths as "adolescents" was that it set them apart from—and considered them not quite ready for—the adult world. If teenagers were not to be treated like small children, but were not yet prepared for work, what were they to do with their time and how were they supposed to channel all the powerful impulses described by Hall into constructive behavior? The logical answer was to keep them in school. Public education became the nation's leading "adolescent-raising institution."[34] Educators would have to remodel their curricula and facilities accordingly. But the mental discipline and moral virtue traditions still reigned, and few urban high schools were in a position to fulfill this new responsibility.

## The High School's Role

Population statistics like those cited above reveal that there were more teenagers in American cities than ever before. But that fact did not necessarily correlate with higher secondary school enrollments. Something beyond poorly-enforced legal decrees had to entice adolescents into the schools. Evidence suggests that a new public attitude toward secondary education was a major influence on the rising high school enrollment. The public began to realize the virtues of expanded education for its young adults. In his seminal study of high schools, historian Edward Krug suggested that the enrollment surge could be explained both by the growing idea that school could lead one to a successful life and the tendency to consider education "a good thing in itself."[35] Similarly, historian Herbert Kliebard discerned that during this period "working people generally began to look to the schools to provide an education that would alleviate their economic anxieties and prepare their children to function successfully in the new industrial regime."[36] In general, the public started to view high schools more positively during the Progressive Era. No longer considered elite "culture factories" for children of privilege, by the early twentieth century common people increasingly perceived the high school to be the type of institution Chicago Superintendent of Public Schools George Howland had called "the Citizen's College"—a vehicle of social improvement that could benefit adolescents of all ethnic backgrounds and social classes.[37]

The high school's elevated status was part of an emerging public trend toward recognizing education's role in maintaining social order and perpetuating cherished ideas like freedom and democracy. John Dewey, the nation's most prominent progressive educator, asserted, "education is the fundamental method of social progress and reform."[38] In *The Promise of American Life*, the quintessential statement of American Progressivism, Herbert Croly preached the significance of education as the salvation of American democracy and the true path to individual self-improvement. "The real vehicle of improvement is education," wrote Croly, "It is by education that the American is trained for such democracy as he possesses; and it is by better education that he proposes to better his democracy."[39] However, although many agreed that education stood as a pillar of American society, problems arose when trying to determine just what education should be offered to the nation's adolescents.

As proponents worked to standardize a multi-tiered system of public education, they also tried to delineate the functions of each level. The primary grades were clearly for imparting basic skills and information, but neither the high school's mission nor its relation to higher education were so sharply distinguished. "Speaking roughly," wrote Yale President Arthur F. Hadley in 1902, "primary education aims to secure the necessary level of general intelligence; technical education aims to secure the necessary level of professional intelligence; secondary education aims at something in excess of these necessary minima."[40]

There was no consensus, however, on what "something in excess" really meant. Educators wrote articles with such titles as, "The High School: Its Necessity and Right to Exist as Part of the True System of Public Education," and "The High School: Its Relation to the Lower Grades of Public Schools," in attempts to resolve the issue of the high school's proper place.[41] Some school officials clung to the earlier nineteenth-century ideal of the high school as a place to train the elite, although "elite" came to mean intellectual more than social. "[T]he chief function of the public high school is to furnish the State with the directive power necessary for its political and social well-being," wrote Philadelphia high school teacher George Stuart in an 1888 article entitled, "The Raison d'Être of the Public High School."[42] He argued that the nation had a selfish interest in nurturing generations of future leaders rather than leaving that obligation "to chance." An alternate viewpoint focused on secondary education as a means for developing individual talents and personal values rather than as a breeding ground for future leaders. Charles F. Thwing, an Ohio professor, outlined this approach. "The obligation of the high school, therefore, first in time and first in importance, let it be at once said, is the duty of teaching students to think," he claimed. "A second obligation of the high school is to promote an intellectual and an intelligent interest in life . . . the high school is under obligation to make every boy and girl continuously interesting, and also to make life itself interesting." Finally, wrote Thwing, "the high school is under another obligation to which I shall simply refer. This duty I shall call a sense of values."[43] Another group of educators called upon the high school to specialize in vocational training to prepare teenagers for their adult jobs. This approach was aimed particularly at working class youths. Under such a program, wrote an educator in 1882, "the poorest and most neglected child is led to feel that there is something in the world for him to do which shall be well worth doing."[44] These viewpoints often conflicted and their tensions were never satisfactorily resolved. But all three perspectives attached a social significance to the high school that did not exist in previous generations.

The high school's heightened status was reflected in the school building's appearance. Architects across the country tried to enhance the visual presentation of their buildings by designing high schools that employed the same architectural language of civic authority as city halls and courthouses. Educators and architects paid more attention to two significant aspects of the school building in the 1890s: its didactic value and its place in the urban landscape. An editorial in the *American School Board Journal* addressed the first issue, exclaiming, "A ramshackle building is a discouragement to educational interests. A plain structure, even, is not stimulating. The outward appearance of a building has its influences which cannot be overestimated."[45] School architects agreed with such assessments. "Few are now found to maintain that the architectural effect of a schoolhouse is an unimportant consideration," wrote school architect Edmund Wheelwright two years later, "and that a beautiful schoolhouse does not do its part in the education of the young."[46] Some educators were particularly adamant about warning the public of bad architecture's ill effects on the nation's youth.[47] William George Bruce, publisher and editor of the influential *American School Board Journal*, expressed common feelings on the subject: "The education of the community is affected by its architecture—hence, an edifice dedicated to the cause of education, above all other public buildings, ought to set the pace for taste, simplicity and dignity in the matter of form and design. If we inculcate the rising generation, by worthy example, with a correct taste in architectural expression, the future will bring forth higher achievements in that direction."[48]

Pronouncements such as these had been rare in architectural and educational journals before 1890. Their proliferation after that date speaks to the high school's growing significance in American society. As a measure of that elevated status, numerous writers advocated a schoolhouse that not only had didactic value, but also symbolized public regard for education, or made integral connections with the urban environment. "Local pride in an educational system finds its gratification in a handsome structure," the *American School Board Journal* stated. "It is something that can be seen, and is regarded as an index to what the rest might be—in fact, serves as a sort of advertisement for many towns."[49] Architect John J. Donovan asserted that "There is nothing more impressive or hopeful in American democracy than the devotion of the people to education. . . . Unconsciously the spirit has been to represent this truly national devotion in the architecture of the public schools."[50]

Several writers placed the schoolhouse among society's most salient cultural buildings. "There are now being built in the towns and cities throughout the country small town halls, libraries, and schools, which are to form the ganglia of a higher public life," wrote C. Howard Walker in 1894.[51] Two years later, in the same journal (*Atlantic Monthly*), editor Horace E. Scudder opined, "The common schoolhouse is in reality the most obvious centre of national unity, and, with the growing custom of making it carry the American flag, it is likely to stand for a long time to come as the most conspicuous mark of a common American life . . . I suggest, as a practical course to be pursued by those persons in any town or village who are earnestly interested in the improvement of education there, that they give their energy to making the schoolhouse the most beautiful public building in the place."[52] Similarly, architectural critic A.D.F. Hamlin cited schoolhouses as "gauges of [a community's] enlightenment," and Kansas City high school principal Gilbert B. Morrison declared the schoolhouse "an infallible index of the educational status of the community in which it is located."[53]

Beyond its local significance, educational architecture could be linked to broader social ideals. "If [the school building] is beautiful," wrote C. H. B. Schaefer, "it will awaken in the youth the desire for refinement that leads to good citizenship."[54] University of Chicago sociologist and City Beautiful advocate Charles Zueblin related the schoolhouse to the success of the urban environment: "If the architecture of the schoolhouse, its decorations and surroundings, impress the child mind with the meaning of the beautiful, he will demand as a citizen a fairer city."[55] And architect Frank Irving Cooper wrote of a model school building that "represents a spiritual ideal. It will represent democracy, free education, hospitality and good-will."[56] These commentators and many others promoted a school architecture that materially embodied the unique mission of public education in a democratic society.[57]

## Order

Despite disputes over the curriculum's proper focus, or the high school's overall goal, most educators realized that the behavioral management of increasingly large numbers of adolescents was becoming a primary focus of American high schools. Chicago's high school enrollment figures reflected the rising popularity of secondary education. The city's high school population grew dramatically between 1880 and 1920. In 1880, 2.5 percent of all fourteen- to seventeen-year-olds in Chicago attended school; by 1915, the figure reached 11.6 percent.[58] The result of this massive enrollment rush was that many teenagers who had no academic inclinations and would not have attended school in previous generations were there at the turn-of-the-century. Public schools administrators, particularly at the high school level, faced the delicate problem of how and what to teach these students. Their response was to reconceive the high school as an "adolescent-raising institution" that exerted more control over students' lives than ever before.

In the Progressive Era, according to historian Thomas Gutowski, the public began to demand more from high schools than teaching academic subjects; "it was also charged with the responsibility for building their character, teaching them socially acceptable behavior, advising them on career selection, monitoring their health, introducing them to worthwhile avocations, making them into loyal citizens, and performing dozens of other tasks."[59] Educators sought these changes as well. The public high school thus became the locus of adolescent socialization and vocational preparation. University of Chicago sociologist Albion Small explained secondary education's new role to a group of teachers at a National Education Association meeting in 1896. Small claimed that the educator's job was not to transmit knowledge but to foster "the completion of the individual;" thus, the goal of education was the "adaptation of the individual to such cooperation with the society in which his lot was cast that he works best with the society in perfecting its own type." In other words, teachers "shall not rate themselves as leaders of children, but as makers of society."[60]

The idea of "making" society resonated with the early twentieth century progressive reformers who attacked the innumerable problems of America's larger cities with an optimistic mixture of enthusiasm and paternalism.[61] Rapid modernization, including rampant industrialization and escalating populations, contributed to health, sanitation, and crime issues as well as increasing ethnic, religious, class, and racial tensions. The progressive desire for change and improvement was rooted in a belief that proper administration and organization could cure the city's ills. Many Americans thought civic and social order could be achieved in the growing metropolis through compassionate, intelligent control by groups of experts. Stated rather simply, countless reform-minded Americans hoped that an orderly physical environment would help guide urban inhabitants toward orderly social behavior. Private reform associations across the country therefore pressed local governments for civic improvements such as better sanitation, less crowded neighborhoods, and more parks and playgrounds. In Chicago, the Civic Federation led the drive for a cleaner, better-organized city. The foundation formed in 1894 as "a protest against prevailing conditions of want, vice, and municipal corruption," and was responsible for instituting a number of social and political reforms.[62] Similarly, the City Club, an upper-class group

Fig. 3.1. Burnham & Bennett, Chicago Plan of 1909.

established in 1903, sought the "investigation and improvement of municipal conditions and public affairs in the City of Chicago."[63]

The impulse to improve cities extended to the fields of architecture and planning as well. Advocates of the City Beautiful movement in the early 1900s attempted to manifest progressive ideals in the physical environment. Architects and planners emphasized the benefits of stately new buildings for cultural and public institutions, often clustered together in "civic centers" and created in tandem with monumental tree-lined boulevards and spacious parks. Beautiful surroundings, it was felt, would stimulate citizens' civic pride, which in turn would cultivate responsible behavior and worker productivity. The ideal City Beautiful environment could "influence the heart, mind, and purse of the citizen."[64]

Daniel Burnham and Edward Bennett's unexecuted Chicago Plan of 1909 personified the City Beautiful movement (Fig. 3.1). In the project, created for the Commercial Club of Chicago, Burnham and Bennett envisioned a radically reconstructed city, with a reorganized street pattern, long blocks of nondescript commercial and residential buildings of uniform height and decoration, an extensive park system along the lakeshore, and a civic center dominated by an extraordinarily large city hall. A goal of plans like this was to order the environment in a way that would infiltrate the inhabitants' minds, helping them develop aesthetic taste and to reinforce orderly behavior.[65] Burnham and Bennett's expansive vision of the future city was actually predated by the remarkable Chicago South Park System. Beginning in 1903, Chicago constructed ten parks (most of them in densely-packed immigrant neighborhoods) throughout the south side. Each park contained athletic fields, playgrounds, swimming pools, and a field house with a library and lecture hall. No other American city before or since has created as much green space inside its boundaries. While relief from crowded, impoverished conditions was the main objective, the parks also provided opportunities for city residents to engage in activities that would enhance their physical, moral, and intellectual development—and so help them become better citizens.[66]

As a companion to the movement to reform American cities, educators and reformers recognized the public schools' unique position in respect to childrens' lives and began to utilize the educational system as a means of organizing and molding students' behavior. The term "social control" describes these actions—"the diverse efforts of social groups to bring the attitudes and behavior of their members into line with accepted and customary social expectations."[67] In the case of Progressive Era education, social control referred to school officials' attempts to shape the behavior of America's youth. Foremost among social control advocates in education was sociologist Edward A. Ross, who achieved recognition with his 1901 book, *Social Control: A Survey of the Foundations of Order*.[68] Like many who were anxious about contemporary trends toward chaos and confusion, Ross dreamed of a not-so-distant future where society was stabilized because every American would have developed "a sense of responsibility by dwelling on the social consequences of conduct."[69] Ross believed that in the pre-industrial past this type of behavior, which arose from man's inherent tendencies, occurred naturally. But in the emerging industrial world man's proclivities toward "sympathy, sociability . . . justice, and individual responsibility" were maladaptive.[70] The complexity of modern civilization required a system of artificial restraints imposed from outside the individual. Unfortunately, according to Ross and others, the traditional institutions for transmitting social values to children—family and church—had been severely weakened by the development of capitalist society. A replacement was therefore needed. Ross turned to public education, which he saw as the perfect tool for inculcating appropriate moral and social principles. The school, not the church or the family, was the most effective institution for instilling "the habit of obedience to external law."[71] He predicted that education would surpass religion "as the method of indirect social restraint."[72] This did not involve simple reflexive discipline, however; instead, Ross was trying to solve a greater dilemma—how to develop a new program of moral training in light of religion's diminished authority in the modern world.

The societal values promoted by Ross and others included obedience, temperance, cleanliness, and, for immigrants, the acquisition of good American habits of mind and action—a process that became known as "Americanization." European immigration to the United States peaked between 1900 and 1910, with millions of foreigners arriving in the "land of opportunity." Urban industrial centers like New York, Pittsburgh, Cleveland, and Chicago bore the brunt of this great exodus. In these cities children who, it was felt, needed to be trained in the ways of their adopted culture (and who, in turn, could help acculturate their older and less malleable family members) flooded the schools. The Americanization programs of urban public school systems sought to integrate these newcomers in the most efficient manner, for the good of society. "Education will solve every problem of our national life, even that of assimilating our foreign element," boasted a New York high school principal in 1902. "The nation has a right to demand intelligence and virtue in every citizen, and to obtain these by force if necessary."[73] While the focus of most Americanization programs was on the lower grades, high schools were also involved in the process. Illiteracy and English language education were the chief priorities, particularly during World War I. School officials around the country opened high school buildings for extensive evening classes targeting adults and working youth.

As architects transformed the high school building from a simple collection of box-like rooms to a large, varied complex, the building out of necessity also became an instrument of control. Rising enrollments created unprecedented organizational and disciplinary problems in the urban schools. The modern school building was a partial solution to these problems, channeling students into architectural spaces where their behavior could be more easily observed and directed.[74]

Planning the school's physical environment with an eye toward regulatory measures was not a novel idea; it had been an integral part of the early nineteenth-century Lancasterian schools.[75] In these "Monitorial" schools, where children were given military-like orders and moved through their lessons in rigid sequences, the building's spatial orderliness complemented the personal regulation sought by society as a whole. The spirit, but not the method, of Lancasterian schools was imported into the nascent public school system. School authorities tried to impose order on boisterous youngsters through a variety of administrative and architectural means.

In the mid-nineteenth century educators had been aware of the connection between architecture and behavior. James Johonnot recognized such a linkage when he wrote, "Certain fixed principles, both of instruction and discipline, are adapted to the different ages and developments of pupils. . . . A true . . . system of education [must apply these] principles in the arrangement of schools, and in the construction of schoolhouses."[76] As schools grew beyond the one-room stage, there was an increasing need for physical environments to facilitate student control and impart order. St. Louis superintendent and future U.S. Commissioner of Education William Torrey Harris expressed the mindset of many educators in 1871: "The first requisite of the school is Order: each pupil must be taught first and foremost to conform his behavior to the general standard."[77] Historian William Reese has noted that "discipline, self-control, [and] adherence to rules and regulations" were imperative in "schools that stressed deference to authority, sanctioned corporal punishment, and tried to integrate apathetic or hostile elements into a single educational system."[78] An example can be found in Dr. Joseph M. Rice's account of a St. Louis elementary school classroom:

> During several daily recitation periods, each of which is from twenty to twenty-five minutes in duration, the children are obliged to stand on the line, perfectly motionless, their bodies erect, their knees touching and feet together, the tips of their shoes touching the edge of a board in the floor. The slightest movement on the part of a child attracts the attention of the teacher . . . I heard one teacher ask a little boy: "How can you learn anything with your knees and toes out of order?" The toes appear to play a more important part than the reasoning faculties.[79]

The imposition of order, as Dr. Rice found during his tour of American schools, was more prevalent in classroom behavior in these years than in architectural design.

By the late nineteenth century educators' interest in using the school building as an instrument of control intensified. An illuminating article from the *American Architect and Building News* is unique in its detailed look at the relationship between architecture and discipline.[80] The author discusses a paper on school planning from the January, 1890 edition of the *Builder*, written by a "Head Master." The earlier article listed the "four chief foes" to school discipline as, "Disorder and Noise," "Bullying," "Petty Larceny," and "Indecent Writing." According to the "Head Master," the school architect can either "greatly aid" in the maintenance of discipline through his design or "can render good discipline almost impossible."[81] The architect might actually foster a lack of discipline by creating a school that has (a) a line of classrooms connected by a dark, narrow corridor, with a few sharp turns; and (b) stone paving in the halls, which enhances noise. Such a design will influence students to run down the long corridors, clash at the angles, and bully each other in the dark corners. The "Head Master's" solution to the discipline problem is worth quoting at length:

> Inside the school-building . . . [disorder, and noise, and bullying] are chiefly promoted by long, dark corridors. With short, wide, straight and well-lighted passageways, which can be supervised at a glance, they can easily be repressed indoors, but the scene of them may be transferred to the playground entrances, or outbuildings, and these must be arranged for easy inspection. Every corner of the playground should be visible from the head-master's room, and from some of the class-rooms: the entrances should be commanded, both from the head-master's room and the janitor's office, and the latter should be placed so that the janitor can oversee, also, the lavatories, and observe every one who enters or leaves them. The existence of the third defect in school discipline [petty larceny] may be said to depend entirely on the architect; if he plans the wardrobes so that they can be easily observed from the class-rooms, there will be no stealing from them: if he does not do so, there will inevitably be pilfering and consequent unhappiness. To meet the fourth evil [indecent writing], corridors should, as before, be few in number, light, and easily supervised; and their walls, as well as those of all lavatories and closets, should be lined with glazed bricks or tiles.[82]

The author, therefore, places a heavy burden on the school architect—the entire issue of student discipline either succeeds or fails because of the school building. While this view might have been extreme, there was a kernel of truth in it. School officials found it easier to manage student behavior once architects began designing schools with wide, well-lighted hallways lined with lockers. In fact, to the outsider the new high school building's most notable interior feature would have been its broad, bright hallways, which contrasted sharply with the old schoolhouse's dark, dusty spaces. When noted social and cultural critic Randolph Bourne visited William Ittner's Ralph Waldo Emerson School in Gary, Indiana, in 1915, the corridors fascinated him; he saw them as "broad halls [that] serve not only as the school streets for the constant passage of the children between their work, but also as centers for the 'application' work, or for informal study. They are so wide that all confusion is avoided, and they suggest to the visitor that they serve the school community in the same way that the agora or the forum did the ancient city."[83] Yet these same spaces served another important purpose—they allowed educators to observe student behavior between classes to a greater degree. When student lockers were added to these hallways, replacing the closet-like wardrobes attached to classrooms in previous generations, the range of student behavior that took place under the authoritarian gaze expanded. Many early twentieth-century schoolhouses also had transom windows in classroom doors, allowing administrators to observe classes from the hall without being in the room. And the typical classroom's physical arrangement, unmodified since the mid-nineteenth century, likewise encouraged and imparted order (Fig. 3.2). As historian Larry Cuban noted, the school system's organizational structure affected pedagogical practices as much as the school building.[84]

The entire system, from age-graded classrooms, to the recitation method, to the classroom layout, with students seated in orderly fashion facing a teacher's desk, was designed to maximize educators' control over student behavior. A 1912 editorial in the *American School Board Journal* illustrated this attitude: "The [modern school's] interior is arranged not only with a view of conserving the comfort and health of the occupants, but also to gain the highest possible amount of efficiency in teaching, management, and discipline. . . . In fact, it may safely be said that the modern schoolhouse is in itself a positive aid to teaching and strong factor in the civil and social advancement of the community."[85]

Fig. 3.2. Schoolroom, 1911.

Disciplinary techniques extended beyond the classroom and the building's floor plan as high schools grew larger and more impersonal. Whereas once there was a family-like spirit in the high schools, reflecting close relations between teachers and students, by the Progressive Era the feeling had dwindled. Increasing enrollments, a new public conception of adolescence that viewed teenagers as separate from adults, and the influence of the corporate model of education altered faculty-student interactions. Teachers began to adopt an air of superiority and separation befitting their professional status. As a demonstration of the changing relationship, Chicago school architects began to include separate faculty restrooms in the high schools during the 1890s. Shortly thereafter, teachers dropped the formal "Mr." or "Miss" when speaking to students. Overall, "a kind of we-they mentality began to appear."[86] Administrators installed locks on schoolroom doors (1888 in Chicago), and enacted rules requiring students to carry hall passes during school hours or eat in the school lunchroom even if they brought a meal from home.[87] Students were aware of the new mood. In Chicago, a Lake View High School student lamented the passing of the "friendly home atmosphere" in 1908, while an Englewood High School student depicted the school's physical education curriculum as "wholesome training in subordination." Some even connected it with the modern school building's architectural aspects, such as when a Hyde Park High School student wrote in 1913 that the brand-new building's "locker lined, cement floored and white ceilinged" halls were "reminiscent of a cell-house in a penitentiary . . . [as] they run their seemingly endless lines into still, cement stairways."[88]

## Educational Reforms

Administrative and curricular changes in the nation's public educational systems, prompted by secondary education's evolution, had an even greater impact on the high school's architectural transformation. Between 1880 and 1920 the public education system's organizational framework in major cities like Chicago was largely restructured and a fundamental shift occurred in the conception and purpose of education. Citizens voted to reform school boards across the country in an effort to rid the educational system of political corruption. A centralized and bureaucratic system, based on corporate models of efficiency, arose with new supervisory positions and stricter control over day-to-day operations. And, more importantly for architectural purposes, educators significantly altered students' studies. Expanded curricula and the addition of manual training and vocational education programs comprised the most visible changes.

These modifications affected the way architects approached school buildings. The evolving educational agenda forced school designers to find ways to accommodate unprecedented spaces in the high school like wood, metal, and print shops, model kitchens, sewing rooms, swimming pools, gymnasiums, and auditoriums. Architects were also confronted with a basic need to enlarge the schoolhouse simply because there were more students. The mixture of compulsory education laws, stricter child labor laws, increased immigration, rural migration, and greater societal interest in education produced an incredible upsurge in high school enrollments.

### Administrative Reforms

"Efficiency" was a particularly popular idea among early twentieth century educators. Efficiency pervaded every aspect of the educational world, from curriculum to organization, testing, and several other areas. In its many guises, efficiency—and its practical application through "scientific management"—influenced educational reform for decades. A very visible outcome of this obsession was the wholesale restructuring of urban public education. Educational systems across the country were "centralized" by reformers who succeeded in altering the size and composition of school boards and changing the administration's organizational structure. The roles of superintendent, principal, and teacher were sharply defined for the first time and each was encouraged to become an expert in his or her field.

Reorganizing the nation's urban school systems along the lines of the "corporate-bureaucratic model" in the late nineteenth century was one of the most significant reforms in American education.[89] Central to this movement was a new idea of administrative control. The reformist model envisioned a small, centralized school board, a superintendent to oversee daily operations, and a professional staff to execute policies. It was intended to replace the ward-based boards of education found in most nineteenth century cities. School boards in America's urban centers tended to be large, cumbersome bodies comprised of politicians and their cronies elected from local wards or districts. Under the traditional ward model each political division in a city provided a member to the board of education—usually a local politician from the small-business and professional classes.[90] These men were accustomed to wielding influence and power. Once ensconced on the board, favoritism and influence-peddling became standard operating procedures. School board members rewarded friends and party members' with teaching positions for their daughters, and made lucrative side deals with dishonest building contractors and textbook manufacturers. Chicago was rife with such corruption.

The middle- and upper-class reformers who advocated for changes in urban systems' organizational structures sought to remove school administration as much as possible from the political arena and implement successful business or corporate principles in the educational realm. These reformers viewed centralized and consolidated school boards as more efficient school boards, just as professional superintendents and business managers—education "experts"—were deemed necessary for the system's smooth operation.[91] The project's widespread appeal was due in part to American society's willingness to embrace the doctrine of efficiency as a tool for social betterment.[92]

The impetus for administrative reorganization has its roots in the 1880s. Massachusetts educator John D. Philbrick promoted the idea that there was "one best way" of educating children—a uniform organization in which curriculum, pedagogy, and administration were standardized across the country—and that implementing this system was crucial to the nation's growth and survival.[93] Philbrick was not alone in his beliefs. Across the country educators and reformers fought to lessen political influence in educational decisions and argued for school systems modeled on the American business, with a centralized decision-making authority (akin to the corporate board of directors), rigid hierarchies of control, and the delegation of duties to "expert" managers.[94] By the 1890s, these struggles began to produce results.

Between 1893 and 1913, the average number of school board members in the nation's twenty-eight largest cities declined from 21.5 to 10.2; by 1923, the median had fallen to seven.[95] The composition of these boards evolved as well; instead of the small businessmen and professionals of the ward system, new board members tended to be "large-scale capitalist businessmen, industrialists, and professionals who increasingly dominated the nation's political economy."[96] Along with this centralization of authority was an attendant increase in superintendents' powers. Developments like these grew out of progressive reformers' efforts to economize by reorganizing urban school systems along the corporate model.

Not all cities, however, were open to this approach. In Chicago, competing political, business, and labor interests hindered efforts to restructure the school system. Even as the city's population exploded, causing significant hardships on the public schools, the centralization movement made little headway. One of the greatest obstacles to progress was a state law that gave the mayor the power to appoint members of the city's school board. Historically, this type of law provided opportunities for mayors to appoint political allies, resulting in much political in-fighting to the detriment of the school systems. Chicago reformers saw that the dangers inherent in this method were not much different from those of the old ward-based school board. But a coalition of educators and activists pressed hard for changes, and in late 1897 they succeeded in persuading Mayor Carter Harrison and the city council to appoint a special commission to review the "educational and business conduct of the school system."[97]

The Educational Commission of the City of Chicago is more popularly known as the "Harper Commission" after its chairman, William Rainey Harper. Harper was an appropriate choice to oversee the commission's work. As president of the University of Chicago and a member of the Chicago Board of Education, he had been attempting to maneuver the university into a position of influence over the public schools.[98] In 1892 for instance, even before the University of Chicago began offering classes, Harper contacted public school superintendent Albert G. Lane about the possibility of coordinating the high school curriculum with the university. Harper thus saw the mayor's special commission as an opportunity both to further the university's influence and to promote the type of educational centralization that he favored.

The Harper Commission sought the advice of educational experts throughout the United States while turning a critical eye toward the Chicago Public Schools. After nearly a year of study, the commission released its final report, which contained the damning criticism that "the school machinery of Chicago is largely defective."[99] The committee recommended shifting to the centralized model of cities like St. Louis and Cleveland. In particular, the commission advocated reducing the school board from twenty-one elected members to eleven appointed members, increasing the superintendent's powers, and hiring a business manager to run the system according to business principles.[100] Reducing the school board's size, said the commission, would require more day-to-day work to be handled by the superintendent and his staff; it might also reduce the number of politically connected board members. Such a move would redirect control of the public schools from politicians to professionals. The Harper Commission also proposed new regulations for teacher preparation: applicants should possess a degree from an accredited college and pass an examination graded by a special examination board. Further recommendations included examinations for teacher promotions and salary increases based on merit.

A bill introduced into the Illinois legislature in 1899 to implement the Harper Commission's suggestions was soundly defeated due to the opposition of powerful ward aldermen and the nascent Chicago Teacher's Federation, which enlisted the Chicago Federation of Labor and the Chicago Woman's Club as allies. The teachers criticized the commission's recommendations on hiring and promotions as elitist proposals that conceded too much control over teachers' work and careers to administrators. They also feared the University of Chicago's meddling, and distrusted a more powerful superintendent.[101]

The Teacher's Federation's opposition to the bill stymied reform efforts for almost two decades. After the state congressional bill was defeated in 1899, Harper tried to get the commission's recommendations incorporated into a new city charter in 1904 and 1905, to no avail. Meanwhile the Chicago Civic Federation unsuccessfully sponsored legislation based on the Harper Commission report in 1901 and 1903; similar bills failed to pass through the Illinois legislature every other year between 1905 and 1909. The Teacher's Federation's own proposal for an elected school board passed a citywide referendum in 1904 but died in the legislature. Finally, in 1917, a bill sponsored by the Public Education Association and supported by the Teacher's Federation (the "Otis Bill," named for school board member Ralph Otis) passed the legislature. The Otis Bill reorganized the school board into eleven appointed members, and instituted a three-member executive arm made up of the superintendent, the school attorney, and the business manager. Despite this victory, the Otis Law was not fully implemented until the 1930s, making Chicago the last major American city to centralize its educational system.[102]

## Curriculum Reforms

If the only significant reforms in American education during the Progressive Era had occurred at the administrative level, high school architecture may not have evolved in the same manner. But the spirit of efficiency that drove administrative reorganization efforts also engaged students more directly, through a curricular revolution in secondary education that produced the "comprehensive" high school, and through the widespread implementation of vocational education by the 1920s. Both developments had significant repercussions for school architects.

Toward the end of the nineteenth century, a strong contingent of humanists continued to champion the traditional academically-oriented curriculum even as reformers tried to expand the course of study to include more practical subjects for those students who were not college-bound. The traditionalists could point to the noteworthy "Committee of Ten" report of 1893 as support for their position. In the previous year, the National Education Association had appointed a Committee on Secondary School Studies to investigate college entrance requirements because diverse standards frustrated high school administrators trying to prepare their students for higher education. In its final report, the Committee of Ten, as it was popularly known, circumvented its original purpose and focused on the high school curriculum rather than collegiate standards. The committee recommended curricular consistency at the high school level. According to historian Edward Krug, it proposed "uniformity of topics, methods, and standards of attainment for any subjects that might be offered or taken."[103] The report suggested four appropriate courses of study: Classical, Latin-Scientific, Modern Languages, and English. The courses were largely differentiated by the amount of foreign language study involved, yet all four courses could equally prepare students for college. The final report also claimed the high school's "main function" was "to prepare for the duties of life that small proportion of all the children in the country—a proportion small in number, but very important to the welfare of the nation—who show themselves able to profit by an education prolonged to the eighteenth year, and whose parents are able to support them while they remain so long at school."[104] Thus, the committee made no distinctions between college-bound and non-college-bound students: everyone had to choose one of the four tracks. So those youths preparing "for the duties of life" would be trained in the same manner as prospective college students.[105] While the Committee of Ten had no binding authority over any school system, its suggestions would influence many educators for decades.

At the end of the nineteenth century, however, more and more school administrators began to loosen their narrowly-focused academic curricula to include alternative courses of study. In Chicago, the school board engaged in a continuous pattern of curricular change. When the college preparatory course outlined in Chapter One was reestablished in 1891 after a seven-year absence, Superintendent George Howland described the board's all-inclusive attitude toward the high school: "The prime purpose of the High School is to prepare those who can go no farther, for the business of life, and to open up to those who would go farther the several avenues of scientific and literary culture which they may hereafter desire to follow."[106] After just five years, however, the school board retracted its support for dual courses of study and reinstated a uniform four-year curriculum for all of the city's high schools. This single course was considerably augmented by the addition of electives in 1900. Seeming to follow an accordion-like pattern, the Chicago board constricted the high school course again in 1905, eliminating most electives, and loosened it in 1910 with the introduction of nine different, vocationally-oriented high school curricula: English, general, science, foreign language, business, builders, manual-training, household arts, and architectural.[107] By 1915, there were an astonishing twenty-two courses of study for Chicago high school students: eleven four-year and eleven two-year programs.[108]

The curricular changes in Chicago reflected a national trend toward "comprehensive" high schools. High schools in this period broadened their focus beyond the traditional academic training, and added general or unspecified courses of study as well as specialized areas. One study of midwestern high schools found that the average school had doubled its courses of study in less than twenty years.[109] The differentiated or comprehensive high school—which provided both academic and vocational education—would become the standard by the onset of the Great Depression. This tendency had been encapsulated in an important report that, like that of the Committee of Ten twenty-five years earlier, both reflected and influenced secondary education in America. The 1918 report of the National Education Association's Commission on the Reorganization of Secondary Education (popularly known as the "Cardinal Principles" report) announced the triumph of "social efficiency" as the guiding force in secondary education.[110] Where the Committee of Ten report had accorded practical training a minor role in comparison to classical education, the Cardinal Principles took training for adult life as the high school's essential purpose. The Cardinal Principles report succinctly stated the principal objectives of secondary education: "1. Health. 2. Command of fundamental processes. 3. Worthy home-membership. 4. Vocation. 5. Citizenship. 6. Worthy use of leisure. 7. Ethical character."[111] The committee proposed that classes dedicated to these objectives would help to create a well-rounded adult citizen; with the possible exception of "Command of fundamental processes," none could be learned through a traditional classical course of study, and none of the goals sought to enhance students' intellectual development. The mental discipline approach was losing support.

Educators inserted the Cardinal Principles into curricula across the nation. Such changes brought to the forefront the high school's evolving role in American society. Once considered an elite training ground for the privileged few, high schools were charged with a new mission—to integrate the masses into adult society. Elwood P. Cubberley of Stanford University divulged the basis for this position when he wrote that urban schools should "give up the exceedingly democratic idea that all are equal, and that our society is devoid of classes. . . . Increasing specialization . . . has divided the people into dozens of more or less clearly defined classes."[112] According to the new philosophy, some students were to be trained for the subordinate roles they were sure to occupy. "If democracy means to try to make all children equal or all men equal, it means to fight nature, and in that fight democracy is sure to be defeated," wrote Harvard President Charles W. Eliot in 1908. "There is no such thing among men as equality of nature, of capacity for training, or of intellectual power."[113] Sociologist Franklin Giddings was equally frank: "High school education should make citizens not learners."[114] The high school's job, in the minds of many, was to prepare adolescents for life rather than exercise their minds.

## Manual Training and Vocational Education

In 1904, Margaret Haley, leader of the powerful Chicago Teacher's Federation, gave a speech at the National Educational Association annual meeting in St. Louis in which she characterized the nature of early twentieth-century public education:

> Two ideals are struggling for supremacy in American life today: one the industrial ideal, dominating thru [sic] the supremacy of commercialism, which subordinates the worker to the product and the machine; the other, the ideal of democracy, the ideal of the educators, which places humanity above all machines, and demands that all activity shall be the expression of life. If this ideal of the educators cannot be carried over into the industrial field, then the ideal of industrialism will be carried over into the school. Those two ideals can no more continue to exist in American life than our nation could have continued half slave and half free. If the school cannot bring joy to the work of the world, the joy must go out of its own life, and work in the school as in the factory will become drudgery.[115]

Haley was targeting the major educational issue of her day: the growth of manual training and vocational education programs. The development of vocationalism dominates the history of American secondary education between 1880 and 1920.

Vocational education was an outgrowth of a manual training movement that began in the late 1870s. Manual training was originally intended to supplement the regular academic curriculum by encouraging students to utilize their hands and their minds to become more well-rounded persons. Proponents stressed how the honest use of tools could serve as an antidote to the corruption of work by an increasingly industrialized society—a type of "moral regeneration."[116] Manual training courses also proved particularly useful for teaching immigrant children a marketable set of skills. But what the early reformers clearly did not want was a program that replaced the traditional academic curriculum with courses teaching specific skills to future factory workers.

Business leaders quickly sensed that these programs presented an opportunity to expand their labor pool and cut costs, since masses of workers conceivably could be trained without expense to them while bypassing labor unions or apprenticeship programs. So businessmen allied themselves with school administrators. The influence of American businesses and their organizations soon tilted many generalized manual education programs toward specific vocational training.

Manual training was increasingly adopted through the 1880s. Public manual or vocational training high schools opened in Baltimore (1884), Philadelphia (1885), Toledo (1885), and Cleveland (1886), while other cities added new classes to their existing secondary curriculum to form comprehensive schools. Vocational education programs, with their need for specialized facilities, made fresh demands on school architecture. Shop rooms required equipment and power sources that were unknown in the traditional schoolhouse. Domestic science rooms called for cooking and ventilation equipment. Art and drafting rooms needed abundant natural light. To guide architects faced with these designing such new types of spaces, educational journals began to offer articles on these topics. Many early shops were in basements or separate buildings, but as vocationalism grew stronger in the late 1890s some cities, like those mentioned above, inaugurated separate manual training or mechanical arts high schools, with most of the rooms dedicated to vocational training.

By 1898, manual training high schools had become prevalent enough for Edmund M. Wheelwright to devote two articles to them in his long-running series on "The American Schoolhouse" in *The Brickbuilder*.[117] Wheelwright identified manual schools as "the most distinctly American development of schoolhouse architecture. . . ."[118] By the early twentieth century these training schools became better adapted to students' and educators' needs. An essay on "The Industrial Arts Department" from 1921 demonstrates how extensive and complicated the design of vocational/manual training spaces could be. The author describes materials and layouts needed for grinding rooms, foundries, and machine, pattern, forge, automobile, printing, electrical, sheet metal, cabinet, and carpentry shops, in what was only a partial listing of the types of trade training available to high school students.[119] The elaborate requirements of such rooms included power sources, proper ventilation, special (and expensive) machines and tools, storerooms, washrooms, and demonstration areas.

Vocational training received a great stimulus in 1906 when the Massachusetts Commission on Industrial and Technical Education (known as the "Douglas Commission") issued its report. The commission criticized Massachusetts' "old-fashioned" curriculum as out of touch with the practical demands of modern society. A declining apprenticeship system in the late nineteenth century had serious repercussions for American industry, and in a series of hearings held across the commonwealth, the Douglas Commission heard numerous complaints about the lack of skilled workers. Manufacturers looked to the public school systems to remedy this problem. The commission chided existing manual training programs, however, for being too narrowly focused on supplementing the academic course of study rather than providing an alternative. A new system should be created, wrote the commission, which would be more in tune with "callings in life . . . professional, commercial, productive and domestic."[120] Appended to the Douglas Commission report was a study of 25,000 fourteen- to sixteen-year-old dropouts—none of whom had ever reached high school—which found that the main reason these children quit school was lack of interest, not economic hardship. Reformers used this evidence to support their call for broader curricula that could adequately train students for the future.[121]

The National Society for the Promotion of Industrial Education (NSPIE) was founded in the same year as the Douglas Commission report. The NSPIE proved instrumental in forming alliances with organizations like the National Education Association and backing state and federal legislation promoting industrial education, including the important Smith-Hughes Act of 1917. The Smith-Hughes Act provided states with federal matching funds for teacher salaries in agriculture, trade and industrial education, and home economics,

Fig. 3.3. Boy's vocational class, Lane Technical High School, early 1900s. By the twentieth century, high school curricula had expanded to include many non-academic courses of study.

as well as $1 million for teacher training in vocational education. This money was specifically meant for secondary schools. Such federal mandates helped change the face of American secondary education; by 1919, all forty-eight states had instituted vocational education programs pursuant to the Smith-Hughes Act.

A manual training school opened in Chicago in 1884, but it was privately-financed by the Commercial Club on Marshall Field's initiative and not part of the public school system. The Commercial Club persuaded the school board to establish a succession of public vocational and technical schools over the years, such as Crane Manual High School (1903), Lane Technical High School (1908), and Tilden Technical High School (1918) (Fig. 3.3). The city's leading businessmen, like many throughout the United States, supported these programs because they perceived a lack of skilled workers.[122] Sympathetic educators attempted to frame big business' support in educational rather than economic terms to avoid criticism that the schools would become publicly-subsidized training programs for American industry. For example, Superintendent Albert G. Lane stated in 1894 that Chicago's

Manual Training School was "in no sense a trade school, but it is laying the foundation for a business education in the elementary knowledge of mathematics, physics, chemistry, mechanical and architectural drawing, and the use of tools upon wood and iron; at the same time it is giving a general education in the use of English, and in history and literature."[123]

Groups like the Chicago Industrial Club, the Illinois Manufacturers Association, and the Chicago Association for Commerce also promoted the democratic aspects of vocational education. They asserted that these programs improved the economic standing of students and enhanced their quality of life. The Commercial Club went so far as to pay former superintendent Edwin G. Cooley to visit European schools and produce a report on vocational education abroad. The 1911 Cooley Plan, derived from that report, advocated parallel educational systems (like that in Germany) where public school children were channeled into either academic or vocational programs depending on their abilities and interests. But Cooley's plan was harshly criticized by the Chicago Federation of Labor, the Chicago Teacher's Federation, the City Club, John Dewey, and others who denounced it as both anti-democratic (because of the way it predetermined children's fate) and anti-union. Defeat in the Illinois legislature on numerous occasions meant the plan was never implemented by the public schools, but it made no real difference because the city already had a de facto dual system that forced sixth graders to choose their career path.

Alongside the development of manual training for boys was a concurrent rise in vocational programs for girls centered on "Domestic Science" and commercial studies (Fig. 3.4).[124] Girls made up the bulk of America's high school population during this period. Nationally, almost 58 percent of all high school pupils in 1890 and 1900 were female, and 56 percent in 1910 and 1920.[125] According to superintendent E. Benjamin Andrews, seven out of ten Chicago high schoolers were female at the turn of the century.[126] Girls also were more likely to graduate; the proportion of high school graduates who were female was 65 percent in 1890, 63 percent in 1900, and 61 percent in 1910 and 1920.[127]

Despite their majority, however, girls' status in the male-centered educational community was low. As late as 1925, a psychologist's description of the "average girl" demonstrates the mindset that influenced girls' education: "What then can be expected of the average girl? There are certain things we know she cannot do; she cannot fill positions requiring the exercise of much

Fig. 3.4. Girl's vocational class, Flower Technical High School for Girls, 1920s. Girls' educational opportunities in the Progressive Era tended to be limited to training for domestic and supporting roles.

initiative or executive ability; she has little capacity for leadership; she can think very little for herself; she follows her leaders blindly . . . she is more easily taught and trained, more apt to make an adjustment to her immediate social environment . . . by virtue of her very lack of intellectual ability she accepts things as she finds them and goes with the crowd."[128] Such beliefs formed the basis for the new vocational curricula. Domestic science and commercial courses taught girls to be efficient homemakers or competent secretaries, maids, cooks, or seamstresses. This was partly a reaction to the increasing number of women in the workplace.[129] Perhaps more significant was the growing importance put on the woman's role in managing domestic life. As historian Jane Powers notes, "advocates of vocational training for young women placed women at the center of significant social and economic change and linked societal change to home economics and preparation for women's trades."[130] In preparation for these roles, high schools taught girls sewing, laundering, cooking, typing, stenography, and bookkeeping. Some of these courses required new types of architectural space. Early-twentieth century high schools began to include fully operational kitchens, model dining rooms and bedrooms, and mock offices. Whereas the Chicago Division high schools had no specialized rooms for "girls training," the 1912 Senn High School had two "Household Arts" rooms, a laundry, model dining, living and bedrooms, and rooms for bookkeeping, typewriting, stenography, and textile arts and sewing. Several cities even opened separate girls' vocational schools to rival industrial arts training for boys, like Chicago's Lucy Flower Technical High School for Girls (established in 1911).

Chicago public high schools occupied a much different position in 1920 than their predecessors. High schools were now called upon to provide adolescents—a special group who were no longer children but not yet adults—with the means to make themselves into law-abiding, hard-working American citizens. Secondary education as a whole opened up to a wider range of students, for a variety of reasons. These students found themselves attending classes more often in monumental, visually striking buildings that stood out in the physical landscape and spoke to a society of the high school's new position in American life.

In these often elaborate settings, the high school curriculum underwent a shift from equality to differentiation. The traditional academic curriculum, which offered a limited course of study and emphasized training students to think, tended to treat all students more or less equally. The "new" curriculum, with its multiple courses of study, intended to better prepare students for their future life tasks based on their abilities and interests; it was the epitome of differentiation. This same transition from equality to differentiation was manifested in physical space inside schoolhouses. Old floor plans with identically sized rooms gave way to new plans with dedicated spaces to accommodate a broad range of subjects. School architects could no longer stack duplicate four- or six-room floor plans on top of each other to create a high school; they now needed to design spaces for laboratories, domestic sciences, art and mechanical drawing, shops, and other activities. The modern high school building had been established.

## Chapter Four

# CHICAGO'S PROGRESSIVE ERA HIGH SCHOOLS

The Chicago Public Schools opened the Robert T. Lindblom Technical High School on the city's southwest side in September 1919 (Fig. 4.1). The massive building dwarfed the surrounding houses in its suburban neighborhood. Lindblom Tech, which occupied an entire city block, was 598 feet long, roughly the length of two football fields laid end-to-end. It could serve the various educational needs of up to 3,000 students. A diverse group of rooms inside the building, laid out in an H-shaped floor plan, accommodated the school's contemporary curriculum: standard classrooms, laboratories equipped with the latest scientific instruments, study rooms, woodworking and machine shops, a foundry and forge, a model kitchen, workrooms, offices, a library, a lunchroom, an auditorium, two gymnasiums, a swimming pool, and more. A giant three-story colonnade with eight Ionic columns dominated Lindblom's grand facade and marked the building as an important social institution. The entire Chicago High School of 1856 could have fit within either of Lindblom's gyms.

Lindblom Tech was a fully mature modern high school building. It featured all of the elements (computers and electronics notwithstanding) that our high schools offer today. Chicago, like other large American cities, had been building these high schools for almost two decades at that point. By 1920, high schools differed dramatically from their 1880s predecessors: they were larger, had greater enrollments, and a wider variety of classes. Archi-

Fig. 4.1. A. F. Hussander, Robert Lindblom Technical High School, 1918.

tecturally, the schools were designed in accord with historical architectural styles, with open floor plans and more diverse room types. Educator Leonard V. Koos performed a study in 1919 that demonstrated the complexity of contemporary high school architecture.[1] Koos analyzed 156 high school floor plans printed in the *American School Board Journal* over a ten-year period. He found an amazing 109 different kinds of rooms. Most of the buildings studied, independent of the size of the community in which they were built, contained at least the following rooms according to Koos: "class- or recitation-rooms, a chemical and physical laboratory, with a lecture or demonstration room for these sciences, an assembly room or auditorium with a stage for same, a library room, a gymnasium, an office for the principal, a room for general storage, and boys' and girls' toilets . . . to this meager list may be added some provision for manual training and domestic science . . . for the larger communities we may also add a laboratory for biology, a mechanical-drawing room, boys' and girls' locker-rooms, and a reception- or waiting-room to the principal's office."[2] Koos advised school administrators to use the entire list—or at least the "minimum essentials" listed above—as a guide when contemplating the construction of a new high school. Undeniably, the diversity and complexity of interior spaces found by Koos firmly differentiated the twentieth-century high school from its earlier counterpart. The high school building had come a long way since Chicago Central.

Fig. 4.2. William B. Mundie, from
*Chicago Tribune*, 18 December 1898.

## William Mundie's Classical Schools

The man who did the most to introduce modern design ideas to Chicago's schools had no particular expertise in educational architecture before becoming board architect. Yet William B. Mundie would hold the position of board architect for five-and-a-half consecutive years, a longer continuous term than any of his predecessors (Fig. 4.2), Mundie was born in 1863 in Hamilton, Ontario. After graduating from the Hamilton Collegiate Institute, he moved to Chicago in 1884 and immediately obtained a job as a draftsman for skyscraper pioneer William LeBaron Jenney. In 1891, Mundie became Jenney's full partner. He had established a name for himself as a first-rate architect of commercial buildings by the time of his appointment as board architect in December 1898.[3] By the end of his tenure, the *American School Board Journal* would praise Mundie's school work, declaring that "the schools that have been erected in recent years in [Chicago] are worthy of the proud and important position Chicago takes among the great and progressive cities of the world. The schools are well planned both as to exterior and interior. They embody many of the best features in

Fig. 4.3. William B. Mundie, Edward Waller High School, 1899. Mundie introduced a historical revival architecture that linked Chicago's high schools to the city's other civic buildings.

the matter of design and orientation and are most practical in the selection of constructive material."[4]

Mundie's first experience with a high school building, however, limited his ability to incorporate new ideas. Upon assuming the board architect position, Mundie inherited the project for another North Division High School, later renamed Robert A. Waller High School (1899), at the corner of Center and Orchard Streets near Lincoln Park (Fig. 4.3). Previous board architect Normand S. Patton had created a U-shaped building with an English Renaissance facade as part of his effort to infuse Chicago's educational architecture with more variety. Patton had been the first school architect in the city to employ historical styles. When Mundie took over the job he made few revisions to the building. He essentially left Patton's plan intact, but transformed the exterior from English Renaissance to classical.[5] To emphasize the building's main entrance, Mundie employed the giant columns that would become a trademark of his educational work.[6] Six white Ionic columns stood out against a background of red brick walls, providing a striking visual contrast and an interesting synthesis of old and new aesthetic concepts. Mundie also introduced at Waller other architectural motifs he would continue to use throughout his term as board architect: the gridded facade with horizontal rows of windows balanced by evenly-spaced vertical pilasters; the five-part facade with a prominent main entry flanked by recessed walls of windows and terminating in pavilions at the building's corners; and the strong horizontal entablature. Mundie's monumental creation was much different from high schools of just a few years earlier.

When Waller High School opened, the board of education praised it in the *Annual Report*: "The general arrangement of the class rooms and special departments has been very carefully studied, until the convenience and equipment will stand on par with the very best examples in the United States."[7] Contrary to the board's opinion, however, the school's interior accommodations showed little progress beyond the decade-old North-West Division High School. Both buildings supplemented standard classrooms with a handful of laboratories and drawing rooms.

## Historical Eclecticism

As the *American School Board Journal* recognized, Mundie's later schools would bring the city's educational architecture in step with the most advanced national trends. His buildings' floor plans were more open than those of previous architects, and although not uncommon for their time, they represented a new direction for Chicago practice. Mundie was also the first school architect in the city to use a classical style, following the lead of Chicago's most recent cultural buildings such as Shepley, Rutan & Coolidge's Chicago Art Institute and Chicago Public Library (1893 and 1897), as well as the World's Columbian Exposition. The exposition, a world's fair held between May and October 1893 in the area that is now Jackson Park and the Hyde Park Midway, was a stirring triumph for Chicago and for a particular type of architecture (Fig. 4.4).[8] Millions of visitors encountered an ensemble of historically-inspired buildings in the Court of Honor—the fair's centerpiece—like none they had seen before. Created by a group of celebrated architects from New York, Boston, and Kansas City, the "White City" buildings (named for their monochrome white exteriors) incorporated elements from the Greek, Roman, and Italian Renaissance past to create a monumental modern classicism. This kind of architecture, known to history as the "Beaux-Arts style" after the French school of architecture that taught it, emphasized historical eclecticism. The Beaux-Arts approach required a scholarly knowledge of architectural history and attention to accurate details, while refraining from outright copying.[9] The

Fig. 4.4. Court of Honor looking west, World's Columbian Exposition, 1893.

method permitted great flexibility, and architects of this period used eclecticism to distance themselves from what they considered the amateurish work of their earlier-century counterparts. Stylistic connections to the past also allowed architects to demonstrate the prestige of certain buildings by visually linking them to eminent historical monuments.

These connections also fulfilled the desire of many architects for an urban landscape of appropriately decorous institutional architecture. That desire was manifested in Chicago just a few years prior to Mundie's hiring, when proposals for a new county courthouse provoked sharp criticism. Responding to a proposal for a new courthouse in the form of a skyscraper, architect Dewitt Taylor-Kennard wrote to the *Chicago Tribune*: "What do we build a courthouse for if it is not to present to the public a building which inspires them with respect for government and justice as well as to be occupied by judicial business?" He continued, expanding on the theme of appropriate civic architecture: "Why do we build public buildings if it is not to inspire and raise to a higher place the hearts and minds of the people to a higher regard for their country and respect for its laws. . . ? Why did we build the Worlds Fair with

Fig. 4.5. William B. Mundie, William McKinley High School, 1900.

its Grecian palaces and Court of Honor? Was it an accident that the architecture was chosen as the embodiment of our highest aims?"[10]

The type of historical eclecticism used by William Mundie and others achieved Taylor-Kennard's goal. Such designs, many thought, inspired citizens to a greater regard for their city, added an air of cultural refinement to the school, and visually related school buildings to socially-important civic buildings like city halls and courthouses. And, as historian Abigail Van Slyck has shown with Progressive Era public libraries, using conservative classical architecture allowed local citizens "to share in the emerging national culture"—to connect with other American communities through similar architectural language. This aspect should not be underestimated when examining an age of great social and technological change and geographic dislocation.[11]

## McKinley and Phillips High Schools

While working on the Waller revisions, Mundie began to conceive his own designs for the first time. The William McKinley and Wendell Phillips High Schools (1900 and 1904) were related, and both exhibited Mundie's mature style. They shared similar floor plans and architectural elements and were much larger than the Division high schools. McKinley, which essentially replaced West Division High School, stood on the corner of Hoyne and Adams west of downtown (Fig. 4.5). The building was created for 1,200

Fig. 4.6. William B. Mundie, Wendell Phillips High School, 1904. Like McKinley, Phillips featured a "zoned" floor plan that grouped together rooms for similar activities.

pupils. Its light-colored brick facade referenced the French Classical tradition with Corinthian columns and pilasters, a robust entablature, and an attic story. The single color scheme made the building look more monolithic than its contemporaries. McKinley's impressive facade surrounded eighteen standard classrooms and fifteen specialized rooms intended for activities like drawing, art, science, and vocational training.

Phillips High School, located on the near south side at 39th Street and Prairie Avenue, was less extravagant. There Mundie returned to the practice of contrasting red brick with light colored stone trim. The building's form was similar to McKinley, but the facade was flatter, lacking its predecessor's three-dimensional columns. The pilasters, which were not based on any historical precedent, gave the school a slight abstract quality. Inside the school were forty-eight classrooms, a lunchroom, a gymnasium, an auditorium, and spaces for extracurricular activities for its 1,500 students (Fig. 4.6).[12] Together, McKinley and Phillips were prime examples of the early stages of the schoolhouse's transformation into a larger, more complex building full of varied spaces—the type of building that would lead Leonard Koos, after examining floor plans from high schools across the country, to exclaim, "Truly, space-provisions in modern high-school buildings are little short of protean!"[13]

This new generation of schools was necessary to accommodate Chicago's evolving secondary school curriculum. After the school board abandoned the college preparatory course of study in 1896, a single curriculum was required of all high school students. But that curriculum was comprised of a broad range of classes. Chicago high school pupils at the end of the century studied Latin or German, rhetoric, English composition and "home reading," algebra, physiology, drawing, vocal music, physical training, English classics, plane geometry, biology, physics, history, history of literature, higher algebra, chemistry, civil government, and political economy, in addition to vocational classes like domestic science or metal shop.[14] Clearly, the old brick cube filled with identical classrooms—like the first generation of Division schools—would not suffice to meet the requirements of most of these subjects; science laboratories and shop classes, for example, needed far different physical spaces than English or algebra classes.

Mundie certainly improved the quality of school architecture in Chicago. His McKinley plan, for instance, incorporated much contemporary thinking about the secondary school—open courtyards, single-loaded corridors, multiple stairways and entrances, and a large centrally-located auditorium. School officials recognized such advances and praised Mundie's work. "In place of the uniform staring brick boxes, with holes punched at regular intervals to permit entrance of light," wrote Superintendent Edwin G. Cooley of Mundie's schools, "buildings are being erected that are a stimulus to the architecture of the neighborhood in which they are placed and a credit to the enterprise of the city of Chicago."[15]

McKinley High School introduced two important architectural innovations to Chicago's public high schools beyond its French Classical style: it was the first high school in the city with a lunchroom, and the first with an assembly hall on the first floor, opposite the building's main entry. This latter fact was significant for social and architectural reasons. Socially, the first-floor assembly hall allowed better public access; structurally, a first-floor assembly hall could be larger than one placed on the top floor because it was not constrained by the size and shape of the roof. Mundie did not originate this practice, however—he was simply following a current trend in school design that had not yet reached the city. In many ways, the auditorium would become the modern high school's physical and spiritual heart, and it often served the same role for the surrounding community. The auditorium was the place where students gathered for school assemblies and graduation, and where local adults heard lectures and watched various entertainment programs. Auditoriums grew into the largest single space in the twentieth-century high school.

## Race and Education

Like McKinley, Mundie's Wendell Phillips High School was significant beyond the way it demonstrated the increasingly sophisticated schoolhouse architecture of the early 1900s. Phillips stood apart as the only Chicago high school that had a noticeable black student population before 1920. Opened in 1902, only thirty-seven out of Phillips's 1,674 students were black in 1910.[16] But the school's black enrollment soared to 20 percent by 1914 and 56 percent by 1918.[17] Englewood and Hyde Park, the only other Chicago high schools with black students, had a mere handful between them.

Despite the extreme localization that made Phillips's black population unique, there was no legal school segregation in Chicago—but not for lack of trying. Segregationists had briefly attempted to gain a foothold in the city with an 1863 law (the "Black School Law") that mandated separate schools for blacks, but it was quickly repealed. In 1874 the Illinois state legislature prohibited elected officials from excluding children from school on the basis of race. The legislation did not stop segregationists from actively pursuing their cause, however, nor did it stimulate racial harmony in the city. White groups repeatedly pressured the school board to segregate the schools in the first two decades of the twentieth century. A *Chicago Record-Herald* editorial, for example, opined that "the color line is a source of continual strife."[18] White schoolchildren started a riot in 1905 after being transferred to a largely black school; three years later, over 150 white students staged a "school strike" by staying home rather than accepting transfer to a school with black students.[19]

While these actions were minor incidents, they hinted at a city seething with racial animosity. Further proof came when fifty-eight black-occupied homes were bombed between 1917 and 1921—many as a result of blacks trying to relocate into white neighborhoods. The enmity boiled over in July 1919, when a black teenager was drowned by white youths in Lake Michigan after he crossed over into the water of a "white" beach. A week-long riot ensued in which white Chicagoans unleashed their pent-up racial hostility. White street gangs invaded the black neighborhoods and blacks retaliated. In a week of brutal violence, twenty-three blacks and fifteen whites were killed, and over 500 people were injured.[20]

In the face of these problems, the board of education resisted segregation. The main reason, then, for the localization of black students in Phillips High School was geography. Phillips was located in the Douglas neighborhood on the South Side, which became the heart of the city's black community. Douglas, bounded by Lake, Clark, 26th, and 39th Streets, was centrally located in the "Black Belt" that began to form in Chicago in the late nineteenth century. Beginning with a colony of blacks clustered around the Illinois Central railroad tracks south of downtown, it spread southward until, by 1920, the area of black population was almost three miles long (extending to roughly 55th Street) and one-quarter mile wide, and confined on all sides by railroad tracks. While the city maintained a relatively small black population during this period (only 1.3 percent of the city's population in 1890 and 4.1 percent in 1920), it was highly concentrated on the south side and grew at a rapid rate. Chicago's black population jumped 148.5 percent between 1910 and 1920. The Douglas neighborhood was three-fourths black by 1920, and 85 percent of the city's 110,000 blacks lived in the Black Belt.[21] In addition to Phillips High School, ten elementary schools were predominantly black by 1920. This racialization of educational space on the south side would only worsen in the subsequent decades, leading Chicago to become one of the most educationally segregated cities in the country.

## Architectural Styles

The desire of architects like William Mundie to enhance the school building's image most likely related to nineteenth-century architectural hierarchy, whereby warehouses, commercial buildings, schools, and other commonplace structures had been considered "minor" or lesser architecture. But as secondary education became more important to American life, school officials felt their buildings should look more significant. The public high school building became increasingly visible in the urban landscape as a consequence, and the discourse on its appearance grew.

There was a great deal of agreement among early twentieth century educators and architects that older school buildings were aesthetically deficient, and that a more honorable architecture was needed to express the high school's significance. In 1907, an editorial in the *American School Board Journal* rejoiced that "all turrets and towers, as well as the high slant roofs, have been abolished. It has been found that dignified and graceful exterior effects can be achieved without resorting to steeples and towers. . . ."[22] A few years later the same journal commented on the dissemination of modern school architecture to rural communities: "The ridiculous roof and useless domes and cupolas are passing away under the developed taste of architects and the appreciation of school officials."[23] Other writers ridiculed older schools' "generally ugly exteriors" or "uninviting, monotonous, dead appearance."[24]

The new school architecture developing throughout American cities rejected familiar "Victorian" elements like steeply-pitched roofs, corner towers, and round-arched windows in favor of overt historical references. But while many architects and educators were willing to discuss the range of acceptable architectural styles, few made recommendations about what style should be used. Boston's Edmund Wheelwright suggested that architects shape schools according to practical requirements (lighting, economy, etc.) and not by style. Since the building's internal arrangements influenced its exterior appearance, and the main consideration in arranging the interior spaces was the penetration and quality of natural light, Wheelwright believed the windows' size, shape, and distribution would have the greatest effect on the facade. In the same vein, the *American School Board Journal* declared that "the modern schoolhouse exterior has lent itself to a maximum of lighting surface."[25] The regularity demanded by lighting concerns thus precluded irregular, picturesque effects, and instead suggested the regularity and orderliness found in Italian Renaissance and Colonial Revival architecture.[26] Wheelwright also felt that these styles, which required little external decoration other than "properly designed brickwork with stone or terracotta trimmings," would help make school construction economical.[27] He created a number of Renaissance-inspired schools in Boston that continued to serve as models for school officials even after his tenure as the city architect ended in 1895 (Fig. 4.7).[28]

Other architects recognized the same constraints imposed by lighting considerations but reached different conclusions regarding their effect on the building's facade. Edmund Wheelwright's successor as the nation's pre-eminent school architect, William B. Ittner of St. Louis, admitted that "the necessities of a schoolhouse interior do not permit much expression of the artistic in exterior design. . . . The demand for the adequate lighting of each classroom calls for a liberal number of windows of certain sizes. These have a tendency to cut up the design, and for a certain treatment of the exterior, which does not cultivate the highest ideals in architectural expression."[29] Unlike Wheelwright, however, Ittner believed that these limitations did not preclude the use of non-classical styles. He personally found "the Old English, the Dutch and the Flemish feeling" to be the "most suitable for public school

Fig. 4.7. Wheelwright & Haven, Brighton High School, Boston, Massachusetts, 1894.

buildings."[30] Ittner relied on these styles for the bulk of his more than 500 school projects across the country (Fig. 4.8).

The Colonial style also had its adherents, especially in New England. Architect Ernest Sibley advocated the Colonial in an article entitled, "Why I Prefer the Colonial Style."[31] The main reason, the author admitted, was personal taste, but he also felt that "when we adapt this style to our school buildings, we link America's most noble institution with the spirit and traditions of the past."[32] This type of nationalism would become common during the 1920s when patriots promoted the Colonial Revival not only as a true American style, but also an Anglo-Saxon style, which was a comfort to many white New Englanders in an era of mass immigration from southern and eastern Europe.[33] Sibley's comments on the Colonial Revival regarding this point echoed those of Alfred Busselle, who had written the following in praise of the Colonial style two years earlier: "Special emphasis is laid upon the traditions of the early building along the Atlantic seaboard, because it is the principles of the Fathers of the Republic *which we are endeavoring to instill into our alien races* (emphasis added)."[34]

Notwithstanding the mixed stylistic advice, a review of contemporary examples reveals that most American school architects designed urban public high school buildings with classical, medieval, or colonial motifs (Figs.

Fig. 4.8. William B. Ittner, Frank Louis Soldan High School, St. Louis, Missouri, 1909.

4.9 and 4.10). Some cities even seemed to carry on stylistic traditions. In St. Louis, William Ittner's high schools were either castellated Gothic or English Tudor; his successor, Rockwell Milligan, made two high schools in the mid-1920s that combined the two styles. There were no classical schools in that city. On the other hand, Chicago board architects favored classicism. William Mundie and A. F. Hussander produced only classically-inspired high schools for over sixteen years, separated by Dwight Perkins's arts and crafts-influenced tenure described below.

Despite widespread agreement on acceptable styles, not everyone was pleased with the high school's new image. Architect Walter Kilham, for example, complained about many buildings' lack of sensitivity to their surroundings: "why do buildings of such hulking proportions have to be constructed in residential districts when they are out of scale with everything in the vicinity? . . .One may well wish that a quiet Collegiate or Georgian type of brick architecture with some vestige of a visible roof might replace the current flat roofed, boxlike designs which, while appropriate to urban surroundings, absolutely fail to correlate themselves with a suburban landscape."[35] Kilham's criticism bears on the Chicago high school buildings like Lindblom Tech; as in other cities around the country, schools of this era were located predominately in residential neighborhoods where their towering presence over the surrounding rows of houses was often jarring. Normand Patton had been

Fig. 4.9. J. Walter Stevens, Thomas Hughes High School, Cincinnati, Ohio, 1908.

aware of this problem years before. He told a *Chicago Tribune* reporter in 1897: "It is my object to introduce in Chicago a greater variety in design, not from mere caprice, but to make each building adapted to the locality in which it is erected. In thickly built parts of the city, where the site is surrounded with high structures with flat roofs, it is proper that schools should partake somewhat of their environments. The massive shape and flat roof are most appropriate. But in suburban localities, where schools will be seen more from a distance than near at hand, there should be picturesque outlines and steep roofs."[36] But Patton's theory remained speculative; his school buildings were in residential neighborhoods near downtown. His successors achieved varying degrees of integration with their surroundings but did not seem to prioritize site and context in the same way.

## Board Architects

Patton was unable to fully implement his ideas in Chicago because he did not last very long as board architect. And while William Mundie advanced the condition of Chicago's educational architecture, he failed to avoid the fate of most of his predecessors. The position proved to be very unstable before the 1920s (see Table 2). Board architects had to deal with a firmly-entrenched power structure and patronage system that impacted school building con-

Fig. 4.10. Edgar Blair, Benjamin Franklin High School, Seattle, Washington, 1912.

struction, and the mayor's ability to appoint board of education members created an atmosphere rife with corruption and graft. This appointment method, wrote George Counts in 1928, "bound the school system to the city hall and has subordinated the interests of education to the vagaries and vicissitudes of partisan politics."[37]

The school board began to establish the parameters of the architect's position in early 1881. It insisted that its architect "give diligent superintendence" to all buildings under construction and be held responsible for all work certified.[38] A foreshadowing of future problems occurred, however, in February of that year when architect Augustus Bauer wrote a "disrespectful" letter to the board concerning the Cottage Grove School. The board returned his letter and censured Bauer for his "gross and unwarranted attack upon a member of the Board."[39]

The position "Architect and Superintendent of Construction" for the Chicago Board of Education was officially recognized later in 1881, and during that school year the board held its first elections. Frederic Baumann defeated a field of eight other candidates in February 1882, after the board had voted unsuccessfully eight times in the previous five months. Baumann resigned in June and was replaced by Julius Ender. He lasted a mere four months before the committee on buildings and grounds determined Ender "did not inspire confidence in his ability to satisfactorily secure the interests of the Board. . . ."[40] Ender's replacement, James R. Willett, signed a one-year contract.

In January 1884, John J. Flanders inaugurated the first period of stability in the board architect's office. Flanders had a good relationship with the board of education, as demonstrated by his serving two terms as board architect (1884–88 and 1891–93) and by the board's comment that his buildings "contain many features, especially in the matter of light and ventilation, which . . . are a very great advance over the buildings previously erected, and the Committee [of Buildings and Grounds] consider them as model school buildings, fully equal, if not superior, to any in the country."[41] However, not everyone agreed with this assessment. An 1888 editorial in the *Chicago Tribune* entitled, "Wanted—An Architect" called for Flanders's resignation on the grounds that his schools were poorly designed, ornate, and costly.[42]

John Flanders was replaced in February 1893 by August Fiedler, the first full-time board architect. The board took the opportunity to clarify the architect's job duties. Under the previous system, architects were paid percentages for designing schools and superintending their construction. The board had no control over the architect's staff, no records were kept, and the architect was not required to attend all board meetings. In an effort to achieve "entire control" over the building process, the board of education amended its rules. The architect now earned a handsome salary ($6,000), was provided with an office in City Hall and a staff, and was required to provide a full accounting of his actions.[43] These changes not only gave the board a tighter reign over the architecture department, they also saved money. According to the Committee on Buildings and Grounds report, "from a standpoint of economy, a saving has been accomplished in the architect's department of from ten to fifteen thousand dollars per year."[44]

Fiedler may have been the first full-time board architect, but he was not the first person in that position to be subjected to the board of education's political wrangling. At one point he ran afoul of the board and it began to investigate the architecture department's finances; in particular there were rumors that Fiedler may have accepted bribes. The *Chicago Tribune*, however, implied that the problems may have stemmed from "crooked contractors" dissatisfied with Fiedler's honesty.[45] A special committee was formed to probe Fiedler's actions in the summer of 1896. By autumn, the board had voted to restrict Fiedler's ability to exercise independent judgment in securing subcontractors. Fiedler fought the new rules. The last three months of his tenure were most likely very difficult.[46]

When August Fiedler's appointment expired in December 1896, he refused to run for reelection. His two successors encountered even more problems. The first was Normand S. Patton, a well-respected local architect who specialized in schools—unlike his predecessors—and lasted almost two years before conflict arose. In September 1898, he read a statement to the Committee on Buildings and Grounds which, as described in the *Proceedings of the Board of Education of the City of Chicago*, "contained language which was disrespectful, insulting and impertinent to this committee, and impugned the standing, reputation, integrity and honesty of a member of said committee and of this board. . . ."[47] Patton's offense was to charge the Committee on Buildings and Grounds, especially board trustee Joseph Downey, with favoritism. The committee had passed a resolution (on Downey's motion) requiring all Chicago public schools to be constructed with hydraulic red pressed brick; since only one company in Chicago made this type of brick, Patton detected a monopoly. He also resented the aesthetic restrictions that such a mandate would place on his design process.[48] Downey and the board demanded an apology. Patton refused, and requested a trial. The board complied after charging him with insubordination, conduct in violation of discipline, impugning Downey's honesty and integrity, and willful disobedience.[49] After a three-day hearing in November 1898, the board found Patton guilty of attacking Downey and fired him—thirteen days before his term was to expire.[50]

William Mundie was hired in December to succeed Patton. Early inklings of a difficult relationship appeared in 1902, when Chicago School Board Trustee Thomas Gallagher publicly assailed Mundie for criticizing his employers; the following year a controversy arose involving school desks.[51] Tensions mounted in November, 1903, when board trustee W.A. Kuflewski, as part of a campaign to reform the school system, targeted the Chicago School Board's Building Repair Department (under Mundie's supervision) for elimination and criticized Mundie's salary.[52] Within weeks the department had been severely reduced and its head "laid off." A distraught Mundie told the board that he would retire from his position in December.[53] A few weeks later, however, the *Chicago Tribune* reported that while Mundie would indeed resign, he would continue in office until an investigation of his practices was completed.[54] This item angered the board and prompted another attack; on December 19, school board president Graham H. Harris accused Mundie of "gross extravagancies" and "unbusinesslike conduct."[55] Yet, at virtually the same time, Mundie ran again for architect's position and was reelected. When Mundie finally quit in March 1904, Harris reported that Mundie was leaving "on account of his health."[56]

The historical record suggests that Mundie was forced out of office because of problems with the board's corrupt construction practices. A 1910 editorial in the *Western Architect* commented on the situation: "Mundie served Chicago through its school board for five years and it well nigh ruined his physical health, but his sturdy Scotch-Canadian mentality would not allow the nagging of a politically domineering board to get on his nerves. He finally decided that the game was not worth the candle and resigned."[57] None of this had been mentioned in an article on Mundie written five years earlier, but that previous author made a veiled reference to possible problems: "For years political affiliations were of paramount importance and a little merit here and there was somewhat essential. Today merit rules and politics is outside the [architectural] department, but not so of the board of education. Political parties pay off their political debts by appointments; and questions of nationality, sectional denominations, capital and labor, in fact any pact or organization of vote getting power is given consideration for seats upon the board and here friction and faction bother the heads of the executive department."[58] This political "friction" between the Chicago Board of Education and its architect would reach its zenith during the tenure of Dwight Heald Perkins.

## Dwight Perkins's Alternative Vision

Dwight Heald Perkins replaced William Mundie as board architect in 1905 and created over forty public schools in Chicago before being fired in a widely-publicized scandal. He continued Mundie's practice of creating school buildings around ideas of health and safety and curriculum adaptation while expanding Mundie's classical language. Within a few years Perkins would be recognized as one of the preeminent school architects in the country.[59]

Dwight Perkins was born in Memphis in 1867 and moved to Chicago as a youth (Fig. 4.11). He studied architecture at M.I.T. for two years and briefly worked for the famous Boston architect H.H. Richardson before returning to Chicago in 1888. There he obtained a job with the prominent firm Burnham and Root and quickly became one of the office's chief administrators. In 1894,

Fig. 4.11. Joseph P. Magrady, Dwight H. Perkins (center), and A. F. Hussander, 1908.
Magrady headed the board of education's school repair department.

he opened his own practice. In the early 1900s, Perkins was a leading figure in
the development of Chicago's extensive park system. While serving as school
board architect from 1905–1910, Perkins carried out a private practice in partnership with John L. Hamilton; after his dismissal, the firm added William K.
Fellows. Perkins, Fellows and Hamilton designed schools across the country,
although Perkins cut back on his work for health reasons in 1925. His son,
Lawrence B. Perkins, became a famous educational architect in his own right
with the firm Perkins, Wheeler and Will, as we shall see in Chapter Five.[60]

Dwight Perkins came to the board architect's position with a reputation as
a reformer. He had worked at Jane Addams' Hull House, designed settlement
houses for the University of Chicago and Northwestern University, and helped
found the reform-oriented City Club. In fact, Perkins may have taken the civil
service exam to qualify for the board architect post at the urging of fellow City
Club members. Perkins entered the world of Chicago education at the peak
of progressive influence. The year he was chosen to be board architect, Democratic Judge Edward F. Dunne was elected mayor. Dunne had campaigned
with strong support from the Chicago Teachers' Federation. Upon taking office,
he appointed the most liberal school board in the city's history. The new board

members included Jane Addams, famous settlement house founder and champion of the downtrodden, and Louis F. Post, editor of the progressive magazine, *The Public*. Dunne's radical board tried to give Chicago's citizens and teachers more representation in educational policy matters. And in a controversial move, they embarked on a campaign to fund the schools by collecting unpaid taxes and renegotiating long-term real estate leases of school property at prices far below market value awarded by the previous board to many of the city's powerful business interests. The *Chicago Tribune*—a beneficiary of one of those favorable leases—responded by labeling the new board members "freaks, cranks, monomaniacs, and boodlers."[61] The board also clashed with Superintendent Cooley, who sided with the city's commercial giants on the issue of vocational education.

Progressive domination of the school board was short-lived, ending with Dunne's defeat in the 1907 mayoral election by Republican Fred A. Busse. After virtually ignoring the education issue during his campaign, Busse struck quickly after assuming office, demanding the resignations of twelve of the twenty-one school board members. He replaced them with conservative men from business and industry who had no tolerance for the type of liberal issues favored by the Dunne board.

Working in this milieu, Perkins would prove to be the most innovative of Chicago's board architects. He set out to devise standardized grammar schools that could be built inexpensively anywhere in the city, an important approach at a time when the school system's financial circumstances were particularly dire. Perkins developed two variations of the grammar school, an expandable building and a complete building. The prototypes shared architectural elements based on what Perkins believed were the most important considerations for Chicago's schools, like fireproof construction, twenty-six rooms, standardized classroom size (874.5 square feet), first-floor assembly halls, third-floor gymnasiums, basement rooms for manual and domestic training, toilets on each floor, and abundant playground space outside.[62] In these projects and others, Perkins would also exhibit a fondness for unique, non-historical architectural styles.

## Lane Technical High School

Perkins's first opportunity to apply his aesthetic ideas to a Chicago high school came in 1908 with the Albert G. Lane Technical High School (Fig. 4.12).[63] Lane Tech was an outgrowth of a vocational training movement that

Fig. 4.12. Dwight H. Perkins, Albert G. Lane Technical High School, 1908. Perkins's first high school constructed in Chicago reflected his interest in a more abstract, less historically accurate form of classicism than his predecessor, William Mundie.

reshaped secondary education in the early twentieth century. Technical high schools multiplied in cities across the country, offering more opportunities to learn crafts and trades for those students unwilling or unable to prepare for college. Chicago educators had embraced the vocational training movement with enthusiasm, despite labor opposition, and Lane Tech would become the city's most visible symbol of that commitment. It was the most recent in a long line of technical high schools.[64]

The Chicago Board of Education intended Lane Tech to be the city's preeminent vocational school. The *Chicago Record-Herald* described the building, erected at the corner of Sedgwick and Division Streets, as "the most expensive public school structure in the West."[65] Perkins's E-shaped floor plan was more open than previous Chicago high schools, which had tended to be either square or rectangular. He placed rooms along the outer edge of a main corridor, bent back the building's ends, and put an assembly hall in the center to form the E (Fig. 4.13). Heavy equipment was located in the basement shops, while the upper floors mainly were comprised of classrooms. The five-story central portion contained an auditorium and gallery, a lunchroom, a gymnasium, and a small running track and lockers on the top floor.

Lane Tech's floor plan was an example of an "open plan," so named after the way it cracked open the formerly closed cubic box that dominated school architecture for most of the nineteenth century. The open plan and the differentiation of room type and use found in schools like Lane Tech were the most significant factors that distinguished the early twentieth-century schoolhouse from its nineteenth-century forefathers. Such schools showed the extent to which increased attention to lighting, heating, and ventilation, along with the demands of an expanded curriculum, profoundly affected the school building's development. When William B. Ittner reflected on educational architecture near the end of a long, illustrious career, he attempted to summarize the turn-of-the-century schoolhouse's transformation. "The fundamental change in schoolhouse planning was initiated about 1899 when the so-called "closed" plan gave way to the open and semi open plan," wrote Ittner. "The enrichment of the educational program which came about gradually from this time on gave emphasis to the flexibility and possibilities of the open type of plan."[66]

Open plans took many forms, but all were intended to expose the building's interior spaces to air and natural light. For most of the nineteenth century schools had resembled an "egg crate"; in other words, a cubical or rectangular shell was filled with similar or identical multipurpose rooms, and hallways and interior corridors were small or nonexistent. There were no open-air spaces within the confines of the exterior walls. The floor plans of these buildings tended to fall into three general categories. One group of smaller buildings had no internal hallways; individual rooms on upper floors were accessed through corner or central staircases (like Chicago Central). A second group contained a single hallway running through the building, usually lengthwise if the building was rectangular (like North and South Division high schools). The third group had intersecting cross- or T-shaped corridors (e.g., West Division II). These closed designs prevented natural light and outside air from penetrating very far into the building. Some architects recognized the limitations of the "egg crate" plan and began to stretch buildings lengthwise, lining rooms along both sides of a central corridor, which maximized light in the classrooms but left the hall illuminated only by end windows. Ittner described a typical building plan of this period: "In this country it is almost universal to flank the two sides of the corridor with classrooms and depend upon the classroom doors and transoms and windows at the ends for light. In Germany, the prevailing custom places the classrooms on one side only, giving

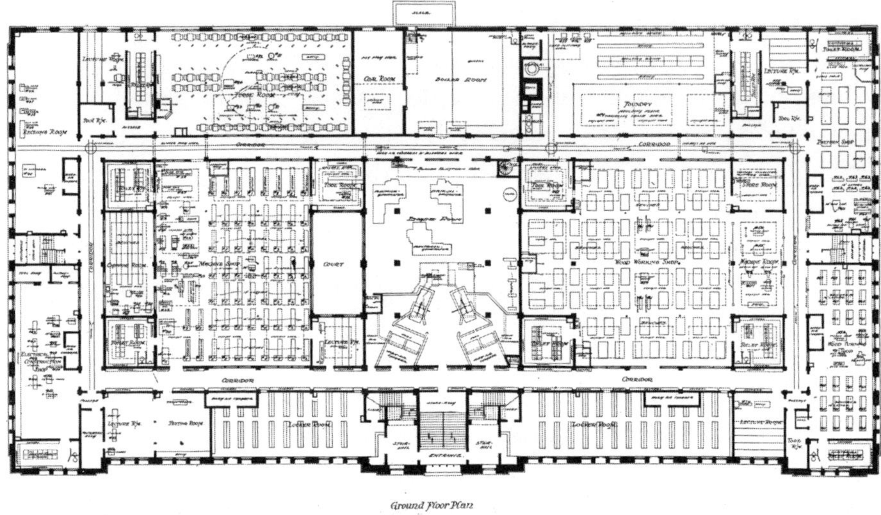



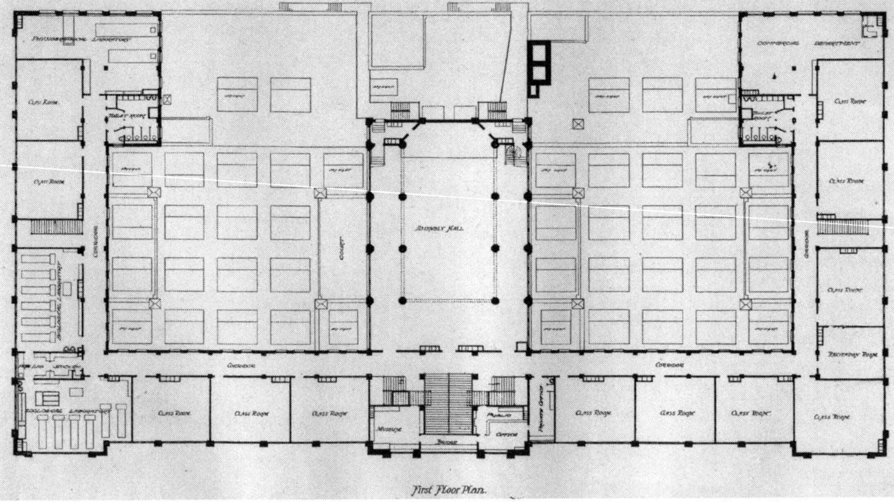



Fig. 4.13. Ground- and first-floor plans, Lane Technical High School. These plans illustrate the significant number of new spaces needed for the modern vocational school.

direct outside lighting in the corridor. While the American custom gives a more compact and economical building, it is accomplished at the sacrifice of proper lighting and attractiveness, and is one of the weakest points about our school plan."[67] During the 1880s, there had been some progress toward opening school building interiors. Architects often accomplished this by vertically expanding the hallway into a multi-story atrium. The larger spaces in the center of buildings were sometimes lit by skylights. School officials could use these atria as assembly halls in schools that did not have a large room specifically for that purpose. Students sat on the ground floor and the upper floors acted as balconies. Such designs, however, proved deadly in the event of fire, providing a flue that channeled fire rapidly up through the building.

Another trend in the 1880s was to experiment with open plans to improve lighting and ventilation. The Boston Latin and English High School was one of the first American school buildings to contain an interior courtyard. As mentioned above, German schools that John Philbrick visited during a European tour inspired the Boston Latin and English High School. Architects of the time also had access to more illustrations of open and semi-open school plans in British architect E. R. Robson's book, *School Architecture*.[68] Most floor plans in the American architectural and educational journals were closed plans, however, until the 1900s.

Architects like Dwight Perkins creating open plan buildings were almost unanimous in placing the auditorium along the building's main axis, perpendicular to the central hallway and directly across from the main entrance, as in the McKinley, Phillips, and Lane Tech schools. Locating the auditorium in such a place on the first floor moved the large, multistoried space out of the main circulation patterns and allowed the building to be symmetrical. Light courts on either side of the auditorium provided needed light and air to the corridors and rooms of either wing. Architects sometimes combined auditoriums with gymnasiums or locker rooms in a vertical stack (or, in some cases, horizontally, with the auditorium stage serving as the gymnasium). School architects combined these practical considerations with a recognition of the school's emerging status in the community. As William B. Ittner stated in a speech at the National Education Association annual meeting, "The growing demand for the use of high-school auditoriums for evening lectures and purposes other than strictly school use demands that they be located on the ground or first floor, and near the main entrance of the building."[69]

In a 1925 report on schoolhouse planning, Frank Irving Cooper listed eight types of school plans, based on extensive nationwide research, that architects had used in the previous two decades (Fig. 4.14).[70] Cooper's taxonomy divided floor plans into two types: closed and open. Closed plans were identified as the "solid rectangle" (the form used for Chicago's Division high schools), the "hollow rectangle," and the "rectangle with interior auditorium and courts" (such as McKinley and Phillips). Open plans included the "small I," the "large I," "T," "U" (Waller) and the "E" (Lane Tech). (The text also listed the "H" plan, which was used at Lindblom High School). Cooper outlined the main considerations in choosing one of these plans as: "1. Orientation 2. Natural Light & Natural Ventilation 3. Expansiveness 4. Flexibility 5. Light Corridors 6. Efficient Supervision 7. Reduction of Vertical Travel 8. Aesthetic Fitness 9. Economy."[71] While the report made no specific recommendations, a review of the floor plans of school buildings in published journals uncovers a definite trend away from closed plans and toward open plans between 1890 and 1920. The most popular high school floor plans by far in the 1910s were the "rectangle with interior auditorium and courts," the "E," and the "H." By the early 1920s, closed plans were almost nonexistent in urban public schools. The open floor plan had triumphed because of its superior ability to provide natural light and fresh air to the schoolhouse and its flexibility for future expansion.

Dwight Perkins's high school designs advanced the open plan beyond the experiments of his Chicago predecessors. His aesthetic for Lane Tech was also new. Most important was the building's lack of historical details. Perkins referenced William Mundie by decorating Lane Tech's roofline, uniting multiple stories with giant pilasters, and using a gridded facade with strong horizontal and vertical elements. But Perkins's column capitals were modernistic and ahistorical, the pilasters were made of brick to match the rest of the facade rather than standing apart, and they reflected the steel-frame structure behind them to a greater extent than any of Mundie's schools. He also substituted fireproof terra cotta for the traditional stone trim. The overall result was an abstract, stripped-down type of classicism that contrasted greatly with the florid Beaux-Arts mode popularized by the World's Columbian Exposition. One contemporary writer described Lane Tech's appearance as "plain to severity" without intending this as a criticism.[72] A few years later, architectural critic Peter B. Wight praised Perkins's school facades (including Lane Tech)

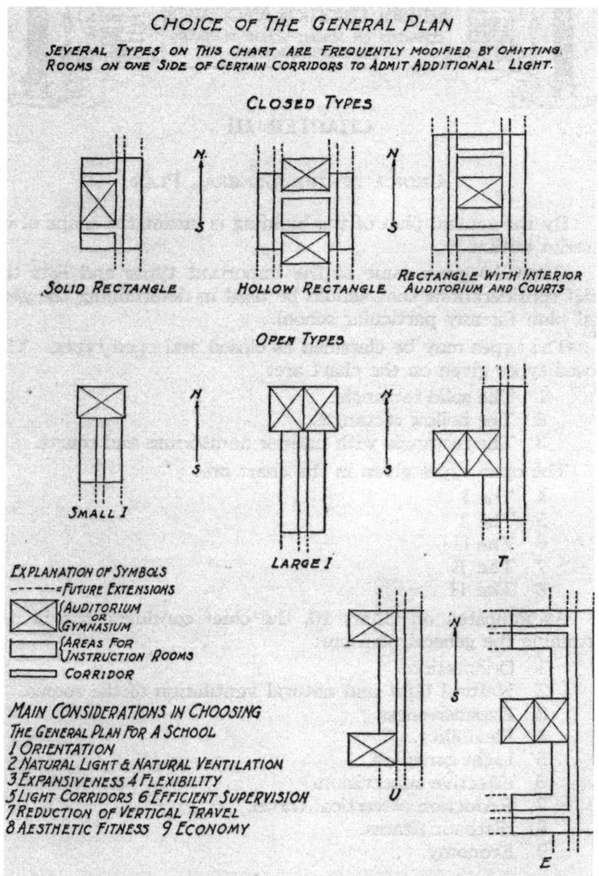


Fig. 4.14. "Choice of the General Plan." This chart, prepared by a National Education Association committee in 1925, illustrates the most popular choices for open floor plans in school buildings.

as "extremely rational developments of the grand plans in brick and stone, without any attempt to introduce extraneous ornament."[73]

One factor that undoubtedly influenced Perkins's minimal and non-historical style was the tight budget allotted for school construction. By this time the general public recognized high schools as social investments and sources of civic pride, but that rarely materialized into financial support. As a consequence, school boards never seemed to have the money needed to build new schools. Financial constraints often forced school architects to create muted versions of classical or Gothic buildings, with a multi-columned temple front on an otherwise plain brick facade, or a curved or crenellated roofline and a few pointed arches. Even the most elaborately classical or medieval-styled schools had minimal decoration compared to other civic and religious buildings. And only a handful of high schools around the United States had any form of architectural sculpture during this period, although it was considered de rigueur for major civic commissions.[74] Restricted budgets limited most school decorations to abstract terra cotta patterns on the exterior and perhaps a mural in the lobby or auditorium.[75]

Dwight Perkins's grammar schools were particularly affected by a board campaign to cut school construction costs in the wake of severe overcrowding problems. Beginning in early 1909, a concerted effort to attack Perkins and his department was carried out by Committee on Buildings and Grounds chairman Joseph Downey and later joined by Chicago Board of Education President Alfred Urion. For seven months, these two men continually chastised Perkins for creating unjustifiably expensive school buildings, despite the fact that he was cutting costs wherever possible. Downey, a former builder and head of the city building commission who was involved in the dismissals of both Normand Patton and William Mundie, alleged that schools could be built for 25 percent less than current costs. He questioned Perkins as to why school buildings cost more than those constructed in the 1890s. Perkins responded that material and labor costs had risen, the board had made more specific requests for spaces or equipment in school buildings, and the city building ordinance had changed in the wake of the 1903 Iroquois Theater fire and now required, among other things, the use of terra cotta in place of limestone for greater fire protection.[76] Urion demonstrated his ignorance of the state of the city's school architecture with comments such as, "The board of education has been wasting $500,000 a year on frills and gargoyles. One-eighth of its available building funds has been frittered away on decoration."[77] Perkins vigorously defended his position, but worried about the possible aesthetic consequences of further constraints. "Factory buildings can scarcely be built cheaper than we have built schoolhouses," he told Urion. "The buildings I have planned are so near factory buildings in appearance that I have feared criticism on that account."[78] In the end the two sides reached a compromise and Perkins agreed to reduce the costs of new school construction by $25-

65,000 per building. But the animosity that developed between Perkins and Urion during the struggle would not disappear.

## Bowen and Schurz High Schools

The combination of economic restrictions and Perkins's architectural philosophy led him to utilize geometric simplicity to impart visual interest and avoid historicist ornamentation. Some of his grammar schools for Chicago were monolithic, undecorated structures whose visual effects were limited to their formal qualities and multi-colored brickwork. In a 1912 speech he outlined his alternative vision for educational architecture: "[W]hen the public demands such schools as these it will have become so intelligent that it will no longer permit architects to inflict designs executed in old, dead, and inappropriate styles; that eventually the imperialism of Rome and the debasing sham of American galvanized-iron imitations of Rome will be rejected to be replaced by a style at once direct, honest, modest, sensible, enduring, and beautiful."[79] At least one Chicago newspaper agreed with Perkins. When the school board attempted to "apologize for the plainness and simplicity" of Perkins's "economical type" school buildings, the *Chicago Record-Herald* countered that such an apology was "unnecessary and even impertinent." "There is no reason why our public school structures should be fanciful or individualistic," stated the writer. "They perform a public and official service, and they should be set above the gusts of passing architectural fashions. . . . If good taste can be reached, with a saving on each building of from $50,000 to $60,000, why should not the board of education and the architects alike be congratulated?"[80]

During this period of turmoil Perkins produced his two most unique high schools for Chicago, named for Carl Schurz and James Bowen. Both were comprehensive schools rather than vocational schools like Lane Tech, and they represented the culmination of Perkins's attempt to merge the latest advances in school architecture with a new non-historical expression—one that, in fact, was actually regressive, for Schurz and Bowen displayed the then-old-fashioned image of the school as house (Figs. 4.15-4.16). Both buildings featured massive gabled roofs that marked them as oversized domestic symbols and related them to their surrounding neighborhoods.[81] Additionally, they contained no historical details. Instead, the buildings' appeal

Fig. 4.15. Dwight H. Perkins, Carl Schurz High School, 1910.

Fig. 4.16. Dwight H. Perkins, James Bowen High School, 1910. Schurz and Bowen bear a resemblance to Frank Lloyd Wright's "Prairie School" style of the early 1900s.

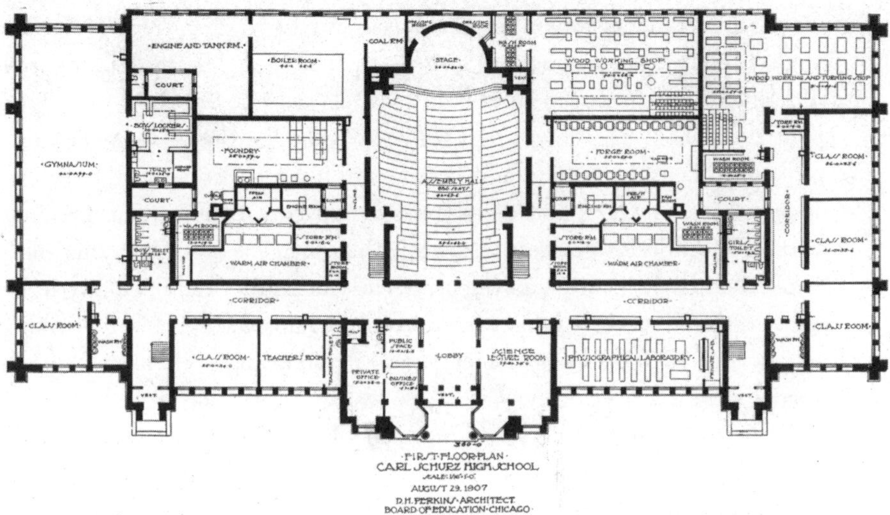

Fig. 4.17. First-floor plan, Schurz High School.

derived from attractive forms, crisp brickwork with contrasting terra cotta, overpowering roofs, and grand scale. The schools were, as one historian has written, "monumental without being formidable."[82]

Many in the architectural world consider Schurz High School to be Perkins's best educational work in Chicago. Although known for its striking form, Schurz's floor plans demonstrate the room variety and planning adaptations of the fully-evolved modern school building (Fig. 4.17). It continued early experiments by Flanders, Patton, and Mundie with zoning, or teaching different subject areas in different parts of the building. Perkins carried the idea to its logical conclusion with Schurz. The building occupied a triangular lot at the intersection of Milwaukee and Addison. The E-shaped plan included technical shops on the ground floor to minimize disruption from the heavy equipment. The west wing contained the gymnasium and second-story running track. Perkins placed science laboratories along the front of the building on the upper floors, while the girls' vocational training rooms (textile making, sewing and fitting, domestic science—with a model dining room) where all on the third floor. Most of the fourth floor was devoted to rooms for artistic and mechanical drawing. A lunchroom inhabited the fifth-floor attic beneath the huge gabled roof.

Architectural historians in the 1960s and 1970s characterized Schurz High School as a rare institutional example of the "Prairie School" style (Bowen, Schurz's nearly identical sister school, was ignored) and a part of the "Chicago School" movement that anticipated modernism.[83] It may be more accurate to consider Schurz and Bowen—in light of Perkins's other school designs—as anomalies, outside of styles or movements other than Perkins's own predilection for progressive ideas. While their massive, sheltering roofs invoke home and family and impart a sense of comfort and stability in an age of dislocation, there is no evidence that Perkins was specifically looking back to the "school as house" metaphor. His other high school in Chicago besides Lane Tech—Englewood (1908)—was English Tudor style.[84] And his only other attempt at a domestic-type school was in nearby Whiting, Indiana, where he designed a 1908 building similar to Schurz but with a smaller, hipped roof and boxy rectangular shape. His post-1910 schools were significantly more historical, especially those of the 1920s.[85]

Bowen and Schurz high schools are best evaluated in light of Perkins's quest to economize school architecture and his association with the arts and crafts movement. Begun in England in the early nineteenth century and popularized by John Ruskin and William Morris, the arts and crafts movement in its original form advocated a denunciation of modern industrialization and a return to pre-industrial craft traditions. As a corollary of these ideas, English architects promoted a vernacular or everyday historicism, focused on domestic architecture, over the leading academic styles of the day. The movement jumped to America where Chicagoans formed one of the first arts and crafts societies in the country in 1897. Dwight Perkins, along with Frank Lloyd Wright, was an early member. Wright's famous Prairie-style houses captured the essence of arts and crafts architecture through their emphasis on natural materials, their floor plans that endeavored to reinforce family cohesiveness, their simplicity and rejection of traditional "high" styles, and their attempt to harmonize architecture with nature. Perkins, though sometimes considered a member of the Prairie School, went his own way architecturally despite his friendship with Wright. He never resorted to Wright-copying, unlike some of his Chicago contemporaries, but did design public and private buildings, like Schurz and Bowen, that evoked  arts and crafts principles. These two school buildings were essentially large-scale  arts and crafts bungalows adapted to the high school's distinctive functional needs.[86]

Perkins's experiments with an alternative educational architecture were cut short by omnipresent political conflicts. In 1909, a mere eight days after Perkins had apparently resolved the school cost conflict and a *Chicago Record-Herald* article entitled, "Schools to Cost Less; Hatchet Now Buried" appeared, school board president Alfred R. Urion gave notice that the ill will between the two men had not waned.[87] Urion attacked again on new territory, charging Perkins during a Committee on Buildings and Grounds meeting with "extravagant office expenditures and delays in making reports."[88] The battle escalated over the following months until Urion ordered Perkins to either give up his outside architectural practice or resign his position. When Perkins refused, Urion suspended him on charges of "incompetence, extravagance, and insubordination."[89] Urion, who was also corporate counsel for the powerful Armour Industries, believed in running the schools like a business; in 1910, he said "As long as I remain the president of the board of education it will be conducted on economical corporation lines."[90] He claimed Perkins was refusing to "fit in" with his system by creating buildings that were costly and poorly designed while devoting too much time to his own practice.

Perkins was tried in a public hearing that began in March 1910 and lasted more than three weeks. The trial seemed to polarize many of Chicago's organizations. Perkins gained the support of the Illinois Chapter of the American Institute of Architects, the Chicago Architects' Business Association, the Chicago Architectural Club, the Chicago Estimators Club, the City Club, and the Municipal Art League, among others, and the Chicago Federation of Labor exerted pressure for a fair hearing. During the inquiry, William B. Ittner of St. Louis was brought to town to view some of Perkins's buildings and testify to his competence and ability. Contrary to public and press opinion, however, the board found Perkins guilty of extravagance and removed him from office on May 1, 1910.[91]

## A. F. Hussander's Monumental School Plants

After the Perkins scandal, the Chicago Board of Education toyed with the idea of eliminating the board architect position, but eventually settled on a replacement.[92] Arthur F. Hussander, Perkins's former assistant, worked as "acting" board architect until achieving permanent status four years later. Little is known about A. F. Hussander other than that he was born in Chicago in 1865 and received an architectural degree from Cornell University. Hussander would serve the school board for over a decade, which was significant given that none of his predecessors lasted longer than five-and-a-half years.

The scandal surrounding Dwight Perkins's ouster had residual effects on the relationship between the board and the architecture department, as demonstrated by Hussander's first published statement in the *Annual Report*:

> Upon my election to office, the Board, through its Committee on Buildings and Grounds, instituted a most thorough inquiry along practical lines looking to a more economical administration in connection with the erection of buildings, and after many conferences of the committee and the members of the Board of Education, a demand was made for a less expensive type of school building which could be duplicated as necessity required on new sites thereby saving, in the first instance, the cost of making new plans as well as a saving in the cost of construction of the building itself; the new type of building to contain ample light, the most modern heating and ventilating apparatus that can be procured, a thorough school equipment; eliminating nothing that would decrease the safety or limit the comfort of the pupils or impair the educational efficiency of the school plant. *The change in style of the building to be along lines of simplicity and strength of construction, keeping in mind, beauty of outline, harmony of color, etc.* (emphasis added).[93]

These remarks seem intended to appease Hussander's superiors, who had charged Perkins with creating "monuments to himself."[94] Shortly before the attack on Perkins, Alfred Urion had declared an end to elaborate school architecture, leading a *Chicago Tribune* writer to exult, "The knell of the ornate public school building, with its tall columns, terra cotta capitals, and fluted cornices, was sounded in Chicago yesterday."[95] Ironically, this description refers to William Mundie's style of architecture, not Perkins's, which makes the last sentence of Hussander's statement particularly interesting. Hussander would actually reject Perkins's simpler abstract and home-like styles for his school designs in favor of an even more monumental type of classicism than Mundie.[96]

A.F. Hussander's Chicago high schools were of a type: Roman classical grandeur on the outside, and sophisticated explorations of open plans and

Fig. 4.18. A. F. Hussander, Nicholas Senn High School, 1912.

zoned areas inside. He presided over the period of Chicago's greatest high school enrollment surge up to that point. Between 1910 and 1920, the number of high school students more than doubled, increasing from 17,800 to 36,433.[97] Increasing enrollments and expanding curricula necessitated larger buildings. One of Hussander's first high schools, Nicholas Senn High School (1912), at the intersection of Southport Avenue and Francis Place on the city's far north side, exemplifies his high school work (Fig. 4.18). Senn High School was a massive building, roughly 240' x 440'. Some of the city's 1880s Division high schools were smaller than Senn's auditorium. The school was three stories high with no basement, which Hussander believed were unsanitary and a waste of space.[98] Its gray brick exterior reintroduced and accentuated William Mundie's classical language. Six giant Ionic columns signaled Senn's central pavilion, and a large entablature ran around the building supported by a multitude of Ionic pilasters. Square pavilions anchored the building at the four corners. An attic story capped the building and a pediment and lunette window rose above the central block. In an article on Chicago schools, the *American School Board Journal*'s William C. Bruce praised Senn High School's appearance as "classic in design and truly monumental as is befitting a high school."[99]

Fig. 4.19. A. F. Hussander, Hyde Park High School, 1913. Compare with John Flanders's Hyde Park High School of two decades earlier (see Fig. 2.8).

Senn's floor plan combined open and closed planning ideas. The first floor was actually a solid rectangle with the entrance on one of the long sides. In contemporary fashion, the entry vestibule opened onto a cross-corridor and auditorium. Also on the first floor, in addition to offices and classrooms, were the athletic facilities (a full gymnasium, a small gymnasium or calisthenics room, and a swimming pool), lunchroom, two science rooms, and shops for vocational training courses. Stairs were located at the middle and end of each long corridor. A U-shaped second floor was dominated by classrooms; Hussander also included the library and more business education rooms for bookkeeping, stenography, and typing. The U-shape continued on the third floor, which contained most of Senn's science laboratories, rooms for drawing and modeling, "household arts" rooms, a textile arts and sewing room, a large lecture room; and more classrooms. A small fourth-floor choral room capped the building.

Hussander created Senn at approximately the same time as two other high school buildings—Hyde Park High School (1913) on Stony Island Avenue near the University of Chicago, and Carter Harrison High School

Fig. 4.20. A. F. Hussander, Carter Harrison High School, 1912.

(1912) at Marshall Boulevard and W. 24th Street (Figs. 4.19 and 4.20). Both schools had immense monumental facades. Harrison closely resembled the Field Museum of Natural History (D. H. Burnham & Co., 1909–12), which opened on the downtown lakefront at almost the same time. Harrison's floor plan was extremely sophisticated (Fig. 4.21). The building was shaped like a hollowed square. The spaces on each floor were strictly zoned. Classrooms and offices were located around the front and sides of the first floor, with shop classes in the rear and a recreational core formed by the auditorium in the center flanked by boys and girls' gymnasiums and a swimming pool. Stairwells were located in the four corner pavilions and at the interior angles of the auditorium. Science rooms lined the front, classrooms were arranged along the sides, and a sizeable lunchroom filled the rear. On the third and highest floor, more science rooms, domestic science rooms and classrooms ringed the open court, and drafting and drawing rooms formed a row across the back. A two-story shop annex extended from the rear corner of the main block.

School construction ground to a halt in Chicago and other cities during the 1917–18 academic year because of America's entry into World War I. When construction resumed, Hussander produced another grand building of

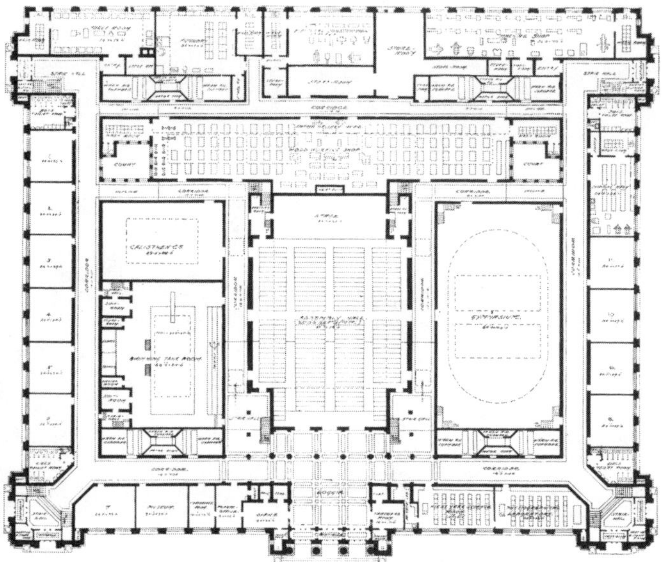



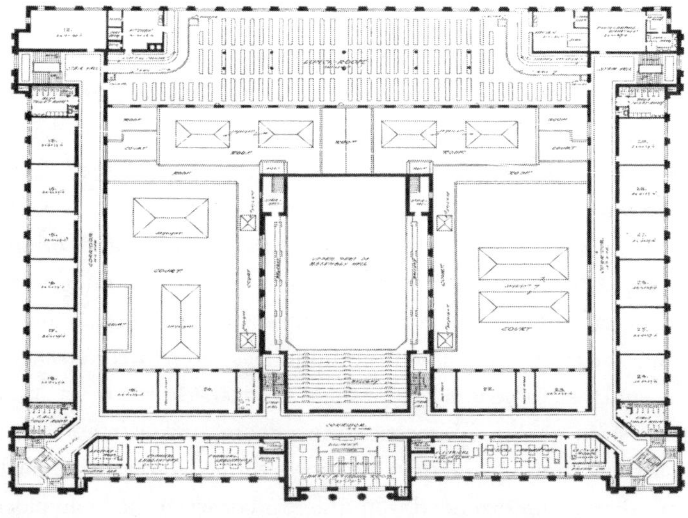



Fig. 4.21. First- and second-floor plans, Harrison High School.

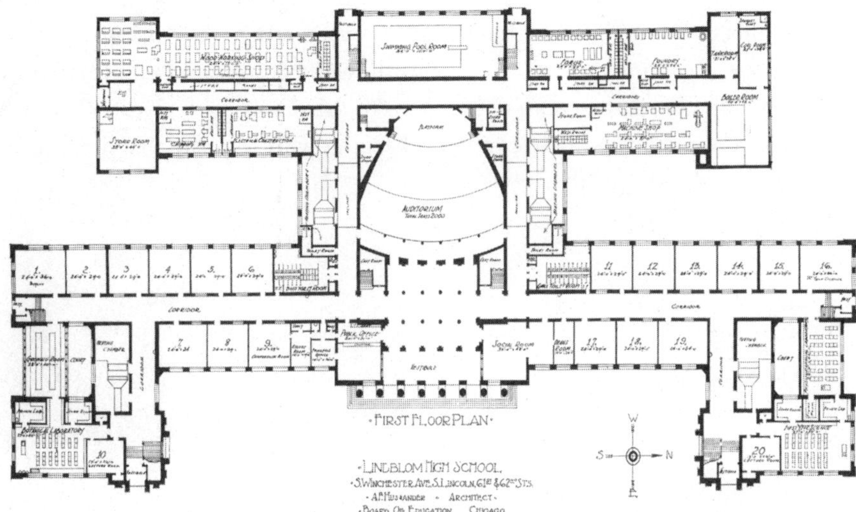

Fig. 4.22. First-floor plan, Lindblom High School.

the same type, Robert Lindblom Technical High School (1919) (see Fig. 4.1). The site was a suburban block at Lincoln Avenue and 61st Street on the near southwest side. As described at the beginning of this chapter, Lindblom was an expansive building designed for over 2,000 students. It followed the same model as Hussander's pre-war buildings and shared formal and planning characteristics—monumental classical exteriors and open plans with areas zoned according to use (Fig. 4.22). The "noise producing departments" (gymnasiums, shops, swimming pool, music room, and power plant) were located in the rear of the H-shaped plan, with the academic and administrative areas concentrated in the front. In an article in the *American School Board Journal*, Hussander noted with pride that the building had no interior courts—"The space between the two wings is so wide that the light is entirely adequate"— and boasted that "one superintendent of schools who visited the building and who made an especial effort to study the lighting, admitted that several hours of inspection failed to find a single dark corner in the entire building."[100]

The nineteenth-century schoolhouse's transformation into the twentieth-century school building was complete by 1920. A. F. Hussander's grand educational palaces were a far cry from the subdued brick boxes of the first

Division schools. Chicago's post-World War I high schools were the kinds of buildings contemplated by the writer of a 1920 article in *Architecture*: "With very few exceptions, the new buildings show the desire, both upon the part of the architect and the community, to make the school something of a monument, a source of local civic pride in keeping with the part that architecture plays in our national life."[101]

# PART III
# DEVELOPMENT

The components of the modern high school building were largely determined and in place by 1920; thereafter the few modifications to school architecture that occurred entailed either new arrangements of those parts or changes to the classroom's basic layout. Until the 1950s, high school buildings across the country were typically monumental structures in historical styles. In the two decades preceding World War II, scandals and economic depression hindered Chicago's school system. After World War II soaring student enrollments and inadequate resources forced the city's school officials to deal with a new set of issues. Chicago's educators initiated a series of building campaigns to create a generation of schools in the modernist manner, rejecting the previous generation's grand monuments. The modernist high schools were intentionally more "casual" in form and layout. Inside these structures the "differentiated curriculum," stressing personal development over traditional academic learning, remained the norm. High school construction slowed in the 1960s, but resumed in the 1970s. By then, school buildings experienced stylistic changes while novel pedagogical experiments altered some of the interior spaces. By the 1980s, the Chicago Public Schools again were crippled, this time by the mixture of shifting demographics, decreasing enrollments, poor student performance, financial problems, and administrative mismanagement. The city government took control of the schools and instituted programs to raise the quality of instruction and improve the buildings. Some of these new measures tied Chicago to a nationwide "back to basics" curriculum reform movement. School architecture, as always inseparable from educational reform, also began to look to the past for guidance.

# Chapter Five

# ROARING TWENTIES, DEPRESSION, AND WAR

By 1920, the ultimate form of the modern high school building had been established in cities like Chicago, New York, and Boston. Large, symmetrical, multistoried buildings with prominent central entrances, specialized rooms laid out around wide corridors, gymnasiums, swimming pools, and grand auditoriums existed across the country, clothed in English Tudor, Gothic Revival, Colonial Revival, or classical styles. These buildings had evolved in response to a changing curriculum and a growing public interest in secondary education. The architects and educators who created them were unaware just how popular the high school would become, as the next two decades brought an unprecedented enrollment explosion that strained the resources of urban public school systems. Further architectural innovation would be eclipsed by practical necessity; as a result, high school architecture in larger cities like Chicago remained virtually unchanged from the early-1900s until the late 1940s.

In 1920 there were 36,433 students enrolled in Chicago public high schools. A decade later, the number had nearly tripled to over 100,000, and by 1940 there were 144,671 high schoolers in the city (see Table 1A).[1] This spectacular rise echoed nationwide statistics. American high school enrollment increased from just over two million in 1920 to over 6.5 million in 1940—the greatest period of growth in history.[2] In relative terms, the percentage of fourteen- to seventeen-year-olds enrolled in high schools across the country during that period increased from 31 percent to 72 percent.[3] According to

Chicago school administrator Don C. Rogers, the great upsurge was initiated by five factors: the average family's improved economic status; compulsory school attendance; the economic depression, which eliminated work as an option for most teenagers; an increasing city population; and an enlarged curriculum that "lured large numbers of young people."[4] George S. Counts, famed critic of the Chicago schools, believed the enrollment increase happened because "There is practically no place in modern industry for a child under sixteen or seventeen years of age."[5] Whatever the reasons for the enrollment boom, it necessitated new facilities. Chicagoans in the two decades between 1920 and 1940 saw more high school buildings rise across the city than at any time before or since.

## The Roaring Twenties

In the early twenties educators and architects considered Chicago high school buildings to be efficient machines in the service of education. Board of education architect A. F. Hussander wrote in the *American School Board Journal*, "From whatever angle it may be considered *the school building is first and last the tool or instrument of the school* and its sole purpose is to provide proper housing for the school so that the latter may most efficiently and comfortably carry on the work of education (emphasis added)."[6] Unfortunately, the crush of students interfered with the building's ability to fulfill this mission. Consistent room and seat shortages forced educators to seek relief by juggling half-day sessions and adding night classes and off-site locations. Many thought a partial solution might lie in the creation of junior high schools.

### The Junior High School Experiment
Junior high schools were becoming a national trend at the time, their popularity driven by both educational and economic motives. Educators and psychologists had singled out early adolescents as a group with special needs; they believed that placing these youngsters together in their own school without the interference of younger or older classmates would stimulate their development. The junior high could also help to ease those children into the types of subjects and classes they would encounter in high school. And junior high school systems would allow educators to begin the process of vocational chan-

neling or "tracking" students into different courses of study, based on their interests and abilities, at a much earlier age. Similarly, American business supported junior high schools because they promised an inexpensive way to train the growing non-college-bound workforce, with the desirable side effect of weakening the apprentice system and, consequently, the labor unions.[7]

Chicago began its flirtation with junior high schools in 1917 upon the recommendation of the school board's Committee on Educational Survey. Junior high schools could provide specialized instruction for seventh and eighth graders and possibly encourage those large numbers of children who dropped out after the eighth grade to remain in school. They could also reduce high school overcrowding.

Three junior high schools with just over 300 total pupils opened in September 1917. But the program really began in earnest under the leadership of a new superintendent. William McAndrew had been hired by Mayor William E. Dever in 1924 for his reputation as a reformer and efficiency expert. One of McAndrew's first campaigns was to suggest a special educational commission to study the junior high school situation. The commission recommended the large-scale implementation of junior high's for the city's seventh-through-ninth graders, "primarily upon the belief that the junior high school affords the greatest opportunity to provide effectively and economically the educational advantages which children of the early adolescent period need most to promote their immediate and future well-being and happiness and their usefulness as citizens."[8] The board approved the proposal despite resistance by labor unions that perceived the junior high system as a means of creating a permanent underclass of wage laborers, and the Chicago Teachers' Federation, which opposed new examinations for potential junior high school teachers.[9] In 1924 the first five junior high schools of McAndrew's tenure opened in remodeled elementary and high schools for seventh- through ninth-graders. Two years later the first purpose-built junior high's opened. The city eventually operated twenty-nine junior high schools before the system was abolished, for financial reasons, in 1933.[10]

Chicago's junior high schools, many of which became senior high schools after 1933, employed standardization as a means of cost-efficiency. They were generally designed as slightly smaller versions of the existing high schools. Most junior high schools had U- or E-shaped floor plans, with interior areas zoned by activity (Figs. 5.1 and 5.2). Their facades were brick with

Fig. 5.1. Paul Gerhardt, Frederick von Steuben Junior High School, 1930. Chicago's brief experiment with junior high schools in the 1920s produced a number of structures that became high schools after 1933, such as von Steuben.

stone or terra cotta trim and large windows. Small pavilions appeared at the buildings' center and ends, and a stone arch often surrounded the main entry. The decorative scheme tended toward an abstracted version of Tudor Gothic, sometimes accented by faux buttresses between windows as the grand classicism of A. F. Hussander's 1910s high schools disappeared. While Assistant Board Architect Ralph W. Yardley claimed in 1931 that "the exteriors of the [junior high] schools vary, depending upon the neighborhood in which they may be placed, the size of the site and the character of their surroundings," there were really few visible differences among this generation of Chicago schools.[11] "The interior arrangement and equipment rooms in all junior high schools is the same," Yardley admitted, and "the standardization of facilities has been found to increase the efficiency of the instruction."[12]

Most of these junior high schools were designed by school board architect John C. Christensen, who took over for Hussander after the latter's resignation in 1922. Christensen's reign over the architecture department would be the longest in city history—except for a hiatus from 1928–31, he would

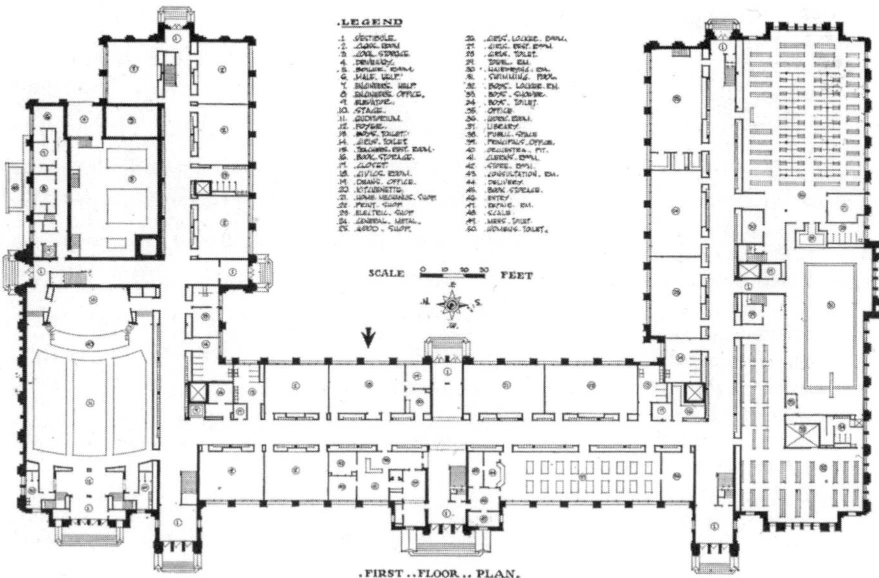

Fig. 5.2. First-floor plan, von Steuben Junior High School.

serve as board architect until 1959.[13] Christensen was the first board architect to work with a new department, the Bureau on Building Survey. Formed by Superintendent McAndrew in 1925 to provide him with information about school buildings and sites, the bureau's staff worked with educators and architects to create floor and building plans. The bureau was born of two desires: to "promote economy and educational efficiency," and to increase administrative involvement in the architectural design process.[14] Both of these goals continued to guide school design for decades.

By the 1930s, the Bureau on Building Survey had evolved into the Bureau of Research and Building Survey (BRBS), an agency responsible for selecting school sites, setting attendance boundaries, establishing branch schools, and recommending new buildings and additions, in addition to providing research on various aspects of the school plant. Don C. Rogers, the directory of the BRBS, boasted that his department had revolutionized school architecture in Chicago: "The year 1924 marked the beginning of scientific planning of Chicago school buildings. Since then the floor space of school buildings has been laid out according to the educational needs in administering the school program."[15]

When the board determined that a new school was needed, the BRBS chose the site. With increasing frequency these sites were in outlying areas some distance from downtown. The 1920s and 1930s junior and senior high schools formed a second ring around Chicago's commercial core and the older schools, extending over ten miles from the Loop in some cases, and blanketing the city's north, west, and south sides. After a building site was selected and purchased, the Educational Department sent its requirements to the Bureau of Architecture. Floor plans were drawn up and submitted to the BRBS; if they were deemed acceptable, the superintendent approved the plans, at which point the Bureau of Architecture was allowed to proceed with elevations, specifications, and working drawings to be submitted to the board.[16]

## Overcrowding and Race

Despite the BRBS' scientific approach to new school planning, overcrowded schools presented an insurmountable problem during the period between world wars as administrators were caught off-guard by the rising enrollments that followed the cessation of school construction during World War I. The board of education's strategy for coping, in addition to rapidly building junior high schools, included creating double- or multiple-shift school days (where children attended either morning or afternoon sessions of three to four hours rather than the entire day), enlarging class sizes, opening branch schools, or renting alternative spaces. There was a long history of these drastic measures, as indicated by an 1896 *Chicago Tribune* article: "Chicago's public school management never turns a pupil away because it hasn't room for him in a public school building," claimed the writer. "It has gone out and rented churches, barns, club-houses, grocery stores, amusement halls, and almost anything else with a roof above it which doesn't leak."[17] In the fall of 1922, fifteen high schools utilized double shifts to try to handle the overflowing classrooms. By 1926, the board estimated a shortage of 428 high school rooms; the following year, BRBS Director Don C. Rogers reported that twenty-one of the city's twenty-four public high schools were seriously overcrowded.[18] A team of outside evaluators found an incredible 39,771-seat shortage in the high schools in 1932.[19]

Chicago's black neighborhoods were the hardest hit by such conditions. Jean Baptiste Point DuSable High School, opened in 1935 on South

Fig. 5.3. John C. Christensen, Jean Baptiste Point DuSable High School, 1935.

State Street in the heart of the "Black Belt," was full almost immediately (Fig. 5.3). A reporter for the *Chicago Defender*, the city's preeminent black newspaper, visited the school three years later and found classes "held in assembly halls, store rooms, lunch rooms, corridors, special gymnasium, and ante rooms to the faculty lavatories."[20] By 1941 conditions in the city's two majority black high schools were appalling: DuSable crammed 4,000 students in a building meant for 2,400, while Phillips had 3,600 students in a structure meant for 1,500.[21]

Overcrowding was not the only problem with the DuSable building. The black community saw it as a symbol of the Chicago Public Schools' racist policies. *Chicago Defender* reporter Metz T.P. Lochard called DuSable a "fiasco" and chastised the school board for failing to adequately design and equip the building. "This school has been operating for four years without proper facilities," wrote Lochard. "Students in the mechanical department are without tools of modern machinery. In the automobile shop they are using old cars bought and hauled from some police stations.... The drawing room is without benches. There are no book cases, no waste baskets in the classrooms. The ceiling in the natatorium has been fixed three times in the space of three years and is in a deplorable condition.... There are even no facilities for such an emergency as illness."[22] The board's neglect extended to DuSable's exterior as well. Its unembellished brick facade was certainly less attractive than the contemporary junior high schools and far below the quality of the grandiose Lane Technical High School, then being constructed as a national showpiece on the city's near-north side (see below). "It presents a more unattractive aspect than any of the new school buildings," Lochard claimed. "In fact, it looks more like a structure in some backward community."[23]

The creation of public high schools like DuSable with overwhelmingly black enrollments was a relatively new phenomenon in Chicago. Between the end of the Civil War and the beginning of World War I, Chicago's schools were fully, if not easily, integrated. A series of events and conditions after 1915, however, created de facto segregation by 1940. Phillips High School, the city's first public high school to become majority black, saw its black student population soar from one-sixth to three-fourths between 1915 and 1921, while the total number of segregated black public schools grew from six to twenty-six in the 1920s.[24] The main catalysts for this radical change were black population growth and geographical segregation. According to historian Michael W. Homel, "The small pre-World War I black district quickly spread on the South Side after 1915, and the rise of the ghetto combined with the practice of basing school assignment on home address, placed most of Chicago's black children in 90-100 percent black [elementary] schools by the 1930s."[25]

## The Depression

While the Chicago Public Schools tended to ignore the black community's complaints, the Great Depression brought unavoidable challenges to the system. Chicago's schools were in trouble even before the Depression began due to widespread corruption and incompetence. For years, property tax assessments were kept artificially (and illegally) low by a succession of mayors in league with powerful businessmen, thus starving the school system of its major source of revenue. Then enrollments continued to increase while funds dwindled. In the belt-tightening period that followed the stock market crash of 1929, school building projects were among the first to be cancelled. The steadily increasing flow of students, however, assured that some construction had to continue.

## Economic Crisis

In an effort to decrease expenses, Chicago Board of Education Architect John Christensen and Superintendent William J. Bogan devised a plan to save approximately $200,000 on future high school construction. They recommended that future buildings have a diminished overall student capacity and that such areas as the central foyer, kitchen, and auditorium be reduced, lockers made smaller, and "corrective gymnasiums" (for posture exercises), conservatories, and electric and automobile shops be eliminated.[26] Non-architectural measures were more serious. Between 1931 and 1933, the board paid Chicago's teachers less than half their normal salary, and they were paid in warrants, which could only be redeemed at less than face value, rather than checks. The school budget was so tight that the school board actually considered the possibility of closing all of the city's public high schools in 1932. That extreme step was never taken, but in the summer of that year the board announced major budget cuts, including the elimination of all junior high schools, all athletic teams, bands, orchestras, manual and household arts classes; suspension of textbook purchases; closing swimming pools and kindergartens; and a 50 percent reduction in the number of high school physical education teachers—all without the superintendent's approval, and without reducing any of the system's many patronage and non-instructional jobs. An ensuing public protest rally attended by approximately 25,000 Chicagoans and numerous lawsuits failed to sway the board. After the schools opened for the fall term the board reversed some of its decisions, but the majority of the cuts remained in place, including the loss of over 1,000 teaching jobs. Only state and federal government intervention saved the Chicago schools from further drastic measures. The Illinois legislature managed to increase funding, which meant less of a reliance on local property taxes (during a time when property values dwindled), while the federal government passed a new law in early 1934 that allowed school boards in larger cities to mortgage school lands as security for bond sales.[27]

## Educational Scandals

Economic disaster was not the only crisis facing the Chicago schools in the early 1930s. Criticisms from two important outside entities focused public attention on serious problems with the high schools' accreditation and the architectural department's practices. In 1932, the school board arranged for a system-wide evaluation by George D. Strayer, a Columbia University educator known for his many lectures and writings on efficiency and highly regarded for his school surveys. The "Strayer Commission," a group of university education professors, was charged with examining five aspects of the Chicago public schools, including the status of the city's school buildings.[28]

Their scathing final report, in the words of historian Mary Herrick, "clearly demonstrated that the schools were being exploited for political profit."[29] Most significantly, the Strayer Commission called for the expansion of the superintendent's powers so that he or she could have more direct control over the school system. And in a volume devoted entirely to school buildings, the commission also attacked the quality of construction and the method of creating new schools. It recommended eliminating the board's powerful Committee on Buildings and Grounds (and all other standing committees); reducing the steps needed between the BRBS, the Bureau of Architecture, and the Educational Department when designing and approving new buildings; and dramatically improving the quality of school buildings while lowering their cost. The commission raised major concerns over issues such as the thirty-two new Chicago schools that were constructed so badly between 1925 and 1927 that over $700,000 in repairs were necessary, and an architectural department that cost over half-a-million dollars per year despite an economically-related stoppage of new designs. On the "Strayer scorecard," which measured the conditions of various aspects of school facilities, almost 100 school buildings across the city failed, including two high schools (Lake View and Waller) whose scores were so low they fell into the "Can't Be Saved" category.[30] Additionally, sixteen of the city's twenty-one other high school buildings were found to need some sort of improvement.

In the final recommendation section, the commission displayed its dissatisfaction with the architecture department with a suggestion that presaged events two decades later: "[The commission recommends] that the Board of Education so organize its bureau of architecture when building operations are renewed that the talent available in private practice may be drawn upon for their contribution to the service. It is the opinion of the survey staff that no less than 50 per cent of all new work should be commissioned to private firms."[31]

A year after the Strayer Report was released, the dismal state of the public school system was further flaunted in the news when the North Central Association of Colleges and Secondary Schools (NCA)—the body that governed public schools in the Midwest—threatened to strip Chicago's high schools of their accreditation, a potentially embarrassing action. When the board abolished the junior high school system it had shifted ten high schools into former junior high buildings. The NCA refused to recognize these high schools and further warned that in the city's other high schools'"services were below standard."[32] Later in the decade, the NCA censured all Chicago high schools for overcrowding, once again threatening to revoke accreditation.

In response to the pressures exerted by these critical outside surveys, the superintendent appointed an internal team to evaluate the city's high school facilities. According to promotional literature, these inspectors "were directed to inspect every room of every high school building and branch in the city."[33] In contrast to the Strayer Report, the inspectors' report outlined a number of relatively minor but widespread deficiencies, like insufficient libraries, inadequate science laboratory equipment, not enough shower rooms and study halls, and the need for renovated hallways and auditoriums, all at a price of $1.25 million. The board of education approved the request and work commenced in the late 1930s.

## The World's Largest High School

Another move to deflect criticism, and provide needed space, was the creation of a new Albert G. Lane Technical High School. The original building, designed by Dwight H. Perkins and opened in 1908, had been an enormous success (see Fig. 4.11). But Lane Tech's enrollment was over 7,000 by the early 1930s—approximately three times the building's original capacity. Overcrowding forced the school to expand beyond the Perkins building into portable rooms and nearby elementary school buildings. This popularity was prompted by the changing circumstances of urban life and the city's enlarged vocational curriculum. "The rapid growth of our cities with the resulting decrease in opportunities for boys to aid in the many manual tasks on farms and in rural homes, the high value a machine age placed upon the services of skilled workmen, and the natural urge of live, healthy American boys to do things" stimulated the success of schools like Lane Tech according to Thomas J. Higgins, the Assistant Director of the BRBS.[34]

The first Lane Tech building lacked the size and equipment to deal with the deluge of students and the evolving curriculum. Since it was opened, "educational theory was keeping pace with the changing world," wrote Higgins. "No longer was it thought sufficient to offer one course to which all boys must adapt themselves. A newer educational philosophy advocated the fitting of the school to the boy. With this thought came a diversification of courses and subjects."[35] This created a problem, for Higgins claimed Perkins's building "was not originally planned nor equipped to allow such diversification."[36] So the school board announced bold plans for "the world's largest high school"—a $6.5 million replacement building on a thirty-acre golf course along the north branch of the Chicago River west of Lincoln Park. A groundbreaking gala in the summer of 1930 brought thousands of spectators and dignitaries to watch a parade from Wrigley Field to the school site. "Lane has taken a place in the educational system that is national and international," proclaimed Grant Beebe, the school's principal.[37]

Chicago School Board Architect Paul Gerhardt designed the new Lane Tech to display both the school's importance to the city and vocational education's significance in 1930s America (Fig. 5.4). The huge building's sprawling floor plan formed a modified "H," dominated by a large interior courtyard and four end pavilions (Fig. 5.5). Inside were a diverse group of spaces to accommodate the demands of a curriculum that included classes in fifty-six different subjects. "With the opening of the new school, under the principalship of Charles E. Lang, the courses offered to the north-side boys of Chicago have been expanded to meet modern industrial and civic demands, and to embody the education best suited to the individual needs and capacities of the pupils," wrote Higgins.[38] Lane Tech held an impressive fifty-three classrooms in addition to a multitude of shops and laboratories for the technical courses. In typical fashion for the time the floor plan was symmetrical around a main axis that ran through the front door; it was also symmetrical about a cross-axis perpendicular to the entry. Gerhardt separated the two largest interior spaces—the auditorium and two of three gymnasiums—from each other at opposite ends of the building. The first floor contained offices, shops and laboratories, as well as the entries to the main gym and the auditorium seating 2,200 people. At the rear of the school was a lunchroom for 1,200 students. On the second floor, spaces were evenly distributed between shops,

Fig. 5.4. Paul Gerhardt, Albert G. Lane Technical High School, 1934.

labs, and classrooms, with a two-story library above the administrative offices. Classrooms dominated the third floor, while Gerhardt reserved the fourth for music and art rooms and biology laboratories.

Lane Tech's classrooms and shops were similar to those of earlier-century schools, except for electric lighting and updated equipment. The building's interior spaces differed from those of its predecessors, however, by being embellished with a substantial art collection—the largest of any Chicago public school. Fifty murals, including some dating back to the original 1908 school, adorned the walls of the first and second floors. In the first floor lobby visitors encountered scenes of a steel mill, a shipping dock, and a construction site. Panels representing the forty-eight states, taken from the General Motors Pavilion at Chicago's 1933–34 Century of Progress Exposition, were placed in the first floor corridors. Outside the second-floor library students could view scenes of Native American life. Sixteen more murals would be added to the library, auditorium, and cafeteria within the next few years.[39] The extensive art program further evidenced Lane Tech's status as the city's marquee high school.

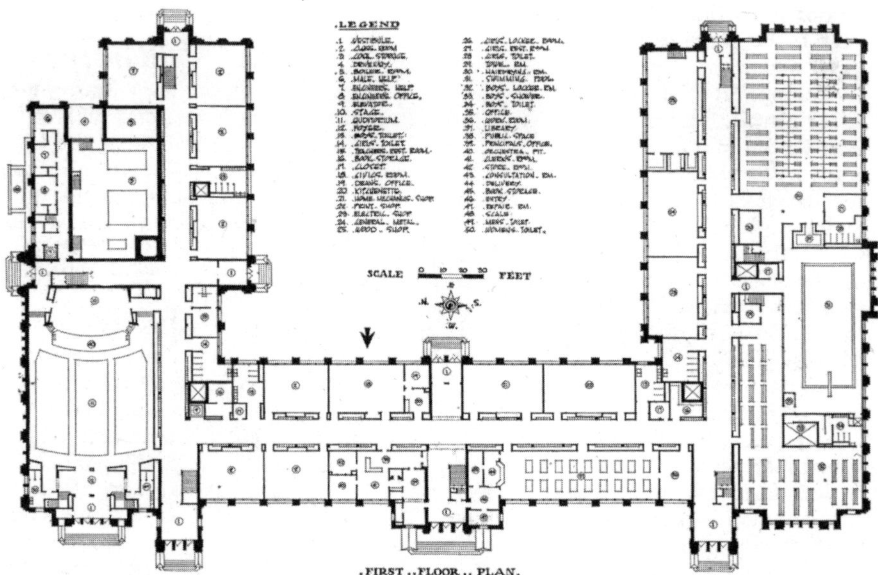


Fig. 5.5. First-floor plan, Lane Technical High School. The building accommodated a vast array of vocational equipment and programs. Although larger than its predecessors, the plan utilized the same design strategies as buildings from three decades earlier.

Gerhardt chose a Tudor Gothic style for Lane's exterior. A red brick skin with stone trim and accents covered the building's steel frame. The Gothic motif was carried inside to the foyer with plaster decoration on the ceilings and lancet-arched windows in the main lobby. While capably designed, there was an odd dissonance between the Gothic style's ancient connotations and the modernity of the industrial education curriculum. Lane Tech thus mirrored the tension between old and new that was coalescing into a contemporary debate among school architects. As it was being constructed, the first intimations of an alternative school architecture began to appear in educational and architectural journals.

## Early Modernism

Modernist architecture began to appear in  the educational and architectural literature in the early 1930s. Educators seem to have been initially attracted to modernist rhetoric highlighting functionality because of the way it meshed with the educational efficiency movement that had held sway for decades.[40] The *American School Board Journal's* William C. Bruce, for example, claimed in 1932 that "The planning of schoolhouses has for many years centered about the idea of the function of each unit—classroom, shop, auditorium, and special area.... It seems to be entirely logical that the functional idea should be carried over from the planning of the school building to the inseparable element of the expression of the form of the whole, so that the building may reflect in every way its true character."[41]

Bruce was not endorsing what came to be known as International Style modernism, exemplified to Americans by buildings like the Dessau Bauhaus and architects like Walter Gropius and Ludwig Mies van der Rohe; his enthusiasm for "modernistic" design, like others of his generation, was directed toward what we know as art moderne or art deco. Similarly, in 1930, the year ground was broken for the new Lane Tech project, Dwight H. Perkins, who had rebounded from his Chicago ordeal to become a nationally-renowned school architect, published a short article in the *American School Board Journal* on "Modern Architectural Design and Its Application to the Schools of Today." Perkins used the term "modern" as did most architects of the time, to refer to a type of design that adapted historical forms to contemporary needs, not as a description of a machine-influenced, European-derived architecture that rejected historical precedent. He wrote about the significance of both plan and elevation: "The composition of the plan has quite as much of the artistic element in it as has the elevations. No good-appearing building can be erected from a poor plan. The plan must be expressed in the elevations and the nature of the material must be recognized." This may have resembled the rhetoric of contemporary European modernists like Le Corbusier, who famously claimed, "The plan is the generator," but Perkins's intent was different.[42] Perkins's traditional approach emphasized that beauty—judged by traditional standards—was equally as important as function. Thus the architect must consider such issues, according to Perkins, as "the relation of solid mass to void, the proportion of plain wall to ornament, the sky line, the use of color."[43]

Three years after Perkins's article, educators' growing interest in modern design was illustrated in an issue of *American School and University*. Architect Guy Study and the Museum of Modern Art's Philip Johnson (who was not yet an architect) contributed opposing essays on the topic, "Architecture for School and College Buildings—Period Styles or Contemporary?" Both writers built their arguments around the concept of functionality. Study, in support of period styles, began by introducing the established Ecole des Beaux-Arts notion of the importance of a building's "character," then proceeded to explain how character is a functional aspect of school design since it can help develop the student's character.[44] "A school building is well designed when it successfully fills its purpose. The whole school plant should work towards the education of youth and help to cultivate appreciation of the finer things in life," he wrote. Study followed in the footsteps of nineteenth century predecessors like Henry Barnard, who felt a schoolhouse should be a teaching tool "calculated to inspire children and the community generally with respect for the object to which it is devoted."[45] In his only mention of planning, Study criticized recent German school architecture, "which seems to be concerned solely with the thought of supplying pupils with light and air" while failing to develop plans based on "what we in this country know as intelligent school administration." The essay then returned to the school building's appearance, with Study arguing in favor of the time-honored styles, particularly Tudor Gothic and Colonial. He concluded the article with a broader view. "In the development of the youth of our land it is well to acquaint them with the great cultures of the past and to cherish the spirit of the founders of the nation:" the best way to do this, according to Study, was through "the two traditional styles of architecture, the Tudor and the Colonial, which fortunately have become our true heritage."[46]

Philip Johnson's retort, entitled "Modern Architecture for Efficiency," lashed out at the type of architecture study prescribed:

> Architects have been more concerned with the system of design which they learned by heart in architectural school than with the functional needs of the building which they were planning. The results were bad lighting, bad planning and high costs. Carefully spaced Georgian windows or Gothic slits did not afford sufficient light for modern interiors; monumental vestibules and dark corridors took up too much space; libraries, offices, gymnasiums and classrooms were all forced into a symmetrical shell regardless of their varying size, shape and function. Classical cornices or cut-stone window

mullions, marble staircases and Georgian belfries ate up the appropriations
of the community which might have been applied to teachers' salaries.[47]

The paradox of period styles, wrote Johnson, is that copying a historical style
correctly makes for an "uneconomic and functionally inefficient modern
school," while adapting historical styles to accommodate the functions of
contemporary schools leaves "no resemblance in letter or spirit to the original
style." Although the short essay put much emphasis on economics, Johnson
also argued that modern schools could be judged beautiful according to the
same criteria as historic styles—proportioning, detail, and materials. However, "in contrast to the imitative monumentality of structures built with an
eye to the past, modern buildings have a cleanness, lightness and simplicity
which accord well with our machine civilization. To surround the growing
generation with bad parodies of dead architecture is a foolish anachronism."[48]

Demonstrating how nebulous the concept of "efficiency" was in 1930s
architectural circles, Chicago School Board Architect John C. Christensen
invoked it in describing the new Lane Tech building—a school Philip Johnson would most certainly consider a structure of "imitative monumentality . . . built with an eye to the past." In an essay in Lane's dedication booklet
Christensen asserted, "The efficiency of any school depends largely upon the
planning of the building. The real test of success of a school building is its
efficiency. If a school building plan is successful in meeting the diversified
educational program, then the architect has achieved his goal."[49] Christensen
believed this had been achieved at Lane Tech through "an adaptation of Tudor Gothic architecture to the needs of a modern high school building."[50]

The efficiency and style debate was not merely an argument over degrees, with traditionalists advocating efficient floor plans wrapped in historical garb versus modernists seeking to extend the plan's efficiency to the
building's exteriors. Rather it was a disagreement over what efficiency really
meant. Traditionalists believed the school model that developed in the early
twentieth century under architects like William B. Ittner to be perfectly
adapted to contemporary educational needs, while modernists advocated
a total rethinking of the school building inside and out. The debate would
remain unresolved, however, during the difficult times of the Depression.

## The 1940s

The rapid rise in Chicago high school enrollment came to a grinding halt and then actually reversed during the 1940s. During the decade enrollment dropped 33 percent, far outdistancing the national plunge of 13 percent (see Table 1B).[51] The numbers plummeted because student-age youths enlisted in the armed forces, the birth rate declined, wartime defense jobs became available to teenagers, and the economy was resurrected after World War II. As a consequence of economic depression and war, high school construction almost ceased during the decade. Those few buildings that were built reflected a national trend toward using increasingly abstracted historical styles with no significant interior innovations.

### More Scandals

Scandals and bad publicity at times overshadowed Chicago's high school enrollment reversal in the 1940s. The problems peaked at mid-decade, when a series of reports, widely covered by the city's newspapers, castigated the system. First, beginning in 1943, the National Education Association (NEA) began to investigate the actions of the board of education and its superintendent, William H. Johnson. The inquiry resulted in a long list of illegalities and abuses of power, along with a series of recommendations, principally that the superintendent be given control over the entire school system rather than just its instructional aspects. As a result of this scathing report, the NEA expelled Johnson for unprofessional conduct, but he kept his job as Chicago's superintendent.

The city council convened a special committee to hold a public hearing in response to the NEA charges. After hearing testimony from a variety of organizations supporting the NEA recommendations, the committee, made up of aldermen loyal to Mayor Edward J. Kelly, responded that nothing was wrong with the school system and pointed to their NCA accreditation status as evidence. Ironically, the next day the NCA released its own report on the city's high schools outlining serious mismanagement and once again threatening to revoke accreditation unless the superintendent's powers were expanded. The ensuing scandal forced Kelly to create a special advisory committee made up of local university presidents and an NCA representative;

after months of investigation, the committee recommended the superintendent and the entire board resign. Superintendent Johnson and one board member did quit, with three more board members following a few months later. Although Kelly complied with all the advisory committee suggestions, including many political concessions, it was too late—the scandals played a large part in undermining his reelection campaign. In 1947 Chicagoans elected businessman Martin Kennelly, who presented school reform as a major plank of his platform, as their mayor.

Perhaps the most important outcome of the scandals was that the Illinois legislature passed a law in 1947 creating the post of General Superintendent of Schools of Chicago. The law capped a long campaign to put more administrative control in the superintendent's hands and lessen the mayor-appointed school board's influence. In Chicago, the corruption within the nation's second largest school system had reached absurd levels during the twenties and thirties. A series of grand jury investigations, supported by various citizens' organizations like the Municipal Voters' League, produced evidence of the graft, waste, and favoritism in the school system that Chicagoans had long suspected. These problems were blamed in part on a partisan school board hand-picked by the mayor according to the recently passed Otis Law; the board, in turn, chose the superintendent. Accordingly, there was what educational critic George S. Counts called an "intimate union" which made "the board of education a creature of the municipal government."[52] The 1947 reform law showed Chicago to be nearly a half-century behind other major cities in the country in terms of addressing school-political connections.

## The "most modern and best equipped trade school in the United States"

The board of education constructed few school buildings during the course of these scandals. The most prominent was the Chicago Vocational High School (CVS), which symbolized the end of an era in high school architecture (Fig. 5.6). Intended as a south side counterpart to Lane Tech, CVS was built between 1938 and 1940 with federal assistance. The massive structure was expected to accommodate 4,000 students, and its main facade was almost as long as three football fields. Early in its history, students nicknamed CVS "The Palace" in recognition of its impressive size and appearance.

Fig. 5.6. John C. Christensen, Chicago Vocational High School. 1940.

On an awkward triangular site, board architect John Christensen took a traditional "hollow rectangle" plan, extended it with large end pavilions, and added a pair of two-story spines, one along Chappel Avenue perpendicular to the main facade, and the other corresponding to the triangle's hypotenuse on Anthony Avenue (Fig. 5.7). The spines contained the school's unique workshops. Aligned along two sides of a central corridor, and intended for eighteen students each, these workshops were the highlight of the building. The rooms were forty-by-seventy foot rectangles (Fig. 5.8). Glass dominated three sides of the workshop to accommodate natural light. In these rooms, students could study such trades as aircraft or automobile repair, mold making, patternmaking, die making, or boiler making, blacksmithing, milling, air-conditioning or refrigeration repair, woodworking, mechanical drawing, and printing. Small classrooms, tool rooms, washrooms, and storage space occupied the areas between workshops. The building also held a library, an assembly hall, a lunchroom, a swimming pool, and six gymnasiums of various sizes. While not as elaborately decorated inside as Lane Tech, CVS did include art deco-style inlaid floors, light fixtures, and wall designs, and an impressive series of carved wooden panels in the auditorium with scenes of Chicago buildings and industry.

Except for the workshop spines, the interior spaces of a building like CVS were not drastically different from its turn-of-the-century predecessors. CVS' room layout and variety were almost the same as William Mundie had used in the high schools forty years earlier, and the interior zoning of spaces related back at least three decades. On the exterior, however, changing architectural tastes in the intervening period had ushered in a plainer, less monumental look. Often described as "stripped" or "modernized" classicism, the style, as displayed in buildings like CVS, presented large expanses of plain, unornamented stone, with minimal decoration. These decorations often

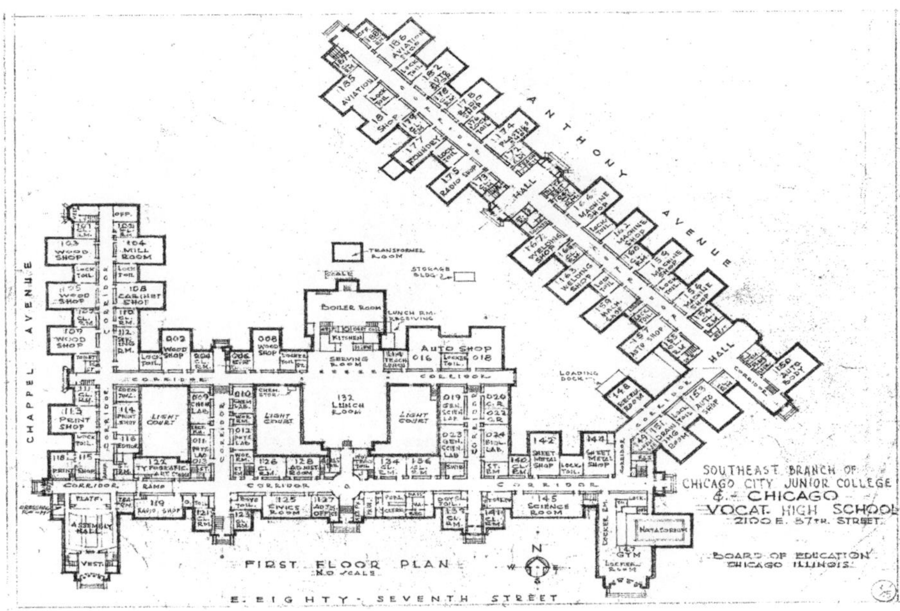

Fig. 5.7. First-floor plan, Chicago Vocational High School (altered by the author). The unique workshops can be seen along the building's outer edges.

consisted of non-historical columns and relief sculpture incised into the wall surface. At CVS, for example, the cornice line of the main facade and primary and end pavilion entrances along 87th Street contained small sculptures depicting some of the subjects taught in the school—chemistry, foundry work, woodworking, bricklaying, drafting, weaving, electronics, etc. Stripped, or abstract, classicism had become the semi-official style of the United States government, appearing in courthouses, post offices, and other government buildings around the country, marking such civic buildings as important through timeless classical references while reflecting both diminished economic times and the growing cultural fascination with the machine age.[53]

The Chicago Board of Education obviously appreciated John Christensen's efforts in introducing the style to the city's schools, writing in 1941, "The school architect has demonstrated that it is possible to have first-class architectural design combined with sound educational features. Modern school building construction embodies economy, utility, simplicity, and a pleasing appearance, minus any lavish architecture to attain ornamentation at educational or financial sacrifice."[54] But an editorial in the *Chicago Tribune*

Fig. 5.8. Workshops, Chicago Vocational High School.

a few years later painted a different picture. "A lot of money has been spent in this and other communities for school buildings; certainly enough to buy better designed structures than most of them are," wrote the author. "Architects have told us that the ungainly appearance of school buildings results in considerable part from the legal requirements of very high ceilings in schoolrooms. . . . Schoolrooms forced into this mold tend to be cold and uninviting. At the same time, the high ceilings impose a monumental scale on the exteriors which some of the architects have tried to relieve with flossy decoration and others have merely ignored. It is hard to say which is worse. The decoration, when it is used, is usually uninteresting; and the absence of it merely accentuates the awkwardness of the mass."[55] The editorial concluded with what may have been a common conviction: "The school is usually the principal building in its community. It is a shame to build unsightly ones when, with a little more thought and study and quite probably a saving of money, genuinely attractive structures could be erected."[56] The writer also may have been reacting to Christensen's two other Chicago high schools of the decade, which were plain, inexpensive brick buildings lacking decoration (Fig. 5.9).

Fig. 5.9. John C. Christensen, South Shore High School, 1940.

When CVS was completed in the summer of 1940 the *Chicago Tribune* called it "the most modern and best equipped trade school in the United States."[57] The school board sang the praises of the curriculum in a pamphlet created to celebrate the groundbreaking ceremony: "Vocational schools furnish training required by skilled workers, foremen, and junior engineer executives, and these groups in turn furnish higher executives and leaders, for industry. Industrial efficiency is not alone a matter of machines. Better industrial relations, public relations, and knowledge of markets, can be obtained by organized study than in the absence of such study."[58] This all would take place in an impressive building that could hold up to 6,000 students, but still lacked necessary mechanical equipment. Possibly because the federal government had contributed almost half of the building's total cost, the Chicago Public Schools offered the building to the government upon completion. Progress was slow in transferring the school, however, and it was not until summer 1941—after sitting vacant for a year—that the U.S. Navy began using CVS to train aviation mechanics. The building was not returned to the public school system until 1946.

Chicago then had two mammoth vocational schools, further evidence of the prominent role vocational education was playing in American secondary education. Overall, during the period from 1920 to 1950, Chicago added more than twenty new high school buildings. Those built in the forties differed from their turn-of-the-century predecessors only in their exterior dressing—the basic elements of the modern high school had all been prescribed by an earlier generation of school architects. In the ensuing decades, however, practical considerations and changing architectural tastes would steer the city's high school buildings in a different direction.

# Chapter Six

# MODERNISM AND EDUCATION

After World War II, school architecture in Chicago and around the country changed as building design was reconsidered, influenced by the lessons of dramatic population flux, the impact of architectural modernism, and educators' pedagogical experiments. But one thing did not change—the American high school's basic components remained the same in the postwar era as they had been in the 1910s, even as architects introduced new materials or educators experimented with novel arrangements of the school's parts.

## A New Type of School for the Postwar Era

The Crow Island School in Winnetka, Illinois, a suburb north of Chicago, heralded a new era in American educational architecture (Fig. 6.1). An elementary school, Crow Island seamlessly meshed the architectural modernism and educational progressivism of its time, and would stand as a model for schools of all levels for decades.

Crow Island's design was a group effort. Officially the project was a joint venture between the young, unknown local architectural firm of Perkins, Wheeler and Will, and the famous architect Eliel Saarinen. Also joining in the building's development were Winnetka's superintendent, Carleton Washburne, who enjoyed a national reputation as a progressive reformer,

Fig. 6.1. Perkins, Wheeler & Will with Saarinen & Saarinen, Crow Island Elementary
School, Winnetka, Illinois, 1940.

along with the school's teachers, students, janitors, and the local school
board.[1] Together this ensemble crafted a school building that proved innovative educational architecture had not reached a dead end in the early twentieth century. With the support of a reformist superintendent and school
board, the designers sought to integrate the school building with student
activities in an unprecedented way. The process began with architect Lawrence B. Perkins—son of former Chicago School Board Architect Dwight
H. Perkins—sitting in on classes in the Winnetka schools to gain firsthand
knowledge of teachers' practices and students' behaviors. Perkins experienced
Winnetka's progressive curriculum, which extended beyond the traditional
"three R's" to develop children's citizenship skills, individuality, and emo-
tional well-being through four main types of school activities: individual
and group academic work, and individual and group non-academic work.[2]
Perkins took these four activities, added two essential elements of school life
from his observations (handling of clothing—coats, boots, etc.—and toilet-
ing) and used them as the basis for shaping the classrooms.

Although the evidence is mixed, it appears that the Perkins, Wheeler
and Will firm probably was responsible for most if not all of Crow Island's
formal planning while the Saarinen team, consisting of Eliel; his wife Loja, a

weaver; his soon-to-be-famous architect son Eero; and Eero's fiancée Lillian Swann, a ceramicist, developed the building's aesthetics. Crow Island's footprint formed a slightly straightened "Z" shape. Interior space was divided into separate areas for administration, communal activities (auditorium, library, art room, and playroom), kindergarten and nursery, lower grades (1–2), and upper grades (3–6). Each grading group had its own wing, classrooms, and playground to minimize interaction between younger and older children. The wings consisted of spines of single- or double-loaded corridors lined with L-shaped classrooms. These classrooms contained both traditional learning space and active work space, each occupying one arm of the "L," and the two areas could be separated by sliding doors. The classrooms' main sections were intended for group and individual academic work and group non-academic projects. Two walls made almost entirely of glass let in abundant natural light and visually connected the children with the outdoors. Moveable furniture gave the teachers freedom to arrange desks and tables for different activities. One large wall opposite the windows was covered with pine and could be used as a bulletin board. Workspaces also contained toilets and closets. And Eliel and Eero Saarinen created a different decorative scheme, full of bright colors, for each room.

Crow Island rejected most of the conventions of contemporary school buildings. It was one-story where they were multi-storied; it was asymmetrical and non-axial where they were formal and dominated by central and cross-axes; its classrooms were L-shaped instead of rectangular, and they ignored the nineteenth-century uniform source rule for lighting by allowing light to enter through windows in more than one wall. Also, the classroom ceilings were only nine feet rather than twelve feet high; toilets were located within the classrooms rather than grouped together in the hallway; workspaces were integrated into the classrooms rather than being in separate rooms; classroom and hallway walls were covered with wood paneling; and, very shocking at the time, all of the furniture was moveable. These various innovations connected the building to the school's progressive curriculum and pedagogy. Unique features like lower ceilings, classroom toilets, wood-paneled walls, and child-sized furniture indicated the planners' attempt to make the spaces less institutional and more homelike. Frances Presler, Crow Island's director of school activities, called the classrooms "school homes" to reinforce this message.[3]

Within a year of opening Crow Island had been publicized with a fourteen-page spread in *Architectural Forum*, the most widely-read and progressive architectural journal in America, and an article in the *American School Board Journal*.[4] Within a decade, elementary schools had been revolutionized, partly because of Crow Island. Architects and educators also began to consider how Crow Island's lessons might be adapted to the high school's more complex requirements. This represented a distinct difference from the pre-war era, when high school buildings were the innovators and elementary schools followed their lead. Educator Walter Cocking recognized this when he wrote, in 1956, "Undoubtedly, the refreshing designs of new elementary schools and the general approval which greeted them helped to give architects courage to consider design innovations for secondary school buildings."[5]

## Architectural Modernism in the 1950s

The success of Crow Island and other early modernist schools across the country stimulated educators' interest in architectural modernism. These schools demonstrated how several of the ideas educators had been discussing for some time could be articulated in architectural terms. Foremost among these was the concept of "flexibility." Architects promoted modernism's inherent flexibility—along with its lower cost—and contrasted it with the rigidity of traditional school architecture. The combination of malleability and inexpensiveness attracted school boards around the country. As a result, by the late 1950s the look and layout of American school buildings had changed drastically.

### Flexibility and Function

"Flexibility" was the most commonly-used word in the educational and architectural literature to describe the postwar school's needs and modernist architecture's advantages. The term itself was elastic; it could represent the ability to allow for different pedagogical techniques within the same space, the building's capacity to adjust to significant expansions or reductions in student populations, the capability of configuring the same space in different ways to accommodate different uses, and many other things. Flexibility's emergence as a key concept was partly due to fluctuating school populations in the previous decades. After World War II, enrollments were the most influential factor affecting school architecture. In Chicago, for example, after high school enrollments rose by over 100 percent in both the 1910s and 1920s, they grew by only 40 percent in the 1930s, and then fell by 33 percent in the 1940s before rising again by 6 percent in the 1950s and 38 percent in the following decade (see Table 1B).[6] Nationally the figures followed the same pattern but the percentage changes were even more dramatic.[7] Educators became keenly attentive to population growth patterns as a result of these surges and recessions, and the future began to play a greater role in their plans. Modernist architecture seemed better able than traditional school design to offer the kind of flexibility needed to meet these varying enrollment demands.

Shifting populations were not, however, the only motivation for educators' to embrace flexibility. Progressive educational ideas from earlier in the century infiltrated the mainstream by the 1940s, influencing educators to make a greater effort to adapt curricula and pedagogical styles to students' individual interests and abilities. The school building was implicated in this effort because reformist educators increasingly viewed older buildings as obsolete. "Modern education seeks to adjust the school program to the child rather than the reverse," wrote Wilmington, Delaware superintendent Ward I. Miller in 1949. "Thus it seems the modern secondary school with a program which utilizes to the fullest the best educational theory requires a building designed especially to suit its purposes. Traditional building styles restrict if they do not altogether prohibit the implementation of good theory. It is to be hoped that working together, architects, engineers, and educators can persuade boards of education and the public that new wine requires new bottles."[8] Kansas City Superintendent Harold E. Moore concurred. He complained that high schools rarely "kept abreast of or reflected changes in the philosophy of education."[9] Education was evolving, and the older generations of buildings, like traditional pedagogical techniques, were proving inadequate. Moore criticized educators and architects who continued to blindly follow custom: "The selection at the onset of a square or rectangular type building, particularly one of the closed type, or one with several stories, curtails the development of instructional units that characterize the needs of the modern secondary school." Modern education required innovative forms, in part because interior spaces had become more complex. According to Moore, "The modern classroom is totally unlike its progenitor. In the first place, it is considerably larger and much more of a workroom or laboratory in design. Work tables, auxiliary spaces, storage, audio-visual materials and equipment, conference facilities, multiple book materials, some degree of comfort, conditioning for color, seeing, sound, and temperature, and other adaptations contrast it with the box-like and rigid lecture or recitation rooms of a few generations ago."[10] Spaces needed to be adaptable, reflecting the new curriculum's supposed freedom from traditional constraints. "Recommended too in modern schools is the opportunity for students to move and change their accommodations to fit their work," wrote Moore. "Flexibility in size of classrooms, laboratories, and shops through the use of movable sound-partitions also characterize modern planning."[11]

One of the foremost proponents of modernist school architecture was Chicago's Lawrence Perkins, who vaulted to national prominence after the Crow Island School's critical success. In their 1949 book, *Schools*, Perkins and co-author Walter D. Cocking explained the principles of a modern school architecture. Perhaps the most important—though by no means novel—idea was that the school building "should provide facilities for the types and kinds of activities necessary for the instructional program which will be carried on."[12] This actually had been the guiding principle behind high school architecture's transformation at the end of the nineteenth century. Like other modernists, however, Perkins and Cocking faulted those earlier school buildings for being too big, too expensive, and not adapted to children's needs. They employed modernist rhetoric to emphasize how contemporary schools were planned with students in mind, unlike their precursors. "The planning and designing of schools during the 1900-1930 period showed many improvements," they wrote. "But schools were still characterized by standardization, topped with lavish front [sic]. Progress had not yet reached the point where the school building was designed for its pupils, tailor-made for its site and built to serve the community with utmost efficiency."[13] But a new day was dawning, characterized by buildings that were flexible, efficient, and beautiful, utilizing modern age materials like steel, reinforced concrete, and large expanses of glass, and incorporating lessons from decades of educational experience.

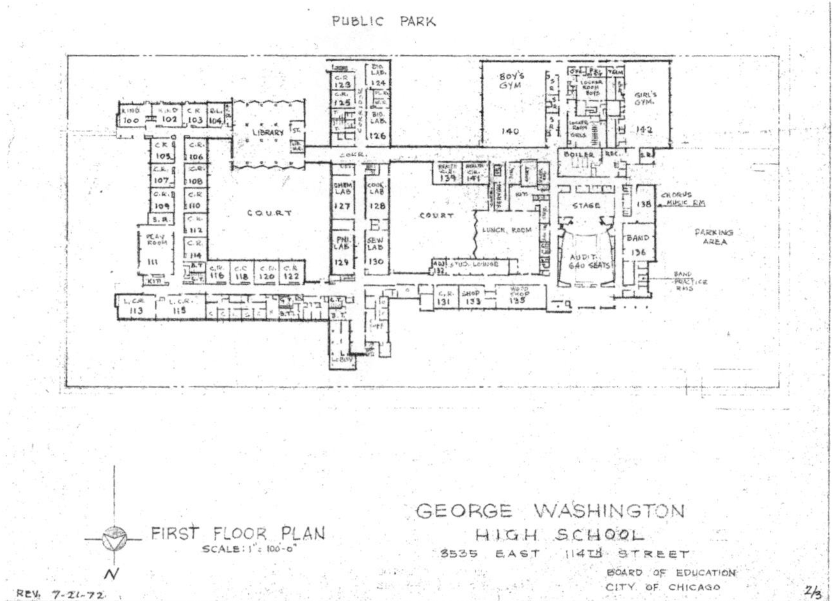


Fig. 6.2. Perkins & Will, modern campus plan, George Washington Elementary & High School, 1957.

Echoing the language of prominent modern architects like Le Corbusier, Perkins and Cocking argued for a school building "planned by its activities" where the building "evolves from the classroom, or from a series of classrooms, each designed specifically for its specific jobs."[14] This next generation of school buildings would share common characteristics. They would have decentralized, campus-like plans, often consisting of multiple buildings connected by covered walkways or breezeways, rather than an entire school in one building (Fig. 6.2). These buildings would be single-story structures for greater safety, lower cost, and less formality (Fig. 6.3). The schools would occupy larger sites to give children more room to congregate or play. Air conditioning would be commonplace. Flexible spaces allowed by moveable partitions and multi-function layouts would dominate floor plans. And, not to be neglected, the modern schools would be beautiful. A building's "true beauty . . . depends on how closely its form follows its function," Perkins and Cocking wrote, echoing Louis Sullivan. "Remember—the building is not an end in itself; it is a tool, an instrument."[15] To insure their appropriateness these tools would be planned not just by architects,

Fig. 6.3. Loebl, Schlossman, Bennett & Dart and A. Epstein & Sons, Inc., Stephen Tyng Mather High School, 1959.

but by a team comprised of architects, administrators, teachers, community representatives, and even janitors.[16]

By the mid-1950s such ideas were becoming mainstream in the school architecture community. Walter Cocking looked back—with obvious bias—on a decade of high school architecture in 1956 and saw profound changes: "Prior to World War II, secondary school buildings were chiefly planned according to structural efficiency, compactness and capacity. Apparently little consideration was given to the characteristics of the youth who would use the buildings or to a program needed by youth. Since World War II there has been a slow but steady awareness of these two factors, and evidence indicates that there is now more emphasis given to them in planning new plants."[17] Cocking listed a series of contemporary trends in high school buildings, including one-story structures, campus plans, larger sites, and a greater connection with nature through the use of courtyards and larger windows. There was also more interest in student and teacher social areas, decentralization of large spaces like lunch rooms, classrooms envisioned as "laboratories for learning or as work spaces," shops created for general rather than specific uses, and an overall flexibility that did not exist before the war.[18] A new approach to educational planning provoked the high school building's evolution, according to Cocking. Prior to the late 1940s, administrative staffs usually helped architects plan school buildings; thereafter, the process was enlarged when the school's entire staff, neighborhood citizens, and special consultants, such as psychologists, anthropologists, and sociologists in addition to educators, became involved.

## Building Campaigns

The modernists' promise of efficient and economical architecture was particularly attractive in the 1950s, when the postwar population explosion began to overburden school systems across the country. Although not reflected in the higher grades until the sixties, the baby boom impacted elementary schools much earlier. Chicago's elementary student enrollment rose by 40 percent in the 1950s even as the city's population began to shrink due to a suburban exodus. The school board and Superintendent Herold C. Hunt countered this expansion with a major school building campaign intended to rectify the paucity of school construction during the Depression and war. Their proposal for an unprecedented $50 million school building bond issue was approved by Chicago voters in June 1951. The four-year building plan proposed only one new high school, as elementary schools were clearly the priority; most high school work involved alterations or minor rehabilitations. When Hunt's successor, Benjamin C. Willis, took over in 1953, twenty-five of the city's forty-seven high schools were being worked on in some fashion.

School architecture in Chicago would be influenced for over a decade by the dynamic Willis. After arriving from the Yonkers, New York, school system, Willis proved so successful in initiating school construction that he earned the nickname, "Big Ben the Builder." Over the course of his thirteen years the Chicago Public Schools would construct more than 200 elementary schools or additions and at least thirteen high school buildings or additions.[19] Writing in his first *Annual Report*, Willis demonstrated his understanding of the space problem: "we need more and different school buildings; we need additions to existing school buildings; and we need the modernization and rehabilitation of many others. Always, it is essential that we remember that all buildings must be planned, built, modernized, or rehabilitated with one objective in mind—housing the educational program that best meets the needs of children."[20] Following the latest trend in school planning, Willis advocated the team approach. "In planning for the individual school plant, parents of children who will use the buildings, teachers and administrators, and neighbors who live "just across the street"—will be consulted as to the needs of the community."[21] Additionally, the board studied census records, school attendance records, birth rates, building permits and real estate trends when planning buildings to make sure they were located in the right places and were large enough to handle future enrollments.

Willis also inaugurated a new feature into the school design process in Chicago—the use of private architectural firms. Since the 1880s, the board architect's office had overseen school design and construction. The Strayer Report's 1932 suggestion that private architects be engaged in the process went unheeded until Willis convinced the board to let him solicit outside architects. The primary rationale for this deviation from tradition was the daunting number of schools that needed to be built. Willis believed that private firms could work faster and cheaper than the Bureau of Architecture while adding variety, and he proved to be right. Within five years, twenty-six outside architects or firms were working on Chicago public schools.[22] Consequently, the bureau's emphasis shifted to rehabilitation and expansion projects.

Willis' keen interest in school buildings was evident early in his tenure. He once told a *Chicago Tribune* reporter that he attended the dedication of an elementary school shortly after assuming the superintendent's position and toured the building with a member of the board's architecture department. "I was interested in saving money," said Willis, "so I asked him why the school had been built with 12-foot-high ceilings, with lots of ornamentation, and other expensive touches which added nothing to the building but additional money."[23] Although apocryphal, since few Chicago elementary schools were built with "lots of ornamentation" in the early 1950s, the story reveals Willis' emphasis on economy. "You keep school construction costs down by attention to every detail," Willis claimed. "You work for top utilization of space. You choose materials which are durable but less expensive, such as concrete blocks instead of lath and plaster. You work for multiple use of space, such as cafeterias which can be turned into libraries, and auditorium-gymnasiums."[24] But his opinion of school buildings was not strictly utilitarian—he also recognized architecture's inspirational and pedagogical properties. At times Willis described the schools as "Laboratories for Learning" and stressed the need to make them "cheerful, friendly and attractive both inside and outside" so they would "suggest a path toward desirable attitudes, values, skills and habits."[25]

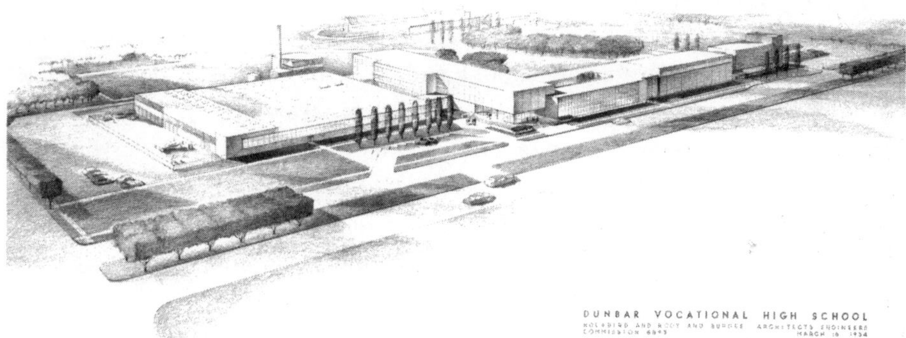


Fig. 6.4. Holabird, Root & Burgee, Paul Laurence Dunbar Vocational High School, 1956.

Expediency, budgetary restrictions, and the modernist aesthetic affected the buildings envisioned by Willis and produced by the new group of outside architects. Steel frames coupled with concrete block walls made construction quicker and cheaper. Ceiling heights were lowered, as Willis mentioned above, and most schools were reduced to one story in height. Large expanses of glass cut down on the need for masonry walls. Plaster finishing and wooden trim were eliminated from interior surfaces. Floors were laid directly on concrete foundations. "Every dollar that can be saved without reducing the quality of the building," wrote Willis, "represents a dollar available to improve the effectiveness of instruction through better salaries for teachers and through better equipment."[26]

## Dunbar High School

The first modernist high school constructed according to such principles in Chicago was the Paul Laurence Dunbar Vocational High School (Fig. 6.4). Plans for the Dunbar school were proposed as part of Superintendent Hunt's 1951 building campaign, but ground was not broken for the project on a twelve-acre site south of the Loop on South Parkway (now Martin Luther King Drive) until 1955. Pursuant to Superintendent Willis' latest initiative, a private firm, Holabird, Root & Burgee, created the building.[27]

Dunbar's \$7 million price tag represented a significant investment considering that the city's next three high schools were budgeted at \$3 million each. The design process utilized the team planning approach promoted by Benjamin Willis and other educators. According to a *Chicago Tribune* account, the final building incorporated "hundreds of suggestions by students and faculty members," as well as the school's principal, Clifford J. Campbell, a former draftsman for the school board.[28] The finished Dunbar high school contained all of the necessities for a modern secondary school: classrooms, commercial rooms, drafting rooms, laboratories, two gymnasia, a swimming pool, a large auditorium, and a library. It also featured such non-traditional spaces as visual education rooms (including a radio-television workshop with a closed-circuit television network) and a twelve-room student guidance and counseling center.[29]

These amenities were enclosed in a steel-framed, brick and glass structure, described by the *Chicago Tribune* as "ultra-modern," that sprawled across the site instead of being contained in an orderly square or rectangle.[30] Though not a full-fledged campus plan like some of the suburban high schools being constructed at the time, Dunbar's architects achieved a sense of multiple buildings by varying the heights, surface materials, colors, and window patterns of the school's different sections so that it actually appeared to be five separate, but connected, structures. A square, one-story section housing the shops anchored the school's south end, faced with light-colored brick with a long, continuous horizontal belt of windows. Attached to the square, separated by a small interior courtyard, was the main academic portion, three stories tall and oriented east-to-west. This section continued the shop area's light color and ribbon windows, but here the architects played a curious game with the building; the steel frame made uninterrupted windows possible, along with a slightly cantilevered corner on the ground floor entry that made the building's bulk almost seem to float. But the lightness of that steel frame was also visually contradicted by unnecessarily thick-looking corners and a main facade that presented the viewer with two stories of sheer brick wall (Fig. 6.5). Inside the entry, the building's skeleton construction was reasserted in a large open lobby overlooking the central courtyard, a 139' x 43' green space surrounded by floor-to-ceiling glass walls (Fig. 6.6).

Fig. 6.5. Entrance, Dunbar Vocational High School. Modernist postwar schools rejected the grandiose entrances of their predecessors.

Fig. 6.6. Lobby, Dunbar Vocational High School.

The rest of the building was perpendicular to the main section (Fig. 6.7). Most of Dunbar was two stories, although the gymnasium and auditorium rose higher. Flanking the main entry on the north side, and stepping slightly forward of it, was a two-story section that held the administrative offices on the first floor and a small library above. This section's end wall was sheathed in dark brick while the street facade was aluminum; both materials and colors provided a strong contrast to the main block's light-colored brick. The next portion in line to the north was the gymnasium area, with a wall of brick slightly darker than the main section and a clerestory window. A low connection joined the gymnasia to an auditorium that appeared to be two rectangular masses of different height, color, and surface texture. A covered walkway/porch ran the length of the street between the connecting section and the auditorium. Altogether, Holabird, Root & Burgee had created something that had never been seen in Chicago educational architecture—a single building that appeared to be an ensemble of modernist structures.

Dunbar High School also signified a burgeoning generation of buildings that eschewed the impressive size and aesthetic grandeur of the past. Modernists like Lawrence Perkins and Walter Cocking criticized older schools like those designed by William Mundie or A.F. Hussander as "pompous big boxes" designed to "awe and to give, by their very colossal dignity, something to aspire to. Often, however, the young rebels who were supposed to be impressed aspired only to break windows, a speedy and projected method of thumbing the nose, throwing the snowball at the silk hat."[31] Such schools were "made into monuments by a post-Civil War generation which had yet to learn that monuments are remembered only by pigeons."[32] One way to avoid monumentality was to lower the building's silhouette; this also made the school safer to evacuate in case of fire and easier to expand. Though multistoried, Dunbar High School's appearance was more horizontal than vertical, in contrast to the older schools, and modern architectural devices like flat roofs, long strips of horizontal windows, and a lack of ornamentation enhanced this perception. The building's floor plan further rejected the formality associated with pre-modernist schools; its main entry was not placed in the center of the facade, and the auditorium was not aligned with the school's front doors. In fact, Dunbar's facade abandoned bilateral symmetry altogether.

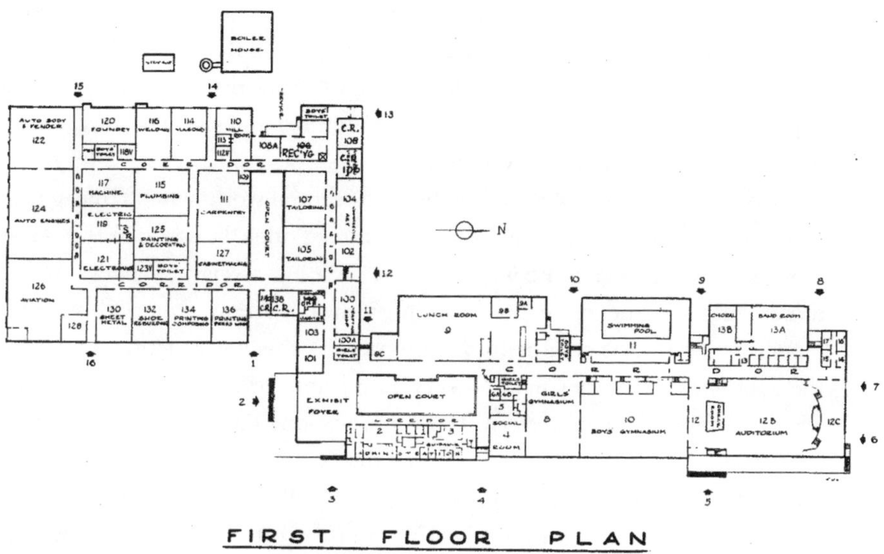


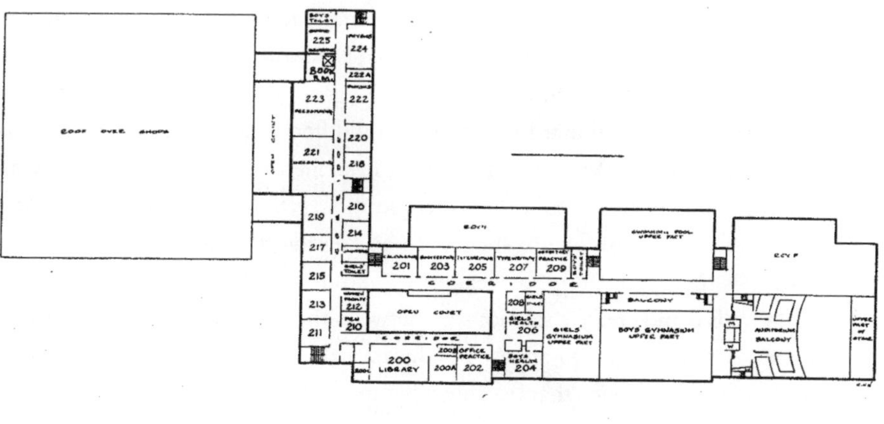


Fig. 6.7. First- and second-floor plans, Dunbar Vocational High School. Dunbar's exterior, which seemed composed of disparate elements, concealed a unified interior plan.

One of the key elements of modernist school architecture was its construction. Nineteenth-century school buildings were made with brick or stone walls that carried the building's weight. As a result, buildings could appear ponderous and thick. The windows' number and size were affected by the need to make sure there was enough wall surface to hold up the building. A major breakthrough occurred in the architectural world when Chicago architects invented and perfected the steel-framed office building in the 1880s. Now an internal skeleton could carry the building's weight, leaving the external surface as no more than a skin or sheath. Many twentieth-century modernist architects sought to directly express this construction system in the building's form. They hailed steel framing and the non-load-bearing wall for the unprecedented freedom those innovations brought to architecture. Steel-frame construction also facilitated the flexibility and expansibility that postwar educators desperately sought. "The building should be skeleton-and-skin construction, without bearing walls," wrote Perkins and Cocking. "The end walls of instructional spaces may have to be altered, so they should be left free: free from load; free from mechanical and utility installations; free from important fenestration."[33]

Because of steel-framing, interior walls no longer carried part of the building's weight; therefore they could easily be made temporary to allow educators a variety of configurations for their rooms. Exterior walls could contain more glass than in previous school buildings. Long, continuous windows like those along the sides of Dunbar High School could flood classrooms and workshops with natural light. Perkins and Cocking described the advantages: "There are many good reasons for continuous fenestration, rather than grouping the windows for each room; one of the chief ones—aside from abundance of natural light—is the opportunity for flexibility."[34] And when used in communal areas, glass walls could create a relationship between the school's interior and the outdoors. Articles began to appear in educational journals promoting courtyards, an architectural device that became a fixture with the rise of the campus plan.[35] Dunbar's spacious lobby area, for example, was celebrated in the board's *Annual Report*: "Glass in the Paul Laurence Dunbar Vocational High School foyer is used to bring the outdoors inside rather than to shut it out. Its lovely central garden is enclosed in glass; on every side it is open for the eye to cherish its beauty. Here, in this tranquil space you know the "green cathedral." With the great, tall panes—your aspirations rise toward the skies" (see Fig. 6.6).[36]

Dunbar was Chicago's first modernist high school building. Older high schools were tall and heavy with thick-looking walls, prominent entrances, ornamentation, and square or E-shaped floor plans. Dunbar incorporated the latest modern school characteristics. The architects intended the building to be efficient and flexible—a "tool" for educators rather than a showplace to instill children with the proper respect for education and an appreciation for fine architecture. Dunbar became one of the city's most lauded postwar schools, winning an Honor Award from the Chicago chapter of the American Institute of Architects and awards from the Chicago Association of Commerce and Industry and the Chicago Association of Consulting Engineers.

## Casual High Schools

The building boom that created Dunbar High School was supported by subsequent $50 million construction bond issues in 1954 and 1957. These campaigns produced a series of high schools that further expressed the modernist characteristics first displayed at Dunbar. The schools built in the 1950s tended to be more campus-like than Dunbar, partly because they were constructed farther from the Loop where land was less expensive and larger sites could be purchased. The John Hancock (Schmidt, Garden, Erikson & Co., architects) and George Washington (Perkins & Will) high schools opened in 1957, John Marshall Harlan (Childs & Smith) in 1958, and the William J. Bogan (Naess & Murphy) and Stephen Tyng Mather (Loebl, Schlossman, Bennett & Dart and A. Epstein & Sons, Inc.) high schools opened in 1959 (Figs. 6.8–6.11).

Washington was an experiment in reducing expenses by consolidating the high school with an elementary school. Financially, the "two-in-one" school would allow the different grades to share facilities, thus cutting both construction and utility costs; on a personal level, attending the same school for thirteen years would foster a sense of community and continuity among the children. Some critics denounced the idea, claiming that the scheduling problems created by the two-in-one school would overshadow its benefits. Architect Lawrence Perkins defended Washington's concept on economic grounds, but offered a warning for the future: "The whole case for or against a twelve-grade school stands or falls on whether it is good to operate elementary and high school classes under the same roof. Sheer bigness in schools rarely pays off. When a school gets beyond 1,500 to 1,800 students, it

Fig. 6.8. Perkins & Will, Washington Elementary & High School, 1957.

ceases to be economical to administer."[37] Washington's initial enrollment was 1,200 students, with less than 1,000 in the high school. The Chicago Board of Education repeated the experiment at John F. Kennedy High School (1965) before dropping the all-in-one school idea.

Mather High School was the last high school constructed under the supervision of John C. Christensen. The long-serving architect finally stepped down as Director of the Bureau of Architecture in 1959; he had been the board architect from 1922–28 and 1931 on, making him the record-holder for longevity in that post. Christensen was also the last board architect to play a major role in shaping the appearance of new schools. His replacement was Saul Samuels, an engineer. Samuels had faithfully served the board for twenty-five years at the time of his appointment.[38] His selection shows the degree to which the position had become more about administrative ability than design prowess. Samuels retained the directorship for seventeen years, reigning over one of the most productive periods, in terms of high school construction, in the Chicago Public Schools' history. Because of the board's near-total reliance on private architectural firms for new designs, however, Samuels left no personal imprint on the city's educational landscape.

Fig. 6.9. Childs and Smith, John Marshall Harlan High School, 1958. In the 1950s, like many other school systems, the Chicago Public Schools ended its policy of having the Board Architect's office design all new school building and began to hire outside firms, resulting in more variety.

Visitors to Chicago high schools like Washington or Mather certainly would have seen something very different from the school buildings of the earlier century. While their predecessors tended to be placed on city blocks surrounded by houses or small commercial buildings, most schools from the 1950s were located in or across from a park. This allusion to suburban spaciousness complemented the sprawling nature of the so-called "California" floor plan. It also reflected architects' recognition of two important postwar considerations: the possible need for future expansion of buildings or campuses, and the accommodation of automobiles via parking lots for students and teachers.

Something else would have seemed odd to those who had experienced their teenage years in the monument-like schools of the early century: a dominant sense of casualness in the school environment, brought on by a new conception of children and their development. America became a "child-centered" society after World War II, and this affected all aspects of children's lives, including their school buildings. Historians Charles Strickland and Andrew Ambrose used the phrase to describe the "high degree of parental preoccupation with the needs and interests of their children" by parents who "placed the welfare of the children at the center of family life"

Fig. 6.10. Naess & Murphy, William J. Bogan High School, 1959.

after the war.[39] The combination of the baby boom (which added seventy-six million American babies between 1946 and 1964), the child-centered society, and the popularization of psychology created a different school environment for teenagers in the 1950s and 1960s. Parents indulged their children to a greater extent than in previous generations as experts espoused the importance of happy and well-adjusted childhoods. From scientific research on developmental psychology to the popularity of psychoanalysis to the ubiquitous Dr. Benjamin Spock's *Common Sense Book of Baby and Child Care* (1946), parents were assailed with messages about how to raise their children. Although the opinions sometimes conflicted, the underlying message was consistent: parents needed to be more permissive than in the past and to pay more attention to their children's wants, needs, and interests.

This led parents to involve themselves in their children's education, and made demands on public school system administrators. And educators tried desperately to accommodate them. As a result, an unprecedented educational attitude arose premised on the belief that educators could maximize students' learning by making school interesting and fun. This approach, which had its roots in the ideas of progressive educators like John Dewey and Fran-

Fig. 6.11. Mather High School. Postwar school designers rejected the massive block building, opting instead for low, one-story structures spread out along the site, but still zoned interior spaces according to use.

cis Parker a half-century before, affected both pedagogy and architecture, at all levels of public school systems. Architects tried to make school spaces less imposing and more pleasant—to create places that did not threaten children or make manifest a rigid order and control. Instead, high schools were scaled down from their predecessors and "humanized:" architects introduced lower ceilings, window curtains, bright, cheerful colors, and even carpeting.

Architects used the forms of these buildings to help materialize the new attitude. Fifties school buildings were low, spread out, flat-roofed, and unimposing—almost casual compared to the grand educational monuments of the earlier generation. Historian Robert L. Hampel described this contrast between postwar American schools and their predecessors: "The new citadels offered friendlier settings than the old museums of virtue. . . . The buildings conveyed the impression of greater accessibility than the schools of early years. . . . On the surface, the architecture announced ranchhouse ease more than cathedral-like solemnity, third-grade playfulness more than college seriousness."[40] This move toward the casual school atmosphere was intentional. "There has been a trend away from monumental features of buildings and toward more simplicity in exterior and interior design," wrote Benjamin Willis. "The net result is less cost, a building with a friendly atmosphere, and an increase in the value of all other property in the community."[41] The word "friendly" appeared with increasing frequency in the superintendent's annual reports of the 1950s and 1960s, reflecting a far different educational ideology than in previous years. School buildings were enlisted to help make education enjoyable to students. This mindset was also reflected in expanding curricula. A writer on high school curricula offered this commonly-held suggestion in 1963: "The appearance of the school should give the impression that the school is a place where it would be fun to live and work."[42]

Designers of the new casual high schools tried hard to make them less imposing. They rejected the monumental schools' weight, bulk, and uniformity. Apart from the large masses of the auditorium and gymnasium, few modernist buildings stood taller than two stories. Also, instead of a single building, the gymnasium, auditorium, classroom and administration spaces, and perhaps shop classes often occupied separate structures, attached to each other by glass-enclosed walkways. The buildings were made with either steel frames encased in brick or concrete block walls. These walls were free of any type of decoration (other than the school's name) and dominated by long rows of uninterrupted or closely-spaced windows. And modern school buildings incorporated other non-traditional materials beyond steel frames. Bogan High School, for instance, featured aluminum window frames, concrete columns, and porcelain wall panels.

Modernist architects rarely positioned building entrances in the center of the facade as in previous generations, which meant, as *American School Board Journal* editor William C. Bruce lamented, "it is sometimes difficult to find the main entrance because so little emphasis in materials or ornament distinguishes it from the rest of the rambling low structure or the complex of structures connected by glassed-in walkways."[43] Entries were often marked by a small platform of a few steps, an overhanging roof, and floor-to-ceiling windows. Once inside the building visitors encountered open lobbies that served as staging areas for further exploration. The main administrative offices tended to be located adjacent to one or more sides of this space. Several schools, like Dunbar, featured an interior courtyard visible through the lobby's glass walls, providing a sense of openness to an enclosed area. Wide cor-

Fig. 6.12. Hallway, Mather High School. Broad, bright hallways with artificial illumination, concrete block or tiled walls, and asbestos-paneled drop ceilings marked the postwar school's radical change from the early century buildings.

ridors led in various directions and offered glimpses into the school's many rooms (Fig. 6.12). A nineteenth-century visitor might consider these corridors odd and, perhaps, unfinished with their bare brick or concrete block walls, lined with lockers. School officials in the 1950s praised such hallways, however, for demonstrating fiscal restraint in an era when administrators found themselves forced to defend occasional "extravagances" such as carpeting (which was justified as sound-absorbing).

The corridors tended to terminate in mass-gathering spaces (auditoriums and gymnasiums) or stairwells. Along the way, stairwells and classrooms were interspersed between lockers. Concrete block walls, sound-absorbent acoustic-tiled ceilings, fluorescent lights, asphalt-tile floors, and large expanses of glass in both exterior and interior walls dominated school interiors from this period. The sizeable windows and improvements in electric lighting had solved most of the previous generation's issues about improper illumination damaging students' eyesight; now more emphasis in educational and architectural journals was given to interior decoration. Walls were to be painted with lively colors (contrary to the opinion of turn-of-the-century "experts") "favorable to learning," in line with the most advanced "indus-

Fig. 6.13. Classroom with moveable walls, Port Huron Northern High School, Michigan. *American School Board Journal* 152 (January 1966).

trial research showing the influence of color on morale and production."[44] Designers outfitted classrooms with curtains to promote a home-like atmosphere and encourage students to relax. The classrooms themselves were the least-changed feature of the modernist school building: they remained rectangular spaces for thirty-to-forty students dominated by large windows and orderly rows of student desks. But some differences did exist. Fifties buildings had larger windows, and some buildings had little or no wall surface in-between the glass. Classroom ceilings were two- to- three-feet lower. Electric lighting provided most of the interior illumination. Painted or tiled concrete block replaced plaster and wooden wainscoting. Student desks were no longer bolted to the floor, nor were chairs and desks always connected. And quite a few classrooms contained new features like movable partitions or small, attached multi-purpose rooms (Fig. 6.13).

Despite the changes in construction materials, furniture, and decorative schemes, one aspect of the high school building continued unabated: rooms were still adapted to particular functions. Lecture rooms, laboratories, and shops were all different in terms of size, equipment, and location. Chicago's 1950s high schools continued the practice, developed over half-a-century earlier, of devoting specialized interior spaces to specialized curricular needs.

## The Differentiated Curriculum

The modernist goal of crafting the school building around the students and their activities was driven in part by the recognition that the content and methods of American high school education evolved after World War II. The nineteenth-century academic high school curriculum, with its emphasis on mental discipline and character training, had disappeared, replaced by a differentiated curriculum aimed at providing adolescents with life-skills.

The 1918 Cardinal Principles report and its seven educational objectives had codified the direction that American high school curricula were beginning to take at the time. In 1933, the NCA reduced the desirable high school goals to four: health and physical fitness; exploring vocations and vocational efficiency; developing successful social relationships; and learning the right use of leisure.[45] Such non-academic pursuits became more important as larger numbers of students attended high school. It was during the Depression and World War II that high school became an integral part of nearly every American teenager's life. In 1900, only 10.2 percent of all adolescents between the ages of fourteen and seventeen were enrolled in high schools across the country. By 1930 that figure had reached 50.7 percent, and by war's end it was over 70 percent (see Table 1B).[46] High schools, which began in the nineteenth century as a privilege for a small percentage of America's youth, had "attained a virtual monopoly over the lives of Americans aged 14-17," and turned into what historians David L. Angus and Jeffrey E. Mirel described as "one of the defining institutions in the lives of American adolescents and a dominant institution in American life"[47]

A new type of postwar high school curriculum furthered the Cardinal Principles report's educational goals and made high school worthwhile for those students not interested in or able to attend college. The "life adjustment" or "life-skills" curriculum emphasized individual fulfillment and societal roles over mental training or mastery of particular subject matter. It was intended to address "real life problems" rather provide an academic foundation. A U.S. Office of Education pamphlet explained the theory behind life-adjustment education: "Most boys and girls are headed for jobs that require little training. These youth need and want an invigorated general education that relates to their everyday lives."[48] Educator A. J. Foy Cross described the basic premises of the orientation in 1956: "A good or successful education program means the application or use of all available learning resources within and outside the school for maximum: a) Personal, individual growth in health, happiness, and well-being; b) Growth among individuals of an active interest in the health and well-being of all other people; c) Continuous growth within individuals of a confidence in their ability to recognize and solve the little and big problems of living in a satisfying and socially acceptable manner."[49]

Educators believed the new studies also were better adapted to adolescents' special needs, which the Illinois Secondary Schools Curriculum Program listed as: "Tools of communication; Strong body, sound attitude toward it; Satisfactory Social Relationships; Competence in and appreciation of improved family living; Knowledge of, practice in, and zeal for democratic processes; Sensitiveness to importance of group action; Effectiveness as consumers; Adjustment to occupation; and Development of meaning for life."[50] "If the products of our schools turn out to be healthy and patriotic citizens who are good husbands, good wives, good fathers, good mothers, good neighbors, good workers, good employers, wise spenders of income, wholesome users of leisure time and so forth," claimed Vernon L. Nickell, Illinois' Superintendent of Public Instruction, "we know that our schools are good."[51]

One of the life-adjustment curriculum's major presumptions was that most students were not talented enough to complete a college preparatory course of study and not interested in the specificity of vocational training (the two traditional branches of high school education since the early 1900s) and therefore needed some general education that was not overly demanding. At a U.S. Office of Education conference on vocational education in Washington, D.C. in 1945, noted educator Charles M. Prosser famously claimed that 60 percent of all high school students fit this description. Conference attendees wholeheartedly agreed and formally adopted Prosser's unproven allegation as a guiding principle. Thereafter life adjustment education caught on quickly. By 1947, just two years after the so-called "Prosser Resolution," the first life adjustment conference was held, chaired by Benjamin Willis, superintendent of schools of Yonkers, New York, and future General Superintendent of the Chicago Public Schools.[52] In December of that year *Time* published an article on the movement, claiming schools in thirty-five states were involved with life-adjustment education.[53]

The Chicago Public Schools likewise embraced life-adjustment education and the Cardinal Principles report. General Superintendent Herold Hunt's *Annual Report* for 1950–51 outlined the theory behind city's high school curriculum, which was titled "The Major Functions of Living." Hunt admitted that "many readers will see the resemblance between [the nine Major Functions] and the seven cardinal principles of education formulated in 1918."[54] Indeed, the two lists, separated by over three decades, were nearly identical. The Chicago schools' functions, calculated to produce individuals who could "fulfill their part in society," were "Practicing American Citizenship" (which corresponded to the Cardinal Principles' "Citizenship"), "Using the Tools of Communication Effectively" (equal to "Command of Fundamental Practices"), "Improving Family Living" ("Worthy Home-Membership"), "Protecting Life and Health" ("Health"), "Building Human Relationships" ("Ethical Character"), "Enjoying Wholesome Leisure" ("Worthy Use of Leisure"), "Meeting Vocational Responsibilities" ("Vocation"), "Satisfying Spiritual and Aesthetic Needs," and "Developing Economic Competence."[55]

Life-adjustment education's grace period was relatively short, however. Criticism was being directed at high schools educators' diminishing interest in traditional academics. The *Chicago Tribune*, for example, published a series of editorials in the 1940s on the poor quality of public education. In 1953, University of Illinois history professor Arthur E. Bestor, Jr.'s book, *Educational Wastelands*, caused a national sensation with its virulent attack on the alleged class-solidifying, undemocratic tendencies of the type of life-adjustment education offered by the Chicago schools. Rather than training students to accept their place in the economic order by directing most of them toward vocational or general education, Bestor argued that "genuine education . . . is intellectual training" in the nineteenth-century tradition, and he emphasized the need for core subjects like math, science, English, history, and foreign languages.[56] Numerous parents and educators agreed. A Gallup poll conducted in 1958 found that almost two-thirds of parents believed every child should have the opportunity to attend college, while a survey of over 1,000 high school principals in the same year divulged that most believed high schools demanded "far too little work of students," contained too many easy classes, and overemphasized extracurricular activities over such fundamentals as reading.[57]

Chicago's movement toward a slightly tougher core curriculum may have been inspired in part by such attitudes. The Chicago Public Schools' "Tentative Report on Secondary Education" refined "The Major Functions of Living" from earlier in the decade. With the goal of striving "to prepare each youth to function in his capacity of citizen, worker, and family member," the report's writers recognized two major content areas in the secondary school curriculum: areas of general education, intended to provide the student "with learning opportunities to develop the common understandings and skills which he shares with other Americans;" and areas of special interest to help students "develop specialized abilities and skills."[58] Following the "Tentative Report" the school board approved the first substantial adjustment to the Chicago high school curriculum in twenty years. The composition of sixteen of the eighteen required units for graduation was reversed: where previously students took six stipulated units and chose ten elective units, now ten units were required with six electives. The board added to those required units an extra year of English and one-to-two years of mathematics. These changes may have been in response to perceived deficiencies in the city's life-adjustment curriculum.

Chicago's curriculum modifications were also prescient, for in October 1957 the Soviet Union launched the first Sputnik satellite, inaugurating the space race and inciting educators across the country to blame public school systems for devaluing academics and allowing the United States to slip behind its arch-enemy in the sciences. Education became a matter of national security as "the curricula of the schools were dragged into the Cold War."[59] By decade's end, however, countless fears had been assuaged by the publication of James B. Conant's book, *The American High School Today*. Conant, a scientist, diplomat, and former president of Harvard University, was a public figure who commanded educators' respect. His survey of comprehensive public high schools found nothing fundamentally wrong with them; "no radical alteration in the basic pattern of American education is necessary in order to improve our public high schools," he wrote.[60] Instead, Conant suggested minor improvements to the existing system but continuing the differentiation of college-bound and non-college-bound students into different courses of study. According to Conant, this format exemplified democracy—contrary to the Soviet system—because it allowed every student to achieve to the best of his or her ability. The "Conant report" was widely-publicized in mass-circulation magazines and newspapers as well as debated in educational journals. Historians David Angus and Jeffrey Mirel argued that Conant's book "essentially ended the raging debate about the high school curriculum in the 1950s and determined how the institution would respond to the challenges of the 1960s and early 1970s."[61] Curricular differentiation was entrenched as the standard high school model.

## Upheaval and Experimentation in the 1960s and 1970s

Construction of public high schools slowed after the 1950s building boom and only a handful were constructed in Chicago in the 1960s. But enrollment problems continued. The furious pace of Superintendent Willis' building campaign was not enough to keep up with the overwhelming tide of public school students. In the 1960s, overcrowding issues and their racial implications would influence the Chicago Public Schools' building programs. And in the 1960s and 1970s, pedagogical experiments and shifting stylistic tastes would affect the schools inside and out.

### Racial Friction

Construction campaigns during the 1950s had focused on the predominantly black neighborhoods on the city's south and west sides. While the new schools led to an overall reduction in class sizes around the city, there was still terrible overcrowding in these areas. Chicago's black population reached nearly 800,000 in 1960 and continued to grow. Although Benjamin Willis refused to provide enrollment data to outside researchers, school board studies showed that while black schools were filled beyond capacity, many white schools had empty seats and classrooms. Moreover, schools in the black neighborhoods tended to be older than those in white neighborhoods, and their conditions were abysmal. A teacher at DuSable High School wrote that "[t]he broken windows were there, along with the torn window shades and broken desk tops, appendages to the badly lighted, worn central hallway."[62] Robert J. Havighurst's 1964 study of Chicago schools, commissioned by the school board, included a critical assessment that echoed the Strayer Report over thirty years before: "There are two levels of discussion for buildings, facilities, and classroom space—the essential level and the desirable level. *Chicago high schools are below the essential level.* The shortage of classroom space is already critical, and is rapidly growing into a major problem (emphasis added)."[63] Havighurst concluded that at least ten additional high school buildings were needed immediately.

A combination of preventable and uncontrollable events created this dismal state of affairs. The main influence, obviously, was a rapidly growing school-age population. At the same time, however, the public school system had depleted its construction funds. After a total of $200 million was raised through bond issues in 1951, 1955, 1957, and 1959, the building campaign ran into a road block when the fifth issue of $25 million passed the legislature but was not offered for public vote until 1966. In the meantime the board's building fund evaporated. And as enrollments increased and funding disappeared, the school system made no effort to redistribute its students. Benjamin Willis made clear when he assumed the superintendent's position in 1953 that he believed every child should attend a school in his or her immediate neighborhood. Throughout the course of his tenure Willis refused to acquiesce to those who advocated busing students out of their home districts to balance enrollments. He further refused to redraw school boundary lines to incorporate black students into white schools with available space and rejected transfer applications. Instead the Chicago Public Schools resorted to a series of traditional and new measures to deal with the black overcrowding problem. Double shifts, branch schools, and leasing commercial properties were traditional Chicago methods. In 1962, for example, many of the city's high school freshmen began to take their first year of secondary education in specially-designated grade schools rather than at their assigned neighborhood high school. The following year, Havighurst found twenty of the thirty-nine high schools studied were using branch sites to educate some or all of their ninth graders.[64] But this was not enough: that same year approximately 40,000 high school students (almost one-third of the city's total) were on a shortened day schedule.[65] By 1966, five high schools (Bowen, Kennedy, Harlan, Marshall, and Hyde Park) were operating at over 150 percent of their student capacity.[66]

Willis's most controversial solution to overcrowding problems involved portable schoolrooms, which critics dubbed "Willis Wagons." Willis persuaded the board to purchase almost 200 of these units in 1961. Each "relocatable classroom" was a prefabricated, 20' x 36' mobile aluminum box that could be delivered to the school site. They included such amenities as air conditioning (which most public school buildings did not have), carpeting, telephones, drinking fountains, and bathrooms. After Willis's resignation acting Superintendent Thaddeus Lubera told *American School and University* the mobile classrooms were cost effective and he hoped they would last ten years.[67] Despite their practicality, Willis Wagons were not acceptable to black families who knew of white schools with empty classrooms just a few miles away. The black community began a campaign to pressure Willis on racial imbalances. The Chicago chapter of the Congress of Racial Equality contacted the Illinois School Problems Commission in 1961 about emerging racial discrepancies in the city, and a few months later the National Association for the Advancement of Colored People claimed that Chicago school board actions "resulted in separate and unequal schools for most Black pupils in the city."[68] A series of protests and student walk-outs in the early 1960s brought more attention to the problems, resulting in a threat from the federal government to withhold funding if a desegregation plan was not implemented. But Willis held fast to his neighborhood school policy until his resignation in 1966, prompted when the board approved the transfer of some black high school students to a white school.[69]

Willis's successor, James F. Redmond, proposed several desegregation plans, all of which met with major resistance.[70] He also criticized his predecessor's "piecemeal" approach to school building, labeling it short-sighted and calling instead for a broader vision—in this case, a five-year, $750 million building program that included the immediate construction of two public high schools.[71] Redmond's massive building project failed to gain approval, and nearly two years passed before funding was once again dedicated to school building. But this time the board bypassed the public, calling off a scheduled construction bond referendum in favor of a new financial arrangement. The public schools formed a partnership with the Chicago Public Building Commission (CPBC) in 1968. This body, formed a decade earlier and headed by the mayor, was authorized to sell bonds to finance public building construction. On the recommendation of the Better Schools Committee (a group of local businessmen interested in education), the board approached the CPBC about a potential partnership. Subsequent negotiations resulted in a plan to borrow $140 million from the CPBC for a two-year building campaign and pay rent to the CPBC until the construction bonds were paid, when title for the property would pass to the board.[72] This financing arrangement would revive school construction in Chicago and serve as the main source for new buildings into the twenty-first century.

## Pedagogical and Spatial Innovations

The mid-century curricular developments discussed above had little overall effect on the form or layout of high school buildings. Curricular differentiation dated back to the late 1800s, and that is when high school architects were forced to adapt the existing building model to accommodate new spaces for previously-unknown subjects. In the subsequent decades the comprehensive high school became ubiquitous, with its constituent parts and general room arrangements long since determined. So by mid-century the types of classes high schools offered no longer affected school architecture, but the manner in which those classes were taught, and the philosophy of education as a whole, did have an impact.

Before World War II, educational spaces tended to be reactive, with architects responding after the fact to curriculum shifts by altering school buildings. In the postwar era, educators seemed to place a greater responsibility for helping to educate students on the physical environment, expecting school spaces to be part of new pedagogical experiments and approaches. This may have been the outcome of having more educators and administrators involved in the design process. Whatever the reason, the result was that many educational experiments pushed architects to re-envision familiar aspects of the school building.

The 1960s was a time of broad social and cultural changes in America, and the educational and architectural worlds were not exempted. An unparalleled spirit of experimentation permeated both fields. The *American School Board Journal*'s William C. Bruce wrote in 1963: "The past five years have witnessed radical changes to the organization and teaching methods of the secondary schools."[73] Educational variations introduced included "open classrooms, free schools, open education, alternative schools, school-within-a-school, personalized education, humanistic schools, mini-schools," and others.[74] Common ideas were reevaluated, often with repercussions for school architecture. For example, there was no longer a consensus on the classroom's proper size or shape. Some educators considered the 24' x 30'

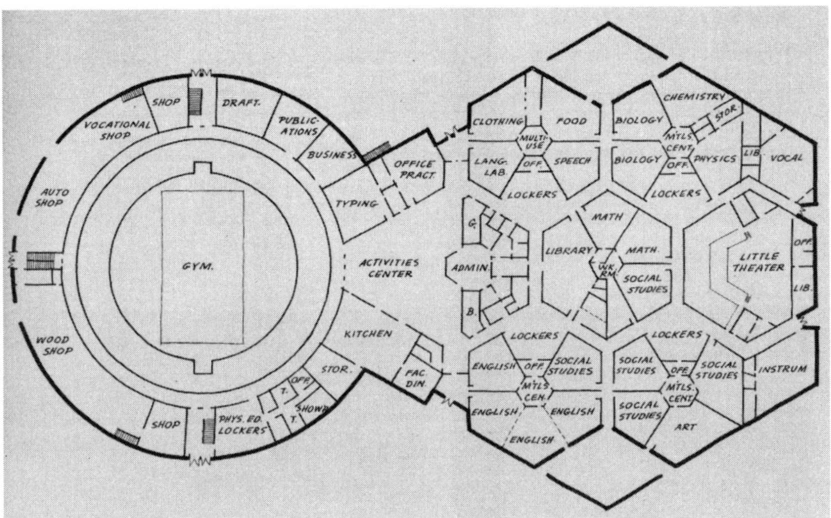


Fig. 6.14. Hexagonal school plan, Educational Facilities Laboratories, 1962

rectangular box, bounded by four immovable walls and a twelve-foot ceiling, having a certain mathematically calculated amount of window area to let in appropriate amounts of natural light, containing orderly rows of desks, and serving only one subject, to be an ancient relic. Every aspect of that old classroom was reexamined and altered. Architects made rooms smaller or larger than the old standards, with lower ceilings and glass walls, better air circulation and lighting, and sometimes with electronic temperature controls. Windowless schools were briefly popular. Other architects and educators experimented with unorthodox room shapes like circles, hexagons, polygons, and ovals (Fig. 6.14). These shapes, intended to invoke the modern school's freedom, were mainly symbolic gestures meant to counter the traditional classroom's constraints.

According to the Educational Facilities Laboratories (EFL), a nonprofit corporation that researched the relationship between education and architecture and spearheaded advancements in school design in the 1960s, educators described older generation schools with such words as "rigidity, isolation, sterility, formality, inaccessibility, uncommodiousness, starkness, immobility, permanence, constraint."[75] Traditional classrooms informed many of these perceptions. "Old walls should not stifle new ideas. Identical boxes must not enforce the same program on all students and teachers; each is a unique individual."[76] Many educators and architects viewed the destruction of the old schoolroom's boxy form as a step toward greater efficiency and a more perfect match between education and architecture. The EFL claimed that "an even greater variety and freedom can be achieved if the right angle is deliberately set aside . . . the non-rectilinear shape begins to serve some of the advanced educational purposes of the coming American high school."[77] Not everyone applauded such developments, however. "The growing practice of planning classrooms with five or six sides is disturbing," wrote William C. Bruce in 1963, "these odd-shaped rooms have an element of inflexibility not found in the older type of quadrilateral rooms."[78]

But no matter how difficult it was to arrange desks or store materials in multi-sided rooms, or how imprecise these calls for unusually-shaped rooms were, educators found themselves attracted to them. Such rooms were believed to be "flexible," especially if they incorporated the non-permanent walls that allowed administrators to reshape interior spaces according to their school's future requirements. Modern skeleton frame construction made these moveable walls or partitions possible since it eliminated the necessity for interior walls to carry any of the building's weight. Non-bearing walls became so popular and varied that the EFL categorized the different types of partitions available: "1. Permanent partitions giving physical integrity to each subject-matter suite as a whole; 2. Relocatable partitions to meet changing program needs; 3. Folding operable partitions for transforming spaces on a minute's notice; and finally, 4. Skiddable-screen walls to define a short-term project area and provide visual privacy without permanence."[79]

Flexible rooms also served multiple purposes rather than being limited to one specific pedagogical experience (e.g., lecture, laboratory) or subject. Architects stretched their imaginations, and schools appeared with auditoriums that could be divided into classrooms, combination library/lunchrooms, and even library/gymnasiums. And a few high schools were adopted with that most radical of the mid-century experiments, the open classroom, where no interior walls existed at all, although this was more common in elementary-level buildings.

A new concept of interior space drove all of these experiments. Architects now conceived school buildings as a series of adjustable spaces wrapped with a thin skin. Flexibility was the ultimate goal. By the mid-1960s, the concept of flexibility was more refined than it had been when Perkins and Cocking praised it two decades earlier. The EFL admitted that "the term has become a catchword, and architects complain that too often it allows educators to shift educational problems to them, without indicating the solutions," but cited positive examples like architect William Caudill (co-designer of Chicago's Martin Luther King High School), who "abandoned the word [flexibility] in favor of more specific terms: expansible space, that can allow for ordered growth; convertible space, that can be economically adapted to program changes; versatile space, that serves many functions; and malleable space, that can be changed "at once and at will."[80] The multifarious concept of interior space represented a step beyond the work of earlier generations of school architects, who sought only to provide appropriate spaces for the subject being taught. Turn-of-the-century high schools had no counterpart to the modern flexible space.

Within the modern high school's new spaces, teachers used an equally innovative array of practices and materials to enhance their students' learning experience. The EFL effectively summarized the dichotomy between older and present-day education:

> Time was when concepts like "teacher," "class," "curriculum," "class period," "textbook," "classroom," and "school" each had an accepted definition. . . . Schools, almost by rote, built a program out of these basic blocks, bringing teachers together with uniform-sized groups of children of a given age, supplying them with syllabus and textbook, chopping up the day into standardized units of time and deploying people and resources throughout the eggcrate buildings. . . . Now, suddenly, each of the old, standard building blocks of the educational program seems to be breaking up into parts, with the resulting release in energy that is the product of fission…In short, the standard components of the instructional program suddenly multiply and become diverse, flexible, variegated. Selection, design, utilization all become more complex—but also, there is reason to hope, more effective. . . .[81]

Educators viewed team teaching (instruction by more than one teacher for the same course) as a way to stimulate student interest and utilize teachers' strengths. Some schools hired teacher's aides to lessen classroom teachers' workloads and increase the opportunities for individualized instruction. Administrators occasionally altered the traditional school period; some schools created shorter "time modules" while others eliminated class periods altogether. A few school officials even adopted the ungraded school, where students advanced along a sequence of courses at their own pace rather than moving en masse through four year-long grades. All of these developments revealed educators' desire to better address students' individual needs, abilities, and interests.

Traditional textbook, lecture, and recitation methods—although still dominant in the postwar era—yielded more and more to seminars, discussions, and small group or individual work. Independent study (often via "programmed learning") also allowed students to proceed at their own natural pace, and was thought to stimulate their interests. Films, filmstrips, overhead projectors, slides, phonograph and audiotape recordings, radios, televisions, and later computers supplemented the teacher's toolkit.[82] Several of these innovations had architectural consequences, as Benjamin Willis recognized when he wrote, "The ideal school is tailored to the teaching methods of its teachers."[83] High schools needed audio-visual centers; libraries increasingly became "resource centers" with requirements beyond book stacks and reading tables; previously unknown rooms like language laboratories emerged; and many schools were built with a version of what one architectural journal labeled "Room A"—an all-purpose room in a central location without a fixed use.[84]

Postwar educational innovations entered the Chicago high schools in a variety of ways. Superintendent Willis's *Annual Report* for 1962–63 featured a graphic listing school improvements over the previous decade; the list read like a sampling of the most popular phrases from national educational journals, including such concepts as "Flexibility," "Team Teaching," "Modern communications media," "Library as instructional materials center," and "Multiple purpose rooms."[85] John F. Kennedy High School (Bureau of Architecture, 1965), for example, was built with an auditorium divisible into four rooms and many double-purpose classrooms. *More Than Bricks and Mortar . . . 1953–1966*, a booklet celebrating Willis' school building campaigns, specifically mentioned such architectural innovations as folding partitions, common areas, and lunchroom-library combinations. Perhaps Chicago's most ambitious high school building of the period was the second South Shore High School (Fridstein & Fitch, 1968). Envisioned as an annex to the existing 1940s building on 76th Street and Bennett Avenue, Willis intended the new South Shore to be a prototype high school for Chicago's future.

Fig. 6.15. Fridstein & Fitch, South Shore High School, 1969.

During construction, numerous newspaper articles promoted the school as "ultra-modern" and highly-sophisticated. From the outside, the finished structure was an unimpressive concrete box with odd window patterns and an open breezeway through the center of the ground floor (Fig. 6.15). Inside the building the architects attempted to incorporate nearly every contemporary educational trend. The ground or "A" level gave access to a 400-seat divisible auditorium and several community gathering rooms; the breezeway held a small, hexagonal, sunken theater. The top three floors included a resource center, classrooms, and science laboratories (Fig. 6.16). On these floors classrooms inhabited the building's core, ringed by locker-lined corridors, with offices or larger rooms relegated to the ends.

Following the EFL's advice, Fridstein & Fitch designed South Shore's classrooms as hexagons. Architect Marvin Fitch claimed in a *Chicago Tribune* article that "6-sided rooms bring students closer to the teaching area without wasting corner space and are more flexible for using with moveable partitions."[86] Each floor contained two "clusters" of six hexagonal "teaching stations," surrounded by hexagonal light wells running vertically throughout the building's three upper floors (Fig. 6.17). Moveable partitions delineated each room/teaching station so the school's administrators could configure each cluster for anywhere from one to six rooms. At the center of each cluster

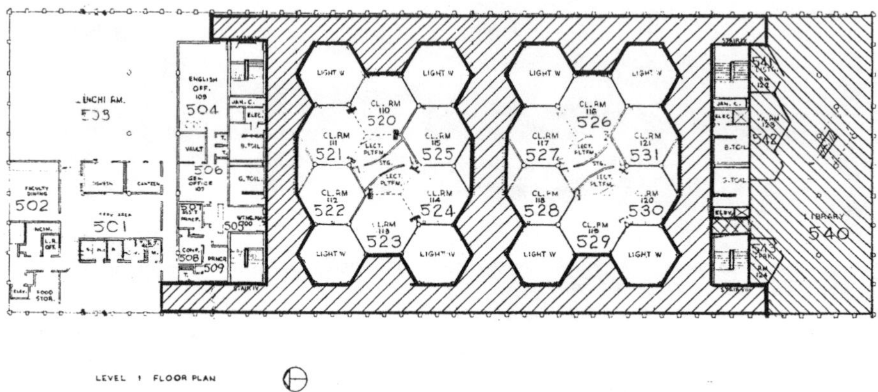

Fig. 6.16. Third-floor plan, South Shore High School (altered by the author). The hexagonal rooms, like those promoted by the EFL, are an example of architects and educators rethinking traditionally accepted norms, such as the rectangular classroom.

was a small stage and "teaching platform" for lectures. The science laboratories also contained twelve-foot revolving circular tables for demonstrations.

Intended by the board to be one of the most advanced high schools in the country and a showpiece for the city, South Shore instead became one of Chicago's most controversial. Its final price tag of $9 million was significantly higher than the original estimates and far beyond any previous school building, and its record of construction delays created bitter feelings in community residents.

South Shore High School, in spite of its unique interior spaces, also personified a weaker feature of postwar school architecture—the demise of physical attractiveness. The building looked defensive with its main floors raised above ground level and its heavy concrete facade, which left little room for windows, and unless visitors moved close to the building they would find no indication of the unique spaces within. *American School Board Journal* editor William C. Bruce launched a campaign to call attention to the often uneasy relationship between modernist educational planning and aesthetics found in buildings like South Shore. "In the architectural design of elementary and secondary school buildings, the sociological and educational aspects of the planning so strongly overshadow the elements of beauty and dignity especially of the exterior," Bruce wrote in 1956, "that few of the newest build-

Fig. 6.17. Hallway showing hexagonal light wells, South Shore High School.

ings really reflect the character of the work carried on in them."[87] A few years later, the problem had not abated: "More than ever, school buildings are designed from the inside with strong emphasis on the efficient uses of teaching areas of assembly and physical instruction spaces, and provisions for quick circulation of student groups. The result has been that exterior design has tended to be rectangular and extremely simple and flat."[88] Bruce continued his critique in 1964: "The exterior design of school buildings has improved very little in recent years. In fact, it is sometimes difficult to find the main entrance because so little emphasis in materials or ornament distinguishes it from the rest of the rambling low structure or the complex of structures connected by glassed-in walkways."[89] And in 1966, capping a decade of criticism, Bruce noted with a hint of exasperation that "Architects are still struggling to give the new forms of schoolhouses the significance and dignity which the school as a most important community structure deserves."[90]

Since Chicago built so few high schools in the 1960s, no defining aesthetic emerged. Those that were built, like South Shore, William Jones Commercial High School (Perkins & Will, 1966), and Kenwood High School (Schmidt, Garden, Erikson & Co., 1969), did demonstrate one commonal-

Fig. 6.18. Schmidt, Garden, Erikson & Co., Kenwood High School, 1969.

ity: the demise of the casual school building (Fig. 6.18).[91] Through growing size and bulk, and the increasingly common use of concrete facades with small windows, these school buildings began to look more institutional than casual, often in contrast to their interior spaces. In this way the sixties high schools took a step back toward their early twentieth century predecessors. The next generation of school buildings in Chicago would continue moving in that reverse direction.

## Another Building Campaign

Because of changing demographics the 1970s proved to be a prolific high school building period in Chicago. The baby boom children that flooded the public elementary schools in the 1960s were working their way through the higher grades. Consequently, high school enrollment climbed through the decade until it peaked at over 147,000 in 1978, a record high. From then on, a downward plunge in public school enrollment began, fueled by declining birthrates and suburban migration.

Stimulated once again by an increase in students and a shortage of classrooms in the older schools in largely black neighborhoods on the south and west sides, the board embarked upon its largest high school building campaign since the 1950s. The project began with the Martin Luther King High School (McCaughey, Erickson, Kristman & Stillwaugh with Caudill,

Rowlett & Scott, 1971). Continuing financial difficulties, however, suspended the building campaign even as high school enrollments climbed. The school system faced severe shortages between 1967 and 1973. The crisis peaked in 1972, with a $98 million debit. Over 1,000 positions were eliminated by the board and the public schools closed for five days before the state legislature approved a new financial package that saved the Chicago schools.[92] A state bailout allowed the board to finish work on four high schools: Marie Curie (Loebl, Schlossman, Bennett & Dart, Inc., with A. Epstein & Sons, Inc., 1973), George Washington Carver (Dubin, Dubin, Black & Moutoussamy, 1973), Roberto Clemente (Office of Mies van der Rohe, 1973) and Rezin Orr (Office of Mies van der Rohe, 1973). The following year saw the completion of the Whitney Young High School (Perkins & Will, 1974), and after that came the George Corliss (Skidmore, Owings & Merrill, 1975) and Percy Julian (Skidmore, Owings & Merrill, 1975) schools. George Collins High School (Andrew Heard & Associates, Ltd., 1976), followed, and the Benito Juarez (Bernheim, Kahn, & Lozano Architects, Ltd., 1977), Paul Robeson (Wendell Campbell Associates, Inc., 1977), and Englewood (Loewenberg & Loewenberg, 1979) high schools closed out the decade. This generation of high schools largely fell into two aesthetic categories—steel and glass or brick—depending upon their most prominent constructive material. All of them, however, continued to reject the low-rise casualness of the fifties campus schools.

## Schools and Parks

Many of the seventies high schools were the fruit of the board of education's new financing arrangement with the CPBC. They also marked the beginnings of a three-way partnership among those two organizations and the Chicago Park District. While the board had attempted to place school buildings near parkland or open space since the early 1900s, a formalized agreement with the park district was not concluded until the late 1940s. The park district and school board either jointly purchased potential school sites, with each entity paying a proportion, or the park district sold some of its existing property to the board at its original cost. These agreements were mutually beneficial—the park district was able to use school property after school hours for programs and activities, while the school utilized the park for playground and athletic purposes. By 1958, thirty-five of these "school-park" cooperative efforts had been constructed or developed.[93] All of the 1950s high schools benefited from the arrangement, with a few, like Dunbar, Harlan, and Washington, being attached to significant acreage.

In the late 1960s the park district and board grew more ambitious and proposed building some schools in established parks. The newly-formed park district/CPBC/board of education team's plans to construct schools in Washington, Douglas, Gately, and Humboldt parks provoked a critical response (the Humboldt project was later dropped in favor of Stanton Park). The *Chicago Tribune*, for example, reported a "simmering controversy" that pitted the educators and city officials on one side and planners, citizens' groups, housing organizations, and conservationists on the other. Promoters advocated the financial savings of making dual-purpose buildings—used by the public schools and the park district—and the inherent goodness of placing children in natural settings. Opponents feared the beginning of a slippery slope whereby more of the city's open space would be lost to schools, public housing projects, or other structures.[94] They approved of schools near parks, but not on parkland. A citizen's group seeking to block the school building projects in Washington and Douglas parks succeeded in reaching the Illinois Supreme Court, where it argued that the CPBC did not have the right to build schools in pubic parks without permission from the state legislature. The Supreme Court, however, ruled in the CPBC's favor, which cleared the way for several projects, including the Collins High School in Douglas Park.[95]

When James F. Redmond succeeded Benjamin Willis as superintendent his administration began to study the plausibility of a different type of park-school environment. At the time a number of cities across the country were considering "educational parks," largely as a way of reducing expenses and battling racial segregation. The idea was to create a "super campus" containing, ideally, an elementary school, junior high school, senior high school, and college in close proximity, along with arts and athletic structures. Each park would draw at least 10,000 students. Economies of scale, obtained by centrally-locating students and facilities, reduced per-child and construction costs, increased facility utilization, and allowed for the savings to be invested in specialized equipment or unique programs. Also important was the large educational campus' ability to draw upon a broader student pool. "A large school complex or facility, when compared with smaller neighborhood schools, has a greater potential for the racial integration of its students," wrote a team studying educational parks. "The neighborhood school draws from a restricted geographic area which, in the city, is quite often characterized by a preponderance of one ethnic group. . . . The larger the attendance area, the greater the chance for student diversity and for flexibility in feeder patterns."[96]

In 1968 the Chicago Board of Education hired Michigan State University professor Donald J. Leu to perform a feasibility study on educational parks. Leu recommended a long-range plan involving thirty-three "cultural educational clusters" or educational parks be built, each costing approximately $60 million. The "star-shaped clusters of educational and cultural institutions" were intended to provide a "greater opportunity for quality education in an increasingly complex society" and "prevent or mitigate against the increasing segregation of the city's public schools."[97] Leu suggested an 18–20,000-student prototype be constructed between the University of Illinois Chicago Circle campus and the Westside Medical Center—near the site of the future Whitney Young High School.[98] The centerpiece of this ensemble would be an 8,000-student public high school, soon to be followed by "magnet schools, primary schools and parochial schools."[99] Despite the backing of organizations like the Chicago Urban League and favorable coverage in the city's newspapers (except for the *Tribune*) the project never materialized. But the magnet school concept would survive.

## From Miesian Modernism to Postmodernism

Although the educational park idea never came to fruition in Chicago, high schools, for the most part, continued to be built adjacent to or in city parks. The high school buildings constructed during the 1970s rejected the experimentation of previous decades and tended toward more uniformity, even though they were designed by different architectural firms.

The 1970s high schools differed from those of the early twentieth century. Besides having dissimilar materials and more open interior spaces, many of the new schools were difficult to distinguish from the average low-rise office building.[100] The idea of using school architecture to inspire young minds to higher things seemed to have vanished. "[F]ew are now found to maintain that the architectural effect of a schoolhouse is an unimportant consideration," wrote school architect Edmund Wheelwright in 1896, "and that a beautiful schoolhouse does not do its part in the education of the young."[101] In 1902, University of Chicago sociologist Charles Zueblin expressed a commonly-held belief when he stated: "If the architecture of the schoolhouse, its decorations and surroundings, impress the child mind with the meaning of the beautiful, he will demand as a citizen a fairer city."[102] By the 1970s, such sentiments had disappeared. None of the educational or architectural journals contained such assertions; the school building now functioned only to properly house the business of learning, and inspirational architecture may not have been necessary to that mission.[103]

The typical new Chicago high school was influenced by an aesthetic popularized by the famous modernist (and Chicago resident) Ludwig Mies van der Rohe. These schools tended to have either visible steel frames and glass walls, or brick facades with smaller windows. Smooth square or rectangular forms were popular with both types. A number of mid-century trademarks had disappeared, such as the low-profile, single-story "California" plan and large open courtyards. Remnants of the campus plan could be seen, however, in the fact that most schools included at least two separate buildings— usually an academic building and a physical education building—joined by an enclosed walkway. Inside, the concept of flexibility still reigned supreme.

The Roberto Clemente and Rezin Orr high schools were notable for being designed by the firm that succeeded Mies van der Rohe upon his death in 1969. Dirk Lohan, Mies' grandson, was the partner-in-charge on both projects. Clemente was a nine-story rectangular tower that adopted Mies' favored facade articulation of a visible steel structure and nearly all glass skin (Fig. 6.19). This unusually tall profile was chosen as a compromise between a restricted site and the desire to have some open space surrounding the school. An athletic building was located across Division Street from the academic tower, connected by an enclosed pedestrian bridge.

Clemente's 3,000 students were divided into four "houses" of 750 students each, according to the most advanced educational thinking. Each house occupied its own floor. The houses—often referred to as "schools-within-schools"—were self-contained units that broke the larger student population into smaller, more intimate communities. Students were assigned to a house in their first year and stayed in it for the remainder of their ten-

Fig. 6.19. Office of Mies van der Rohe, Roberto Clemente High School, 1973.

ure. Educators had been experimenting with house plans or schools-within-schools since the early 1950s. Administrators admired house plans as much for their social and psychological benefits as their organizational advantages. "The idea is for each house to develop its own personality and atmosphere," an EFL publication claimed, "in order to strengthen social relationships, emphasize activities on a human scale, encourage a sense of identity and the kind of group loyalty that helps children toward achievement and success."[104] Each of Clemente High School's houses had its own class and activity spaces and dining/commons areas. The floor plans were as open as possible, with the only fixed elements being the central utility core and the stairways, while all other interior walls were moveable (Fig. 6.20). All four houses shared common spaces for specialized and technological work.

A similar version of the house plan appeared a year later in Perkins & Will's updated version of the modern high school. Whitney Young High School opened on the west side near the University of Illinois Chicago Circle Campus in 1974 (Fig. 6.21). Young was Chicago's first magnet high school. In contrast to the typical high school, which drew students from a predetermined geographic area, magnet schools brought students together from

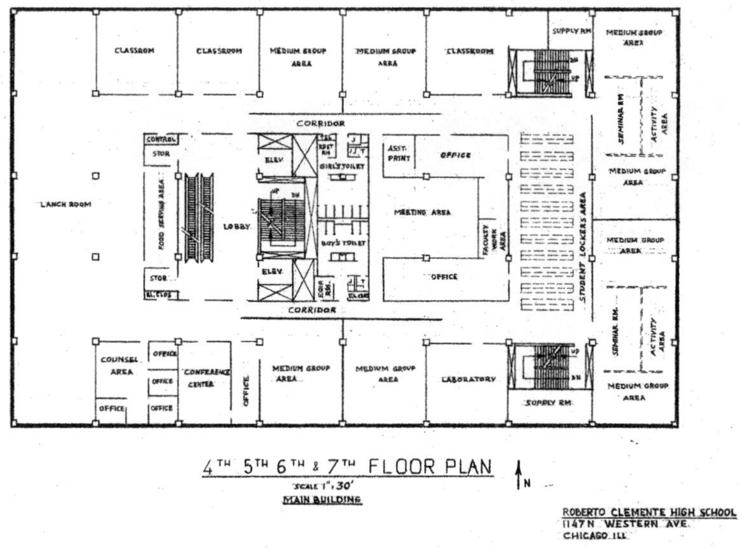

Fig. 6.20. Fourth- through seventh-floor plans, Roberto Clemente High School. An example of the more open floor plan that became popular in the Sixties, with spaces flowing into each other rather than being segregated by walls.

across the city with the lure of special opportunities and free transportation. Young originally offered special programs in medical and physical sciences and performing arts. It also housed a school-within-a-school for hearing-impaired students. When it opened, superintendent James F. Redmond touted Young as "potentially the most exciting and innovative secondary school in urban America," and promised that "[t]his school can fulfill many of our dreams, bringing together students from a wide range of racial and ethnic backgrounds who have diverse academic abilities, interests and talents."[105]

The school charged with accomplishing these lofty goals was designed as a campus of three buildings linked by elevated walkways. The academic building was a three-story enclosed square with a Miesian steel frame and glass curtain walls. The first floor contained administrative offices and the hearing impaired house for 650 students. Second and third floors held 2,000 students in four houses of 500 (Fig. 6.22). Each house had areas for classes, study, lockers, dining and lounging, and counselors, and moveable partition

Fig. 6.21. Perkins & Will, Whitney Young High School, 1974.

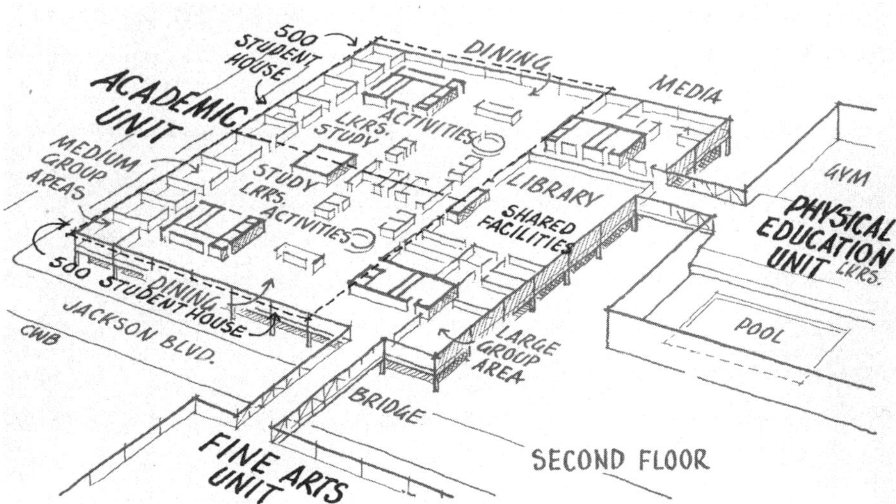


Fig. 6.22. Second-floor plan, Whitney Young High School.

Fig. 6.23. House dining area with library in right background, Whitney Young High School.

walls (Fig. 6.23). All houses used the second-floor resource center and third-floor science areas. A bridge across Van Buren Street led to the two-story Fine Arts Building. On the first floor, facilities for fine arts, communications, and technical and industrial instruction surrounded a 500-seat, multifunctional auditorium-theater. The second floor contained spaces for business and health education. A separate Physical Education Building was home to the gymnasium, swimming pool, and exercise and gymnastics rooms.

The designers of at least one 1970s high school turned to a mild postmodernism as an alternative to the limitations of modernist aesthetics. The Benito Juarez High School, which at first glance appeared to be a simplistic concrete box, was deceptively rich in allusions to Hispanic heritage (Fig. 6.24). Juarez was built in the Latino neighborhood of Pilsen, west of downtown. Community residents had waged a two-year battle with the Chicago Public Schools to get a new high school in the area. When the school was finally approved, architects Bernheim, Kahn & Lozano faced budgetary restrictions and an awkward, severely limited site at the intersection of three major thoroughfares. They responded with a basic two-building plan (one

Fig. 6.24. Bernheim, Kahn, & Lozano Architects, Benito Juarez High School, 1977.

for academics, the other for physical education), enlivened inside and out with references to Hispanic history. The architects created the illusion of banked walls—echoing ancient Mayan and Aztec monuments—on the academic building's exterior through contrasting colors and materials. Inside, a three-story atrium in the building's heart, intended as a gathering place for both students and community in the absence of an auditorium, was reminiscent of traditional Mexican architecture. A series of large murals in the atrium's four corners, begun in the 1980s but planned from the building's conception, featured scenes of Aztec gods and goddesses, Spanish conquistadors, Benito Juarez, and the Pilsen neighborhood, reinforcing the school's connection with its constituents; stained glass windows by students in the atrium and library, paintings and mosaics on hallway walls, and murals on the physical education building continued this project (Fig. 6.25).

This type of individualization would have been abhorred by mid-century modernists, but the postmodern movement had made it acceptable to address culture and history in architecture again. Postmodernism began to emerge in the 1960s, characterized by buildings with overt historical references. Although some versions of postmodern architecture tended to be witty or ironic, in serious hands it significantly expanded the architect's toolkit and allowed for

Fig. 6.25. Atrium, Benito Juarez High School.

greater connections between building and surroundings. At Juarez, the architects were able to inject artistic interest and solidify the connection between building and community by ethnicizing the standard late modernist box in a way that had not occurred with previous Chicago schools. They were able to realize *Chicago Daily News* writer M. W. Newman's call for school architecture that "is supposed to blend with the community instead of being standoffish ... instead of standing grim and immune like forbidding jailhouses."[106]

Throughout the architectural and educational explorations of the sixties and seventies, the Chicago high school curriculum remained deeply invested in both differentiation and personal development. The board continued to follow the advice of advisory organizations like the National Committee on the Reform of Secondary Education (NCRSE), which updated the 1918 Cardinal Principles for the 1970s. The NCRSE's "Content Goals" for high school curricula included semi-traditional concerns such as "Achievement of Computational Skills" and "Proficiency of Critical and Objective Thinking," but the plan was dominated by non-academic "Process Goals" like "Appreciation of Others," "Ability to Adjust to Change," and "Self-knowledge."[107]

Consensus for a change of direction was growing, however, that would alter secondary education in the next decade.

The end of the 1970s marked the beginning of a two-decade hiatus from high school construction in Chicago. During that time some of the older schools were rehabilitated or enlarged, but the city essentially found itself with enough high schools to serve its ever-shrinking student population. When construction renewed at the turn-of-the-century, a very different school system began building high schools that took postmodernism's engagement with the past a step further by reviving some of the fundamental principles of school architecture from one hundred years earlier—at the same time that a "back to basics" movement renewed some traditional educational ideas.

# Chapter Seven

# INTO THE NEW CENTURY

The new century really began for the Chicago Public Schools in the 1980s. That decade saw the schools racked by massive changes. Public student enrollment fell by 50,000 while the city's population dropped by almost a quarter-million.[1] More specifically, the number of public high school students in the city fell by over 30 percent from its peak in the late 1970s. Even worse, the school system had its finances taken over by an outside entity. And the system's administrative structure was dramatically reorganized. During these struggles, secondary school construction ceased; when it began again after a twenty-year hiatus, a new generation of Chicago high schools appeared, updated to the contemporary educational environment but reviving many architectural ideas over a century old.

## Reform and Reorganization

The school system's major problems began when it faced a deficit of over $500 million for the 1978–79 school year, largely caused by underpaid and uncollected taxes. This financial emergency spurred a city bailout that included municipal and state loans, increased tax rates, thousands of layoffs, and the creation of the Chicago School Finance Authority, an oversight entity responsible for controlling all of the board's finances.[2] After the crisis was averted, public attention focused on the dismal state of Chicago education, particularly the high schools. In 1985, statistics showed that 43 percent of the city's high school freshman would never receive a degree; in the inner-city areas, the dropout rate reached 67 percent.[3] A 1987 report published in the *Chicago Tribune* showed that thirty-three of the city's sixty-four high schools scored in the lowest 1 percent of schools nationwide on the ACT exam. Only seven Chicago schools scored higher than the tenth percentile.[4] Chicago high school students' average ACT score of 13.9 (out of thirty-six) was far below the state average of 18.9.[5] Other reports uncovered similar deficiencies. These and other problems led U.S. Education Secretary William Bennett to label Chicago's school district the worst in the nation. "You've got close to educational meltdown here," he said.[6]

Chicago was not alone, however, in its high school problems. *A Nation at Risk*, a 1983 publication by the National Commission on Excellence (NCE), emphasized the doleful state of American secondary education. The authors' main critique was that comprehensive high schools' curricula lacked depth. "Secondary school curricula have been homogenized and diffused to the point that they no longer have a central purpose," they wrote. "In effect, we have a cafeteria-style curriculum in which the appetizers and desserts can easily be mistaken for the main course."[7] The NCE recommended that curricular differentiation—the high school standard since the turn-of-the-century—be abandoned. Instead, schools around the country should employ a standard academic curriculum for all high school students that emphasized "The Five Basics" (English, mathematics, science, social studies, and computer science).

This return to nineteenth century ideals resonated with both educators and the public. Within three years of the report's publication, forty-five states and the District of Columbia had raised high school graduation requirements, and many others had strengthened math and science requirements.[8] Illinois adopted a series of goals for its high school students based on their performance in core academic subjects like mathematics, science, social studies, and language arts. Comprehensive testing was instituted to monitor progress toward these goals. "The context of high school education has changed," wrote G. Alfred Hess, describing the new movement. "The focus has shifted from warehousing and managing the behavior of kids to a focus on student learning . . . a new focus on academic performance."[9]

Reformers persuaded the Illinois legislature not only to address core educational issues like academic standards, dropout rates, and early childhood education but also the governance of Chicago's school system. Some lawmakers attempted to revive the old Harper Report plan for an elected school board; while that proposal failed to garner enough support, an amended bill passed that created Local School Improvement Councils (LSICs) for each Chicago school to review discretionary spending.

In 1989, Illinois changed the management of Chicago schools by enacting P.A. 85-1418, better known as the Chicago School Reform Act, described by historian Jeffrey Mirel as "a truly distinctive decentralization plan."[10] The law strengthened the LSICs and gave them decision-making powers. Each of the city's 542 new councils would consist of eleven members—the school principal, two teachers, six parents, and two community representatives. This group would be responsible for making policy and curriculum decisions and controlling the school's budget. The law also contained provisions for establishing goals for subject matter areas and transferring funds from school systems to individual schools. More specific to Chicago, the law required the city's school board be expanded from eleven to fifteen members and ordered the city to perform a national search for a new superintendent. The mayor, however, retained the right to choose the school board members, assuring continued political control over public education.

These changes helped the public school system but did not solve all of its problems. The reorganization process took a further step in 1995 when the state legislature allowed Mayor Richard M. Daley to take complete control of the schools. Daley appointed a reform team—headed by a chief executive officer in place of the superintendent—and set to work. The team unveiled an unprecedented capital improvement program in 1996 to address the city's aging physical plant. Reducing overcrowding and creating educational environments to aid learning were key points of the program's agenda. The project would prove to be the largest school construction campaign in American history. By the fall of 2005, the city had spent billions of dollars on twenty-one new schools, eight replacement schools, and sixty-one additions and annexes.[11] More than 50,000 seats were added to the system in the first ten years.[12] As a result, Chicago gained a vastly improved set of schools, modernized equipment, and room for more students.[13] The cost was high, however, as the school system relinquished much of its control to the city government.

## Old Ideas for a New Century

The massive injection of attention and money into Chicago's school infrastructure helped publicize a nationwide epidemic of aging school buildings. In the mid-1990s, U.S. Department of Education investigators calculated the average American public school building at forty-two years old.[14] The U.S. General Accounting Office estimated that one-third of all public school students, or about fourteen million children, attended classes in structures that needed "extensive repair or replacement."[15] And just a few years later, the National Trust for Historic Preservation placed "neighborhood schools" on its list of "America's 11 Most Endangered Places," and began a campaign to promote maintenance and renovation over destruction.

As a consequence of the intensive focus on the condition of the nation's public school buildings, construction escalated to levels not seen since the immediate postwar era. Expenditures rose by almost 40 percent between 1990 and 1997, to nearly $25 billion.[16] Chicago followed this trend. As a part of the Capital Improvement Program, the Chicago Public School system began to construct its first new high school buildings in nearly twenty years. During that period, however, an interesting phenomenon occurred: the landscapes of both education and school architecture had changed dramatically, with both educators and architects looking to the past for guidance. *A Nation at Risk* and similar educational critiques spurred a "back to basics" movement with repercussions beyond the high school curriculum. Concurrently, the fashionable postmodern movement in architecture had made historical styles, materials, and models acceptable again after being banished during the reign of high modernism. These two forces combined to produce a new generation of secondary school buildings characterized by traditional ideas like more formal floor plans, tall building profiles, multiple facade colors and textures, extensive use of masonry cladding, and an increased interest in monumentality (although many new schools tended to have smaller student populations).[17] Such qualities related the fin-du-siècle schools more closely to early twentieth-century precedents than the modernist experiments of the postwar era. Veteran school architect Earl Flansburgh summarized the significant transitions in an *Architectural Record* article devoted to school architecture. "Flexibility [in the postwar era] was achieved by such architectural elements as open-plan classrooms with operable partitions (suitable for team

Fig. 7.1. OWP/P Architects, Northside College Preparatory High School, 1999.

teaching), and conference rooms and specific project areas related to clusters of classrooms," said Flansburgh. "Now, with renewed interest in basic education in mathematics, science, English, and history, we don't see this interest in flexibility. . . . We're seeing simple interiors, reflecting a basic educational program. Exterior educational symbolism has replaced interior educational flexibility as a driving force for academic buildings."[18]

The newest Chicago high schools definitely made historical connections. In the tradition of A.F. Hussander's stately entrances, the $50 million Northside College Preparatory High School (OWP/P, design architects, 1999), the city's first new high school structure since the late 1970s, featured an oversized three-story glass entry prominently located in the center of the building, dominated by giant abstracted columns supporting an overhanging roof (Fig. 7.1). Apart from the entry, the facade was downplayed, with its brick surfaces and simple windows providing a striking contrast to the elaborate entrance. Northside's floor plan also harked back to days past, resembling a slightly skewed version of an "I" or in-line plan. A fine and performing arts center and a gymnasium/swimming pool complex anchored

Fig. 7.2. OWP/P Architects, VOA Associates, Inc. (architects of record), North Grand High School, 2004.

the school's two ends, connected by a main corridor, lined with classrooms, which served as the circulation spine. In the center, a two-story media center dominated the plan. The building was thus zoned (separate areas for arts, classrooms and offices, athletics) in the same fashion as William Mundie's or Dwight Perkins's early 1900s high schools. Although the layout and monumentality were traditional, the building was contemporary, with fiber optic cables connecting a school-wide computer network.

Northside College Prep was followed in rapid succession by the Walter Payton College Preparatory High School (De Stefano & Partners; MacLachlan, Cornelius & Filoni, design architects, 2000), Neil Simeon High School (HOH Architects, 2003); North Grand High School (OWP/P, design architects, 2004), and Little Village High School (OWP/P, design architects, 2005) (Figs. 7.2–7.3). All employed monumentality, multi-colored masonry, and functional zoning finessed into variations on long-established floor plans (Simeon an "E" or "T" shape, Little Village a rectangular box with open courtyards). Of this group Little Village was perhaps the most interesting. Constructed in the Mexican community of Little Village on the far west

Fig. 7.3. OWP/P Architects, Gonzalez Hasbrouck, and Guajardo Associates (architects of record), Little Village High School, 2005.

side at 31st Street and Pulaski Avenue, the school was actually a combination of four schools in one, each with its own administration. Continuing the 1970s "school-within-a-school" experiments, Little Village divided students into 450–500 person groups within the main structure. Now, however, instead of one school split up into four groups, there were four separate and independent schools under one roof.[19] Each small school had its own academic facilities but shared the library/media center, two gymnasia, cafeteria, and auditorium. Architecturally, the building's monumental entry echoed that of Northside College Prep (also by OWP/P, Little Village's design architects), and the extended three-story structure housed three interior courtyards.

The general scheme of Little Village resembled other schools around the country. What made it unique is that the architects attempted to incorporate elements of the school's tumultuous founding and its students' ethnic heritage into the material fabric. Little Village High School appeared only after intense local pressure on the school board. The board had long promised neighborhood residents a high school, but never made any progress on the plans. In 2001, fourteen residents forced the board's hand by staging a well-publicized nineteen-day hunger strike. OWP/P memorialized this struggle by embedding the numbers fourteen and nineteen in various places

Fig. 7.4. Courtyard, Little Village High School.

throughout the building. Fourteen trees along the school's main entry signified the strikers, while the school's entrance and a corridor were skewed from the rest of the building at nineteen-degree angles. The architects also worked with local residents to find ways to emphasize their Mexican heritage. The entry plaza was based on similar plazas at Mexican churches. A seventy-foot, cone-shaped solar calendar dominated the school's central courtyard; it was intended to evoke the ancient Aztec's solar calendar (Fig. 7.4). Further Aztec connections appeared in the incorporation of the "Five Worlds" myth: through a unique color scheme, each separate school was associated with earth, fire, wind, and water—the four previous worlds—and the larger school as a whole represented the present world.[20]

Outside of Little Village, these new Chicago high schools contained features that could be seen in other American high school buildings. They combined the monumental and the casual, for example, as if to link the pre-modernist and high modernist pasts of the 1900s and 1950s, respectively. Monumentality showed in large, well-marked entrances, wide corridors (sometimes two stories high), and great expanses of glass wall. Familiar materials like brick and sometimes wood, brought inside the buildings, helped to offset this quality, as did the practice of leaving ducts and pipes exposed in the ceilings as a display of the structure's inner workings. Floor plans were more elongated, less boxlike than in the 1970s, but were simpler than those of schools a century earlier because the new high schools held fewer rooms and no old-fashioned shop spaces. And the campus plan had completely disappeared—all of the schools' spaces had once again been gathered into a compact whole. The same back-to-basics movement that emphasized traditional educational methods such as testing and core subjects had provoked a return to traditional architectural ideas as well. Educational reform thus continued to shape school architecture.

## Chicago High Schools at 150 Years

Chicago's high school scene, like that in other large metropolitan areas, has now splintered into a dizzying array of public, charter, magnet, and specialty schools, centers, and academies, reflecting new directions in secondary education. In 2006, on the 150-year anniversary of the opening of the city's first high school, there were over 100 high schools in Chicago. This group included academic centers, alternative schools, career academies, charter schools, magnet schools, military academies, and technology academies, among others. Even terminology had changed. For example, the word "campus" had taken on a different connotation than in the past; instead of the 1950s-60s meaning of a group of separate but interconnected buildings, the word now meant "multiple, autonomous small schools" in a "large, traditional high school building," like Little Village.[21] And while a school such as Little Village might include truly contemporary spaces which were inconceivable for most of the twentieth century (distance-learning laboratories, daycare centers, computer rooms), it is more like a "traditional" high school building of a century ago than people might realize.

Chicago's newest high school buildings of the early twenty-first century bear little physical resemblance to the city's first high school. But the first and the most recent high school buildings, however separated by time, all reflect the state of secondary education at the time of their creation. All of these schools, from the simple 1880s boxes to the grand monuments of the 1900s, from the casual 1950s schools to the Miesian frames of the 1970s and the neo-traditional buildings of today, record the increasing importance given by American society to the education of its teenagers. They also mark the shifting priorities of educators and administrators regarding what these youngsters should learn and how they should learn it.

The Chicago Public Schools' massive investment in its infrastructure, through the Capital Improvement Program, proves that the city's educational decision makers continue to recognize the importance of school environments to the mission of public secondary education. History shows that the effort to advance education by improving the physical environment is not novel—it was one of the cornerstones of the Progressive Era. But Chicago's undertaking is laudable for its sheer scope. It comes amid a rising interest in school architecture among both architects and educators. A myriad of organizations have formed to investigate school design issues and disseminate ideas, in the tradition of the EFL, including the National Clearinghouse for Educational Facilities, the National Center for the 21st Century Schoolhouse at San Diego State University, America's Schoolhouse Council, DesignShare, and the American Institute of Architects Committee on Architecture for Education. The Chicago Public Schools' design competition "Big Shoulders . . . Small Schools" in 2000-01 stimulated more than 100 entries and generated much publicity for the system and school architecture. Further interest in schools, particularly high schools, arose after Thom Mayne, winner of the 2005 Pritzker Architecture Prize, unveiled his Diamond Ranch High School in Pomona, California. Diamond Ranch has received more publicity than any school in decades, partially because of Mayne's award. Other high-profile architecture firms like Coop Himmelb(l)au, and Arquitectonica have extended their practices to include new high school buildings.

The future holds many possibilities for Chicago's high schools. If the current educational emphasis on testing and basic skills continues, will school buildings shrink (smaller enrollments are definitely seen as better) and will shops and arts rooms disappear, marking the end of the comprehensive school and the return of the undifferentiated box? Specialty schools are already replacing specialty rooms in some cities. Will Diamond Ranch

High School's marquee status invite more experimentation or avant-garde approaches? Will high schools become the fashionable high-status commission of the future, as art museums are today? What affects will distance learning, already so important to higher education institutions, have on secondary schools? How will the sustainable architecture movement change school design? How long will the Capital Improvement Program be able to bolster the city's aging schools?

Whatever happens, one can be sure that high school architecture in cities like Chicago will continue to have an intimate relationship with educational reforms, for they have become equal partners since the early twentieth century in the process of educating America's youth.

# APPENDIX

## Table 1A
## Public High School Enrollments

| Year | Chicago | National |
|---|---|---|
| 1880 | 1,043 | ---- |
| 1890 | 1,701 | 202,963 |
| 1900 | 10,201 | 542,000 |
| 1910 | 17,781 | 1,153,000 |
| 1920 | 36,433 | 2,537,000 |
| 1930 | 103,851 | 4,770,000 |
| 1940 | 144,671 | 6,714,000 |
| 1950 | 96,786 | 5,806,000 |
| 1960 | 102,886 | 8,821,000 |
| 1970 | 141,549 | 13,336,000 |
| 1980 | 132,075 | 13,231,000 |
| 1990 | 102,868 | 11,338,000 |
| 2000 | 94,223 | 13,514,000 |

## Table 1B
## Percentage of Fourteen- to Seventeen-year-olds Enrolled in High School, Nationally

| Year | Percentage |
| --- | --- |
| 1880 | 3.7 |
| 1890 | 5.6 |
| 1900 | 10.5 |
| 1910 | 17.8 |
| 1920 | 35.0 |
| 1930 | 54.9 |
| 1940 | 73.0 |
| 1950 | 76.6 |
| 1960 | 89.0 |
| 1970 | 92.0 |
| 1980 | 90.3 |
| 1990 | 93.7 |
| 2004 | 94.0 |

*Sources*: Board of Education of the City of Chicago *Annual Reports*; Mary J. Herrick, *The Chicago Schools: A Social and Political History* (Beverly Hills and London: Sage Publications, Inc., 1971); David L. Angus and Jeffrey E. Mirel, *The Failed Promise of the American High School, 1890–1995* (New York: Teachers College Press, 1999); *Chicago Public School Facts & Figures* (1972–73 & 1987–88); Elaine M. Allensworth and Shazia Rafiullah Miller, *Declining High School Enrollment: An Exploration of the Causes* (Chicago: Consortium on Chicago School Research, 2002); U.S. Census Bureau, *Statistical Abstract of the United States: 2003* (Washington, DC: United States Government Printing Office, 2004).

# Table 2
## Chicago Board of Education Architects, 1882–1981

| Architect | Tenure |
|---|---|
| Frederic Baumann | February 1882–June 1882 |
| Julius S. Ender | June 1882–October 1882 |
| James R. Willett | October 1882–January 1884 |
| John J. Flanders | January 1884–December 1888 |
| Charles Rudolph | December 1888–December 1890 |
| John J. Flanders | December 1890–February 1893 |
| August Fiedler | February 1893–December 1896 |
| Normand S. Patton | December 1896–November 1898 |
| Fred A. Fiedler | November 1898–December 1898* |
| William B. Mundie | December 1898–March 1904 |
| Robert B. Williamson | April 1904–June 1905* |
| Dwight H. Perkins | June 1905–April 1910 |
| Arthur F. Hussander | February 1910–1914*, 1914–March 1922 |
| John C. Christensen | March 1922–September 1928 |
| Paul Gerhardt | October 1928–April 1931[†] |
| John C. Christensen | April 1931–1959 |
| Saul Samuels | 1959–1976 |
| Kenneth Groggs | 1976–1981 |

* acting architect                    [†] temporary architect

*Note*: The position of Chicago Board of Education Architect was not full-time until the tenure of August Fiedler.

*Sources*: Board of Education of the City of Chicago, *Annual Reports* and *Proceedings of the Board of Education of the City of Chicago*.

# Table 3
## Classroom Types in Chicago Schools, 1856–1915

| High School | Class-rooms | Library | Gyms | Science | Shops | Comm-ercial | Dom-estic | Art | Music |
|---|---|---|---|---|---|---|---|---|---|
| Central | 10 | | | | | | | | |
| West Division | 15 | | | | | | | | |
| North Division | 12 | 1 | | 1 | | | | | |
| South Division | 18 | | | 1 | | | | | |
| West Division | 28 | | | 1 | | | | | |
| North-West Division | 15 | 1 | 1 | 3 | | | | | |
| Hyde Park I | 23 | 1 | 1 | 2 | | | | | |
| Waller | 19 | 1 | 1 | 3 | | 2 | | 2 | |
| McKinley | 24 | 1 | 1 | 5 | 3 | 2 | 3 | 2 | |
| Phillips | 48 | 1 | 2 | 5 | 3 | 4 | 3 | 3 | 1 |
| Schurz | 26 | 1 | 1 | 5 | 4 | 4 | 3 | 5 | 1 |
| Senn | 38 | 1 | 1 | 9 | 5 | 5 | 2 | 6 | 1 |
| Hyde Park II | 48 | 1 | 2 | 9 | 4 | 3 | 2 | 6 | 1 |
| Harrison | 42 | 1 | 2 | 9 | 6 | 4 | 8 | 5 | 1 |

# REFERENCES

## Introduction


1.     See, for example, William W. Cutler, III, "A Preliminary Look at the School-house: The Philadelphia Story, 1870–1920," *Urban Education* 8 (January 1974): 381–99; idem, "Cathedral of Culture: The Schoolhouse in American Educational Thought and Practice since 1820." *History of Education Quarterly* 29 (Spring 1989): 1–40; Lucian August Szlizewski, "Schoolhouse Architecture in America from 1830–1915" (Ph.D. diss., Miami University, 1989); Mohamed Ageli Hammad, "The Impact of Philosophical and Educational Theories on School Architecture (The British and American Experience 1820–1970)" (Ph.D. diss., University of Pennsylvania, 1984); and Jean L. Harchelroad, "The Evolution of Public Elementary School Architecture in Pittsburgh, Pennsylvania, 1835–1915: An Analysis of Changing Styles and Func-tions" (Ph.D. diss., University of Pittsburgh, 1988).

2.     Notable exceptions include Robert A. M. Stern, Gregory Gilmartin, and Robert Montague Massingale. *New York 1900: Metropolitan Architecture and Urban-ism, 1890–1915* (New York: Rizzoli, 1983) (which contains a brief section on *fin de siècle* school); Amy Suzanne Weisser, "Institutional Revisions: Modernism and American Public Schools From the Depression Through the Second World War" (Ph.D. diss., Yale University, 1995); Lisa B. Reitzes, "Moderately Modern: Interpret-ing the Architecture of the Public Works Administration" (Ph.D. diss., University of Delaware, 1989); and Dell Upton, "Lancasterian Schools, Republican Citizenship, and the Spatial Imagination in Early Nineteenth-Century America," *Journal of the Society of Architectural Historians* 55 (September 1996): 238–53.

3.     See, for example, Annmarie Adams, *Medicine By Design: The Architect and the Modern Hospital, 1893–1943* (Minneapolis and London: University of Minnesota

Press, 2008); Carla Yanni, *The Architecture of Madness: Insane Asylums in the United States* (Minneapolis and London: University of Minnesota Press in association with the Center for American Places, 2007); and Abigail A. Van Slyck, *Free to All: Carnegie Libraries & American Culture 1890–1920* (Chicago and London: University of Chicago Press, 1995).

4.    For example, Charles B. J. Snyder designed hundreds of schools in New york City from 1891 until 1922. See Jim Dwyer, "A Builder of Dreams, in Brick and Mortar," *The New York Times* (October 18, 2008): A18.

5.    Useful studies of Chicago education include Mary J. Herrick, *The Chicago Schools: A Social and Political History* (Beverly Hills and London: Sage Publications, Inc., 1971); Julia Wrigley, *Class Politics and Public Schools: Chicago 1900–1950* (New Brunswick, NJ: Rutgers University Press, 1982); David John Hogan, *Class and Reform: School and Society in Chicago, 1880–1930* (Philadelphia: University of Pennsylvania Press, 1985); Dorothy Shipps, *School Reform, Corporate Style: Chicago, 1880–2000* (Lawrence: University Press of Kansas, 2006); Thomas W. Gutowski, "The High School as an Adolescent-Raising Institution: An Inner History of Chicago Public Secondary Education, 1856–1940," (Ph.D. diss., University of Chicago, 1978); and John Wesley Bell, *The Development of the Public High School in Chicago* (Chicago: University of Chicago Libraries, 1939).

6.    The best source to date for such information is Kate Rousmaniere's *City Teachers: Teaching and Social Reform in Historical Perspective* (New York and London: Teachers College Press, 1997), which contains a brief discussion of the physical environment of teaching as recounted by some teachers who worked in the New York City public schools in the 1920s. See, also, Nancy Hoffman, ed., *Woman's "True" Profession: Voices From the History of Teaching*, 2nd ed. (Cambridge, MA: Harvard Education Publishing Group, 2003), and Donald Warren, *American Teachers: Histories of a Profession at Work* (New York: Macmillan Publishing Company, 1989).


## Education and Architecture in Early Chicago


1.    For basic information on the development of the American high school, see William J. Reese, *The Origins of the American High School* (New Haven and London: Yale University Press, 1995); Edward A. Krug, *The Shaping of the American High School, 1880–1920* (New York: Harper & Row, 1964); Krug, *The Shaping of the American High School, 1920–1941* (Madison, WI: University of Wisconsin Press, 1972).

2.    Reese, *Origins of the American High School*, 57.

3.    Ibid., 40.

4.    R. Carlyle Buley, *The Old Northwest Pioneer Period, 1815–1840*, vol. II (Indianapolis: Indiana Historical Society, 1950), 416.

5.    The best source for the history of common schools is Carl F. Kaestle, *Pillars of the Republic: Common Schools and American Society, 1780–1860* (New York: Hill & Wang, 1983).

6.    *A Volume of Records Relating to the Early History of Boston, Containing Boston Town Records, 1814 to 1822* (Boston, 1906), 169–71; quoted in Reese, *Origins of the American High School*, 14.

7.    The quotes are from Thomas J. Schlereth, *Victorian America: Transformations in Everyday life, 1876–1915* (New York: HarperPerennial, 1991), 275. Chapter Three will discuss this "discovery" and its implications for American secondary education.

8.    Priscilla Ferguson Clement, *Growing Pains: Children in the Industrial Age, 1850–1890* (New York: Twayne Publishers, 1997), 145. Clement notes that the figures underrepresented actual employment.

9.    Ibid., 59–79.

10.    "Reducing the School Expenses," *Chicago Tribune*, March 22, 1878.

11.    Kaestle, *Pillars of the Republic*, 121. In a study of St. Louis students in 1880, Selwyn Troen found that 80 percent of the thirteen- to sixteen-year-old sons of professional fathers were enrolled in school, 64 percent of the sons of white collar workers, and only 32 percent of unskilled workers' sons. Selwyn K. Troen, *The Public and the Schools: Shaping the St. Louis System, 1838–1920* (Columbia, MO: University of Missouri Press, 1975), 127. David Labaree looked at students in Philadelphia Central High School for the same year and discerned that 46 percent of the student body came from the middle class compared to 3.5 percent from the working classes. David F. Labaree, *The Making of an American High School: The Credentials Market and the Central High School of Philadelphia, 1838–1939* (New Haven and London: Yale University Press, 1988), 42. See also David L. Angus, "Conflict, Class, and the Nineteenth-Century Public High School in the Cities of the Midwest, 1845–1900," *Curriculum Inquiry* 18:1 (1988): 7–31.

12.    Thomas W. Gutowski, "The High School as an Adolescent-Raising Institution: An Inner History of Chicago Public Secondary Education, 1856–1940," Ph.D. diss., University of Chicago (1978): 15; David L. Angus and Jeffrey E. Mirel, *The Failed Promise of the American High School, 1890–1995* (New York: Teachers College Press, 1999), 203.

13.    National Education Association, *Report of the Committee of Ten on Secondary Schools* (Washington, D. C. : U.S. Government Printing Office, 1893), in *The American Curriculum: A Documentary History*, eds. George W. Willis, William H. Schubert, Robert V. Bullough, Jr., Craig Kridel, and John T. Holton (Westport, CT: Greenwood Press, 1993), 92. Enrollment figures support this description; in Chicago, for example, only 731 of Chicago's 185,000 public school students in 1894 were in their last year of high school (0.39 percent). Mary J. Herrick, *The Chicago Schools: A Social and Political History* (Beverly Hills and London: Sage Publications, Inc., 1971), 82.

14.    The school fund had its origins in the Northwest Ordinance of 1785, which allotted one square mile in every six-mile township in the Northwest Territory for school land. An 1830s Illinois law required land given by the federal government for schools to be sold upon petition of a preponderance of the township's eligible voters. Chicagoans submitted such a petition in October 1833. The original school land in the city was one square mile bounded by State Street on the east and Madison on the north. The land was divided into blocks and sold—except for four blocks—for $38,619. 74. This money was used to establish the school fund. In subsequent years, it was bolstered by state donations of "canal lands" and state income from the sale of government land, and by a city allocation of unpaid river wharf rents. Herrick, *The Chicago Schools*, 22–27.

15.    In 1841, the council passed along the right to choose textbooks and set courses of study to the school inspectors.

16.    Herrick, *The Chicago Schools*, 403.

17.    Ibid., 403, 41.

18.    Bessie L. Pierce, *A History of Chicago: Vol. I., The Beginnings of a City, 1673–1848* (New York: Alfred A. Knopf, 1937), 382.

19.    Herrick, *The Chicago Schools*, 29.

20.    *Proceedings of the Board of School Inspectors of Chicago* (December 27, 1852): 48–52.

21.    Female students actually dominated the nineteenth-century high school ranks in Chicago and other cities around the country. Between the mid-1850s and 1880, they accounted for 60 percent of Chicago's high school graduates. In some cities, the discrepancy was even greater. St. Louis's high school population was 58 percent female in 1870, 77 percent in 1893, and 65 percent in 1900. Reese, *Origins of the American High School*, 243; Karen Graves, *Girls' Schooling During the Progressive Era: From Female Scholar to Domesticated Citizen* (New York and London: Garland Publishing, Inc., 1998), 163.

22.    Because of the large number of rural schools, even at the turn of the century in states like Illinois and Connecticut only 15 percent of all high schools were in separate buildings. Theodore R. Sizer, *Secondary Schools at the Turn of the Century* (New Haven and London: Yale University Press, 1964), 39–40.

23.    Edward M. Miggins, "The Search for the One Best System: Cleveland Public Schools and Educational Reform, 1836–1920," in *Cleveland: A Tradition of Reform*, eds. David D. Van Tassel and John J. Grabowski (Kent, OH: Kent State University Press, 1986), 139; *St. Louis Public Schools: 160 Years of Challenge, Change, and Commitment to the Children of St. Louis, 1838–1998* (St. Louis: St. Louis Board of Education, 1998), 11.

24.    William H. Wells, "Public High School in Chicago," *American Journal of Education* 3 (June 1857): 536.

25.    U.S. Census records, cited in Herrick, *The Chicago Schools*, 403.

26.    *Thirteenth Annual Report of the Board of Education of the City of Chicago* (1867), quoted in John Wesley Bell, *The Development of the Public High School in Chicago* (Chicago: University of Chicago Libraries, 1939), 27.

27.    At the time, the board of education and the city council shared responsibility for purchasing new property and constructing schools. In a very awkward relationship, the board chose the sites and the council purchased them with the board's money. This arrangement would continue for the next half-century. Herrick, *The Chicago Schools*, 43–44.

28.    Bell, *Development of the Public High School in Chicago*, 28.

29.    Ibid., 20, 90. This tripling of enrollment outpaced the city's growth, which doubled during the same time (505,977 to 1,099,850). Herrick, *The Chicago Schools*, 403. High school enrollments rose even more dramatically after 1890; see Appendix A. Bell, *Development of the Public High School in Chicago*, 90–91.

30.    Perry R. Duis, "The Shaping of Chicago," in Alice Sinkevitch, ed., *AIA Guide to Chicago* (San Diego, New York, London: Harcourt Brace & Company, 1993), 7.

31.    *Twenty-Ninth Annual Report of the Board of Education of the City of Chicago* (1882–83) (Chicago: Jameson & Morse, Printers, 1884), 61.

32.    *Twenty-Seventh Annual Report of the Board of Education of the City of Chicago* (1880–81), (Chicago: Jameson & Morse Printers, 1882): 26.

33.    United State Commissioner of Education Report (1873), quoted in David B. Tyack and Elisabeth Hansot, *Learning Together: A History of Coeducation in American Public Schools* (New York: Russell Sage Foundation, 1992), 117.

34.    Gutowski, "The High School as an Adolescent-Raising Institution," 76; Angus and Mirel, *The Failed Promise of the American High School*, 203.

35.    Larry Cuban, *How Teachers Taught: Constancy and Change in American Class-rooms 1890–1990* (New York and London: Teachers College Press, 1993), 31; David I. Macleod, *The Age of the Child: Children in American, 1890–1920*. Joseph M. Hawes and N. Ray Hiner, eds., *Twayne's History of American Childhood* Series, (New York: Twayne Publishers, 1998), 149.

36.    David Nasaw, *Schooled to Order: A Social History of Public Schooling in the United States* (New York: Oxford University Press, 1979), 134. According to David Nasaw, only 14 percent of high school students could afford college in 1890, and those percentages actually dropped (9. 6 percent in 1905 and 5.6 percent in 1909) as enrollments increased, demonstrating the progressive impoverishment of Americans as immigration grew in the early twentieth century. For more information on the background of high school students' parents, see Note 11.

37.    This was a drastic move because Greek was traditionally a college preparatory topic and most colleges included a Greek component in their entrance examinations.

38.    Board of education president Martin A. DeLaney reflected this stance in the *Annual Report*. Responding to "many commentaries of a disparaging nature . . . upon our system of High Schools, as not giving instruction in the more useful branches of learning, and in not fitting young people for 'practical' occupations," DeLaney defended the system for producing "men and women possessing intelligence and moral worth as citizens. " "Neither the state nor the municipality," wrote DeLaney, "is endangered by such intelligence as is imparted to our Grammar or High School pupils. " *Twenty-Eighth Annual Report of the Board of Education of the City of Chicago* (1881–82), (Chicago: George K. Hazlitt & Co., 1883): 20–23.

39.    David K. Cohen, "Practice and Policy: Notes on the History of Instruction," in *American Teachers: Histories of a Profession at Work*, ed. Donald Warren (New York: Macmillan Publishing Company, 1989), 399.

40.    *Sixth Annual Report of the Superintendent of Public Schools of Chicago* (1860–61) (Chicago: Department of Public Instruction, 1860), 27.

41.    *Twenty-Eighth Annual Report* (1881–82), 40.

42.    There has been very little analysis of the history of teaching. Notable exceptions include Cuban, *How Teachers Taught*; Cohen, "Practice and Policy: Notes on the History of Instruction"; and Kate Rousmaniere, *City Teachers: Teaching and Social Reform in Historical Perspective* (New York and London: Teachers College Press, 1997).

43.    Macleod, *The Age of the Child*, 79. See also Cuban, *How Teachers Taught*, 7.

44.    Cuban, *How Teachers Taught*, 35–36.

45.    Dr. Joseph M. Rice, *The Public-School System of the United States* (New York: The Century Company, 1893), 9.

46.    Ibid., 20.

47.    Cuban, *How Teachers Taught*, 38.

48.    B. Edward McClellan, *Moral Education in America: Schools and the Shaping of Character from Colonial Times to the Present* (New York: Teachers College Press, 1999), 16.

49.    James Davison Hunter, *The Death of Character: Moral Education in an Age Without Good or Evil* (New York: Basic Books, 2000), 51.

50.    Ibid., 48.

51.    See Reese, *Origins of the American High School*, 103–22.

52.    Ruth M. Elson, *Guardians of Tradition: American Schoolbooks of the Nineteenth Century* (Lincoln: University of Nebraska Press, 1964), 338.

53.    Henry Barnard, *School Architecture* 2nd ed. (New York: A. S. Barnes & Co., 1848; reprint, ed. Jean and Robert McClintock, New York: Teachers College Press, 1970), 55.

54.    Oliver P. Smith, *The Domestic Architect* (Buffalo: Derby & Co., 1852), iii.

55.    "No child can do his school work thoroughly and completely when packed in a room whose air is vitiated, corrupt, filled with germs of disease, where the light striking him full in the face, half blinds him and gives rise to headaches and other brain disturbance, where the heating is so imperfect that his head is hot and his feet are cold and where oftentimes the sound waves echo and re-echo through the room distracting his thoughts and preventing him from studying, and yet these very conditions exist in thousands and thousands of school rooms all over the country and they will continue to exist as long as school houses are put up according to the whim of the architect and the ignorance and weakness of the board." "A Good School House: Proper Legislation the Means of Getting Them," *American School Board Journal* 6 (April 1894): 2.

56.    The Boston School Committee appointed a committee on ventilation in 1846 to investigate conditions in the Boston schools. See Stanley K. Schultz, *The Culture Factory: Boston Public Schools, 1789–1860* (New York: Oxford University Press, 1973), 96–100.

57.    Troen, *The Public and the Schools*, 16.

58.    *Second Annual Report of the St. Louis Public Schools* (1855), quoted in "System of Public Instruction in St. Louis," *American Journal of Education* 1 (March 1856): 356.

59.    Barnard, *School Architecture*, 55.

60.    Ibid., 55–56.

61.    See Richard Emmons Thursfield, *Henry Barnard's American Journal of Education* (Baltimore: Johns Hopkins Press, 1949), 249.

62.    Reese, *Origins of the American High School*, 82.

63.    "New Central High School, Cleveland," *New England Journal of Education* 8 (September 26, 1878): 192.

64.    Ibid.

65.    A. H. T., "High Schools," *Massachusetts Teacher* 26 (June 1873): 197–98.

66.    "The Week," *New England Journal of Education* 8 (October 3, 1878): 212. The commentary was in response to a previous article on the Cleveland High School. "New Central High School, Cleveland," 192–193.

67.    *Thirty-First Annual Report of the Board of President and Directors of the St. Louis Public Schools* (1884–85) (St. Louis: St. Louis Public Schools, 1886): 108–109.

68.    "The Week," 212.


## The Transformation of the Schoolhouse

1.    John D. Philbrick, "Boston Latin and English High Schools," *American Journal of Education* 31 (July 1881): 401.

2.    I refer to the building in the singular because the two schools occupied separate but connected buildings that mirrored each other.

3.    John Dudley Philbrick (1818–1886) was born in New Hampshire, graduated from Dartmouth College and taught in Roxbury and Boston before becoming principal, or "Master," of Boston's Quincy School in 1847. He left Boston for the Connecticut State Normal School in 1852; the next year, he was appointed state superintendent of schools, a position he held for four years. Philbrick returned to Boston to serve as the city schools superintendent from 1857–74 and 1876–78. He wrote a number of textbooks and educational books, and became recognized nationwide as a leading school administrator. In 1878, Philbrick represented the United States Commissioner of Education at the Paris Exposition. "James Dudley Philbrick," *Biographical Dictionary of American Educators*, vol. 2, ed. John F. Ohles (Westport, CT and London: Greenwood Press, 1978), 1029–30.

4.    As William Cutler points out, however, the one-room schoolhouse remained ubiquitous in rural America even into the 1920s. William W. Cutler, III, "Cathedral of Culture: The Schoolhouse in American Educational Thought and Practice since 1820," *History of Education Quarterly* 29 (Spring 1989): 6.

5.    "The characteristics of the best school-houses in this country were well known to me, and I have some knowledge of school architecture abroad; but it was not until I visited the *Akademische Gymnasium*, in Vienna, at the time of the Universal Exposition of 1873, that I was able to picture in my mind the image of such a building as we wanted in Boston for these two schools. " Philbrick, "Boston Latin and English High Schools," 407.

6.    E. R. Robson, *School Architecture* (London: John Murray, 1874; reprint, New York: Humanities Press, 1972).

7.    I have found no other examples in pattern books or articles in the *American Journal of Education* and the *American Architect and Builder's News.*

8.    Philbrick, "Boston Latin and English High Schools," 425.

9.    These characteristics are: (1) The court plan; (2) The "perfection" of the individual classrooms; (3) The omission of clothes rooms connected to the classrooms; (4) The military drill hall; (5) The gymnasium; (6) The detached chemistry laboratory; (7) The character of the natural science rooms; (8) The libraries; (9) The many conference rooms for teachers and offices for headmasters and janitors; (10) Toilets on each floor; (11) The treatment of the assembly halls; (12) The spacious drawing rooms; (13) Fireproofing; (14) The iron staircases with rubber-padded steps; (15) The lighting, heating and ventilation; and (16) "The composition of the design. " Ibid., 425–429.

10.    Ibid., 410.

11.    Edmund M. Wheelwright, "The American Schoolhouse VII," *The Brickbuilder* 7 (May 1898): 94.

12.    Gilbert B. Morrison, *School Architecture and Hygiene* (Albany: J. B. Lyon Company, 1900), 30.

13.    The phrase is borrowed from William W. Cutler, III, "A Preliminary Look at the Schoolhouse: The Philadelphia Story, 1870–1920," *Urban Education* 8 (January 1974): 381–399.

14.    Quoted in Philbrick, "Boston Latin and English High School," 408.

15.    Robson, *School Architecture*, 45.

16.    Ibid.

17.    Michael Willrich, *City of Courts: Socializing Justice in Progressive Era Chicago* (New York: Cambridge University Press, 2003), xxxi.

18.    "While these buildings are not larger than will eventually—and even soon—be required for High School purposes, they will be at first larger than is necessary; so that they will in part serve the needs of pupils of the primary and grammar grades." *Twenty-Ninth Annual Report of the Board of Education of the City of Chicago* (1882–83) (Chicago: Jameson & Morse, Printers, 1884), 28.

19.    *Twenty-Seventh Annual Report of the Board of Education of the City of Chicago* (1880–81) (Chicago: Jameson & Morse, 1882), 116.

20.    "The Chicago School Board and its Architect," *Inland Architect and News Record* 20 (December 1892): 48.

21.    *Thirty-Third Annual Report of the Board of Education of the City of Chicago* (1886–87) (Chicago: Jameson & Morse, Co., 1888): 106; A. T. Andreas, *History of Chicago From the Earliest Period to the Present Time*, v. 3 (Chicago: A. T. Andreas, 1884), 144.

22.    "Chicago School Board Extravagance," *Chicago Tribune*, December 8, 1885.

23.    *Thirty-First Annual Report of the Board of Education of the City of Chicago* (1884–85) (Chicago: George K. Hazlitt & Co., 1885), 12–13.

24.    G. Stanley Hall, "The Health of School Children as Affected by School Buildings," *Journal of the Proceedings and Addresses of the National Educational Association* (1892) (New York: National Educational Association, 1893): 683.

25.    H. Endemann, "Chemical Examination of the Air of Various Public Buildings," in New York Board of Health, *Third Annual Report, 1872–1873* (New York: New York Board of Health, 1873); J. A. Larrabee, "The Schoolroom a Factor in the Production of Disease," *Journal of the American Medical Association* 11 (1888): 614; Albert P. Marble, *Sanitary Conditions for Schoolhouses*, U.S. Bureau of Education, Circular of Information, No. 3 (Washington, D. C. : U.S. Government Printing Office, 1891); John S. Billings, *Ventilation and Heating* (New York: The Engineering Record, 1893), 410. Carbonic acid is actually made when carbon dioxide is reacts with water

26.    "Ventilation in the Schools," *Chicago Tribune*, November 15, 1874.

27.    Charles P. Dwyer, *The Economy of Church, Parsonage and School Architecture, Adapted to Small Societies and Rural Districts* (Buffalo: Phinney & Co., Publishers, 1856), 57.

28.    James Johonnot, *School-Houses* (New York: J. W. Schermerhorn & Co., 1871), 27.

29.    See, for example, Edmund M. Wheelwright, "The American Schoolhouse VI," *The Brickbuilder* 7 (April 1898): 67–69 (250 cubic feet); Pennsylvania Statue on Schoolhouse Construction (1905), quoted in William George Bruce, *School Architecture: A Handy Manual for the Use of Architects and School Authorities.* (Milwaukee: Johnson Service Company, 1906), 17 (200 cubic feet); Indiana Statue on Schoolhouse Construction (pre-1912), quoted in L. N. Hines, "Response to William B. Ittner, 'School Architecture,'" *Journal of Proceedings and Address of the 50th Annual Meeting of the National Educational Association* (1912): 1223–24 (225 cubic feet). In Chicago the standard was 300 cubic feet.

30.    See, for example, Albert P. Marble, "Facts for Building Committees," *American School Board Journal* 4 (May 1892): 6 (20 ft./min.); "Poisoned Air in the Schools," *St. Louis Post-Dispatch* (October 25, 1896): 6 (33 ft./min.); R. C. Carpenter, "Heating and Ventilating of Schoolhouses," *The Brickbuilder* 9 (January 1900): 52–59 (33 ft./min.); Pennsylvania Statue on Schoolhouse Construction (30 ft./min.); Indiana Statue on Schoolhouse Construction (30 ft./min.); George E. Reed, "Heating and Ventilating," in John J. Donovan, et. al., *School Architecture: Principles and Practices* (New York: The Macmillan Company, 1921), 526 (25–30 ft./min.).

31.    J. D. Sutcliffe, "The Progress of American Schools in Regard to Health Laws," *American Architect* 88 (November 4, 1905): 148. The Smead System was heavily promoted in advertisements in the *American School Board Journal* late in the nineteenth century.

32.    For an excellent summary of early twentieth century heating and ventilation systems, see Wilbur T. Mills, *American School Building Standards* (Columbus: Franklin Educational Publishing Company, 1915), 125–151.

33.    Ethel M. Gardner, "The School Building In Its Reaction On The Teacher's Work," *Addresses and Proceedings of the Fifty-Ninth Annual Meeting of the National Education Association of the United States* 59 (1921): 404–406.

34.    School Survey Committee, *Survey of Public School System, City of New York* (New York: Board of Education of the City of New York, 1924), 347.

35.    Sutcliffe, "The Progress of American Schools in Regard to Health Laws," 148. Waters was first listed as the school board's chief engineer in the *Thirty-First Annual Report* (1884–85). His work in one of William Mundie's schools is described in "Typical Chicago School Heating and Ventilating Plant," *Western Architect* 4 (July 1905): 10–12.

36.    Warren Richard Briggs, *Modern American School Buildings* (New York: John Wiley & Sons, 1899), 119.

37.    Stuart H. Rowe, *The Lighting of School-Rooms* (New York: Longmans, Green, and Co., 1904), 8.

38.    N. R. Baker, "School Room Fenestration," *American School Board Journal* 40 (May 1910): 5; Fletcher B. Dresslar, *School Hygiene* (New York: Macmillan, 1913), 228.

39.    "Poor Eyesight in Chicago Schools," *Chicago Tribune*, November 3, 1900.

40.    Henry Barnard, *School Architecture*, 2nd ed. (New York: A. S. Barnes & Co., 1848; reprint, ed. Jean and Robert McClintock, New York: Teachers College Press, 1970), 56.

41.    Johonnot, *School-Houses*, 34.

42.    *Twenty-First Annual Report of the Board of Education of the City of Chicago* (1874–75) (Chicago: publisher unknown), 75–76. See also Superintendent Louis Soldan's comments on classrooms and lighting in the *Forty-Second Annual Report of the Board of President and Directors of the St. Louis Public Schools* (1895–96) (St Louis: Nixon-Jones Printing Co., 1897): 25–26.

43.    *Twenty-Ninth Annual Report* (1882–83), 16. Bridge wrote that using at least five windows in each classroom increases lighting surface from 10.5 percent to thirteen. Thirteen percent of the floor space, which increases light 25 percent; but this was not ideal, since a twenty-eight by thirty-four foot room for sixty pupils needs not less than 16 percent lighting surface.

44.    Dresslar, *School Hygiene*, 221.

45.    See, e. g., Albert P. Marble, "How to Light School Buildings," *American School Board Journal* 4 (July 1892): 3. Although accepted by most architects, the unilateral source rule was not without challenges. For example, in 1904, Stuart H. Rowe advocated lighting from two sides of the classroom (while also agreeing that unilateral lighting was generally the most practical). Rowe, *The Lighting of School-Rooms*, 34–38. Reviewing photographs and floor plans of schools from the early twentieth century also shows that most buildings contained corner rooms that received light from two directions.

46.    Severance Burrage and Henry Turner Bailey, *School Sanitation and Decoration* (Boston, New York, Chicago: DC Heath and Company, 1899), 54.

47.    Edmund M. Wheelwright, "The American Schoolhouse II," *The Brickbuilder* 6 (December 1897): 267; Burrage and Bailey, *School Sanitation and Decoration*, 83–93; Rowe, *The Lighting of School-Rooms*, 49–51; Bruce, *School Architecture*, 25; Walter J. Kenyon, "The Interior Decoration of Schools," *School Review* 14 (November 1906): 625–634.

48.    "The Eyes of School Children," *Chicago Tribune*, September 28, 1907.

49.    Kenyon, "The Interior Decoration of Schools," 625–626.

50.    See e. g., F. Laurent Godinez, "School Room Lighting," *Architecture and Building* 47 (October and November, 1916): 365–367; 400–402; Romaine W. Myers, "Electrical Installation and Illumination," in Donovan, et. al., *School Architecture*, 557–568; George D. Strayer and Nicholas L. Engelhardt, *Standards for High School Buildings* (New York: Teachers College, Columbia University, 1924), 27.

51.    Rowe, *The Lighting of Schoolrooms*, vii, 68. The educational discourse about proper lighting and ventilation that helped shape the West Division II and North-West Division High Schools related to another influence on turn-of-the-century schoolhouse design. Proper lighting was considered necessary not only for safeguarding students' eyesight, but also for maintaining their general health. For example, in the early twentieth century, "hygiene experts" promoted sunlight's health-giving aspects to educators and architects. One of the best-known hygiene experts was Fletcher B. Dresslar, a professor at Peabody College in Memphis, who stated a prevailing view in 1913. "Direct sunlight is the most economical and practical of all germicides," Dresslar wrote. "Schoolrooms that are kept thoroughly clean and receive a thorough sunning each day are not likely to need much further attention in the matter of disinfection. Cleanliness and sunshine are worth more than any artificial germicides that can be applied to schoolrooms." Dresslar, *School Hygiene*, 359.

52.    Mary J. Herrick, *The Chicago Schools: A Social and Political History* (Beverly Hills and London: Sage Publications, Inc., 1971), 406.

53.    Ibid., 403.

54.    The organizational structure and power relations governing Chicago education were firmly established by this time. Not surprisingly, politics ruled the educational world. The Chicago Board of Education was responsible for day-to-day operations, such as teacher employment, textbook selection, and salary schedules. The superintendent and his staff, appointed by the board, administered much of this work. On the other hand, the city council controlled the public school system's finances. And the mayor selected the board members (with the council's approval). Since, as Dick Simpson explained, "In this era, Chicago had a strong-council weak-mayor form of government," with the mayor subject to the City Council's power, it was the council that ostensibly controlled Chicago education. Dick Simpson, *Rogues, Rebels, and Rubber Stamps: The Politics of the Chicago City Council from 1863 to the Present* (Boulder, CO: Westview Press, 2001), 47. For an overview of the city's educational history and the interactions between the board and the council, see Herrick, *The Chicago Schools*.

55.    In 1895, for example, the school system reported $558,010 in income and $6,334,328 in expenditures. Herrick, *The Chicago Schools*, 75.

56.    Julia Wrigley, *Class Politics and Public Schools: Chicago 1900–1950* (New Brunswick, NJ: Rutgers University Press, 1982), 55.

57.    Ibid.

58.    Ibid. The fads and frills controversy was resolved by dropping drawing, singing, and clay modeling courses from many of the lower grades and having classroom teachers rather than specialists teach physical education.

59.    Herrick, *The Chicago Schools*, 403.

60.    *Fortieth Annual Report of the Board of Education of the City of Chicago* (1892–93) (Chicago: The J. M. W. Jones Stationary and Printing Co., 1894), 123.


## Educational and Societal Reforms


1.    Karin Calvert, "Children in the House, 1890–1930," in Jessica H. Foy and Thomas J. Schlereth, *American Home Life, 1880–1930: A Social History of Spaces and Services* (Knoxville, TN: University of Tennessee Press, 1992), 76.

2.    On the idea of the sheltered childhood, see David I. Macleod, *The Age of the Child: Children in America, 1890–1920*, Twayne's History of American Childhood Series, eds. Joseph M. Hawes and N. Ray Hiner (New York: Twayne Publishers, 1998). Further evidence of a new perspective on the differences between children and adults may be seen in the proliferation of children's hospitals. See David Charles Sloane, "'Not Designed Merely to Heal': Progressive Reformers and Children's Hospitals," *Journal of the Gilded Age and Progressive Era* 4 (October 2005): 331–54.

3.    Ibid., 110, although Macleod also discusses possible problems with these figures.

4.    Mary J. Herrick, *The Chicago Schools: A Social and Political History* (Beverly Hills and London: Sage Publications, Inc., 1971), 62.

5.    Andrew Feffer, *The Chicago Pragmatists and American Progressivism* (Ithaca, NY: Cornell University Press, 1993), 136.

6.    *Eleventh Annual Report of the Board of Education of the City of Chicago* (1864–65), quoted in Herrick, *The Chicago Schools*, 52.

7.    For more on child labor regulation and compulsory education, see David B. Tyack, Thomas James and Aaron Benavot, *Law and the Shaping of Public Education, 1785–1954* (Madison, WI: University of Wisconsin Press, 1987).

8.    *Fifty-First Annual Report of the Board of Education of the City of Chicago* (1904–05) (Chicago: Board of Education, 1906), 176.

9.    Edgar T. Davies, "The Enforcement of Child Labor Legislation in Illinois," in *Child Labor and the Republic* (New York: National Child Labor Committee, 1907), 97.

10.    Tyack, et. al., *Law and the Shaping of Public Education*, 59.

11.    Quoted in Herrick, *The Chicago Schools*, 63.

12.    Edith Abbott and Sophonisba P. Breckenridge, *Truancy and Non-Attendance in the Chicago Schools* (Chicago: University of Chicago Press, 1917), 55.

13.    *Proceedings of the Board of Education of the City of Chicago* (1888–89) (Chicago: Board of Education of the City of Chicago, n. d. ), 75.

14.    See Robert L. McCaul and Peter P. DeBoer, *Annotated List of Chicago Tribune Editorials on Elementary and Secondary Education in the U.S., 1852–1971* (Lewiston, NY: The Edwin Mellen Press, 1992).

15.    E. Benjamin Andrews, "The Public School System of Chicago," *Education* 20 (December 1899): 266.

16.    David B. Tyack, *The One Best System: A History of American Urban Education* (Cambridge and London: Harvard University Press, 1974), 183; Thomas J. Schlereth, *Victorian America: Transformations in Everyday Life, 1876–1915* (New York: Harper-Perennial, 1991), 247.

17.    David L. Angus and Jeffrey E. Mirel, *The Failed Promise of the American High School, 1890–1995* (New York: Teachers College Press, 1999), 203. By 1930, the number was 50. 7 percent; in 1940 it reached 72. 6 percent.

18.    Schlereth, *Victorian America*, 247.

19.    Michael Willrich, *City of Courts: Socializing Justice in Progressive Era Chicago* (New York: Cambridge University Press, 2003), xxxi.

20.    Tyack, *The One Best System*, 230.

21.    Ibid., 2.

22.    There were 30,150 blacks in Chicago in 1900 and 109,540 in 1920. Philip T. K. Daniel, "A History of Discrimination Against Black Students in Chicago Secondary Schools," *History of Education Quarterly* 20 (Summer 1980): 151.

23.    Macleod, *The Age of the Child*, 149.

24.    The phrase comes from Joseph F. Kett, *Rites of Passage: Adolescence in America, 1790 to the Present* (New York: Basic Books, Inc., 1977).

25.    Ibid., 215–16. Kett argues for the permanent effect of these changes: "[T]he institutions created in the early twentieth century survived to become an enduring

form of custody for youth long after the ideas and impulses which created them were laid to rest." Ibid., 217.

26.    G. Stanley Hall, *Adolescence: Its Psychology and Its Relations to Physiology, Anthropology, Sociology, Sex, Crime, Religion and Education*, 2 vols. (New York: D. Appleton, 1905). The child study movement was the first scientific attempt to understand child development in terms of the relative effects of environment and instinct and to use education to nurture children's development. The research was characterized by large compilations of data, usually questionnaires of teachers and parents. Hall's Clark University in Boston was the center of the child study movement. See Herbert M. Kliebard, *The Struggle for the American Curriculum, 1893–1958*. 2nd ed. (New York, London: Routledge, 1995).

27.    G. Stanley Hall, *Youth: Its Education, Regimen, and Hygiene* (New York: D. Appleton, 1907), 135.

28.    Paul Boyer, *Urban Masses and Moral Order in America, 1820–1920* (Cambridge, MA and London: Harvard University Press, 1979), 245–46.

29.    See Dominick J. Cavallo, *Muscles and Morals: Organized Playgrounds and Urban Reform, 1880–1920* (Philadelphia: University of Pennsylvania Press, 1981).

30.    Boyer, *Urban Masses and Moral* Order, 243.

31.    William J. Reese, *Power and the Promise of School Reform: Grass Roots Movements During the Progressive Era* (New York: Teachers College Press, 2002), 151.

32.    Macleod, *The Age of the Child*, 4; Cavallo, *Muscles and Morals*, 54.

33.    Andrews, "The Public School System in Chicago," 269.

34.    Thomas W. Gutowski, "The High School as an Adolescent-Raising Institution: An Inner History of Chicago Public Secondary Education, 1856–1940," Ph. D. diss., University of Chicago (1978): 1.

35.    Edward A. Krug, *The Shaping of the American High School* (New York: Harper & Row, 1964), 170–171.

36.    Herbert M. Kliebard, *Schooled to Work: Vocationalism and the American Curriculum, 1876–1946* (New York and London: Teachers College, Columbia University, 1999), 27.

37.    *Twenty-Ninth Annual Report of the Board of Education of the City of Chicago* (1882–83) (Chicago: Jameson & Morse, Printers, 1884), 61. The phrase "culture factories" is borrowed from Stanley K. Schultz, *The Culture Factory: Boston Public Schools, 1789–1860* (New York: Oxford University Press, 1973). For an account of how, in the nineteenth century, the middle class used seconday education as part of a larger strategy for conserving social status see Mary P. Ryan, *Cradle of the Middle Class: The*

*Family in Oneida County, New York, 1790–1865* (reprint edition, New York and London: Cambridge University Press, 2004). Educators were also paying more attention to the high school. A review of the *Poole's Index of Periodical Literature* for this key time period uncovered a significant rise in the numbers of published articles on high school topics: two before 1882; six between 1882–87; thirteen between1887–92; twenty-six between 1892–96; thirty-six between 1897–1902; and fifty-five between 1902–07.

38.    John Dewey, "My Pedagogic Creed" (1897), *Dewey on Education: Selections*, Introduction and Notes by Martin S. Dworkin, Teachers College Classics in Education No. 3 (New York: Teachers College Press, 1959), 30.

39.    Herbert Croly, *The Promise of American Life* (1909), ed. Arthur M. Schlesinger, Jr. (Cambridge, MA: The Belknap Press of Harvard University Press, 1965).

40.    Arthur T. Hadley, "The Meaning and Purpose of Secondary Education," *The School Review* 10 (December 1902): 732. For a discussion of the confusion surrounding the high school's proper place, see Theodore Sizer, *Secondary Schools at the Turn of the Century* (New Haven and London: Yale University Press, 1964).

41.    Josiah L. Pickard, "The High School: Its Necessity and Right to Exist as Part of the True System of Public Education," *Education* 3 (November 1882): 158–163; John Hancock, "The High School: Its Relation to the Lower Grades of Public Schools," *Education* 3 (November 1882): 164–165.

42.    George Stuart, "The Raison d'Être of the Public High School," *Education* 8 (January 1888): 291.

43.    Charles F. Thwing, "The Obligations and Limitations of the High School, *The School Review* 9 (June 1901): 334, 337, 339, 340.

44.    Hancock, "The High School," 164.

45.    "Costly High Schools," *American School Board Journal* 12 (April 1896): 10.

46.    Edmund M. Wheelwright, "The American Schoolhouse VI," *The Brickbuilder* 7 (April 1898): 76.

47.    See, e. g., A. C. Clas, "Modern School House Architecture," *American School Board Journal* 26 (June 1903): 25; Ira Remson, "School Houses and Beauty," *Architect's and Builder's Journal* 5 (September 1903): 20; F. Treudley, "Public School Structures as Related to Educators," *American School Board Journal* 30 (May 1905): 7.

48.    William George Bruce, *School Architecture: A Handy Manual for the Use of Architects and School Authorities* (Milwaukee: Johnson Service Company, 1906), 4. For later examples of this type of plea, see, e. g., "Our School Architecture," *Architecture* 42 (November 1920): 325; Alfred Busselle, "Domestic Quality in School Design," *Architecture* 43 (April 1921): 121.

49.    "Costly High Schools," 10.

50.    John J. Donovan, "Architecture, Planning and Construction," in John J. Donovan, et. al., *School Architecture: Principles and Practices* (New York: The Macmillan Company, 1921), 18.

51.    C. Howard Walker, "Suggestions on the Architecture of Schoolhouses," *Atlantic Monthly* 74 (December 1894): 826.

52.    Horace E. Scudder, "The Schoolhouse as Centre," *Atlantic Monthly* 77 (January 1896): 103.

53.    A. D. F. Hamlin, "Consideration in Schoolhouse Design," in *Modern School Houses* (New York: The Swetland Publishing Co., 1910), 4; Gilbert B. Morrison, *School Architecture and Hygiene*, Monographs on Education in the United States, No. 9, ed. Nicholas M. Butler (Albany: J. B. Lyon Company, 1900), 3. See also C. H. B. Schaefer, "Styles in School Architecture," *American School Board Journal* 45 (September 1912): 20–21, 54–55; Beverly S. King, "School Architecture as an Influence," *American School Board Journal* 46 (January 1913): 17–19;

54.    Schaefer, "Styles in School Architecture," 20.

55.    Charles Zueblin, *American Municipal Progress: Chapters in Municipal Sociology* (New York: Macmillan, 1902), 240.

56.    Frank Irving Cooper, "Standards of Schoolhouse Planning," in Donovan, et. al., *School Architecture*, 573.

57.    Another factor that may have influenced the high school building's enhanced architectural image, especially in Chicago, was the challenge faced by the public schools from parochial education. From the mid-nineteenth century through today, Chicagoans have supported the largest Catholic school system in the nation. The city's growing Irish and Eastern European populations were particularly partial to parochial education, and with many new immigrants having no educational background (and thus no experience with a state-supported educational system), the church may have seemed a logical and safe source for teaching children. The elaborate architecture of the public high schools after the fin-de-siecle, then, might well have been aimed in part at the working class immigrant ranks, to present an image of tradition, stability, and dignity and therefore to help persuade the masses of the public school system's worth.

58.    Gutowski, "The High School as an Adolescent-Raising Institution," 76.

59.    Ibid., 1.

60.    Albion W. Small, "Demands of Sociology Upon Pedagogy," (1896), quoted in Krug, *The Shaping of the American High School*, 251.

61.    As William J. Reese points out, the traditional story of top-down Progressive Era reform, which celebrates the imposition of controls by the an elite group of wealthy businessmen and their wives, is inaccurate; he persuasively demonstrates that reform during this time was a struggle between "elitism and democracy," where "grass roots" organizations were also responsible for a good deal of "bottom-up" changes in American cities. See *Power and the Promise of School Reform*. See also Peter G. Filene, "An Obituary for 'The Progressive Movement,'" *American Quarterly* 22 (Spring 1970): 20–34; and Robin F. Bachin, *Building the South Side: Urban Space and Civic Culture in Chicago: 1890–1919* (Chicago and London: University of Chicago Press, 2004).

62.    Douglas Sutherland, *Fifty Years on the Civic Front 1893–1943* (Chicago: Civic Federation, 1943), 4.

63.    *City Club of Chicago Yearbook* (1904), quoted in Gary A Cook, *George Herbert Mead: The Making of a Social Pragmatist* (Urbana, IL and Chicago: University of Illinois Press, 1983), 105.

64.    William H. Wilson, *The City Beautiful Movement* (Baltimore and London: Johns Hopkins Press, 1989), 1.

65.    The Chicago Plan was never fully carried out, except for certain portions of lakefront parkland and the street system. See Thomas S. Hines, *Burnham of Chicago: Architect and Planner* (Chicago and London: University of Chicago Press, 1974); Carl Smith, *The Plan of Chicago: Daniel Burnham and the Remaking of the American City* (Chicago: University of Chicago Press, 2006).

66.    For more on the City Beautiful and Chicago parks, see Wilson, *The City Beautiful*; *Prairie in the City: Naturalism in Chicago's Parks, 1870–1940* (Chicago: Chicago Historical Society, 1991), and Daniel Bluestone, *Constructing Chicago* (New Haven and London: Yale University Press, 1991).

67.    Barry M. Franklin, *Building the American Community: The School Curriculum and the Search for Social Control* (London and Philadelphia: The Falmer Press, 1986), 10.

68.    Edward Alsworth Ross, *Social Control: A Survey of the Foundations of Order* (New York: Macmillan, 1901). Similar books by Ross' contemporaries included Charles H. Cooley, *Human Nature and the Social Order* (New York: Scribner's, 1902) and Simon N. Patten, *The New Basis of Civilization* (New York: Macmillan, 1907). For an analysis, see Franklin, *Building the American Community*.

69.    See Boyer, *Urban Masses and Moral Order*, 226.

70.    Franklin, *Building the American Community*, 16.

71.    Ross, *Social Control*, 176, 164.

72.    Ross, *Social Control*, quoted in Krug, *The Shaping of the American High School*, 252.

73.    Cited in Tyack, *The One Best System*, 232.

74.    For an extreme explication of this theory, see Michael B. Katz, *Class, Bureaucracy and Schools* (New York: Praeger Publishers, 1975), xv-xvi.

75.    Dell Upton, "Lancasterian Schools, Republican Citizenship, and the Spatial Imagination in Early Nineteenth-Century America," *Journal of the Society of Architectural Historians* 55 (September 1996): 238–253.

76.    James Johonnot, *Country School-houses: Elevations, Plans, and Specifications* (New York: Ivison and Phinney, 1859), 119.

77.    William Torrey Harris, quoted in Tyack, *The One Best System*, 43. Charles Northend made a similar statement almost twenty years earlier: "If there is any place on the surface of the earth where order is the first, and last, and highest law, that place is the schoolroom." Charles Northend, *The Teacher and the Parent* (1853), quoted in Carl F. Kaestle, *Pillars of the Republic: Common Schools and American Society, 1780–1860* (New York: Hill & Wang, 1983), 96.

78.    Reese, *Power and the Promise of School Reform*, 12.

79.    Dr. Joseph M. Rice, *The Public-School System of the United States* (New York: The Century Company, 1893), 98.

80.    "The Planning of School Buildings," *The American Architect and Building News* 27 (February 8, 1890): 81–82.

81.    Ibid., 81.

82.    Ibid., 81–82.

83.    Randolph S. Bourne, *The Gary Schools* (Boston, New York, Chicago: Houghton Mifflin Company, 1916), 23–24.

84.    Larry Cuban, *How Teachers Taught: Constancy and Change in American Classrooms 1890–1990* (New York and London: Teachers College Press, 1993), 17.

85.    "Progress in School Architecture," *American School Board Journal* 44 (April 1912): 32.

86.    Gutowski, "The High School as an Adolescent-Raising Institution," 142–48; Gutowski, "Student Initiative and the Origins of the High School Extracurriculum: Chicago, 1880–1915," *History of Education Quarterly* 28 (Spring 1988): 54.

87.    See Gutowski, "Student Initiative, 54–55.

88.    Gutowski, "The High School as an Adolescent-Raising Institution," 140, 142.

89.    The phrase comes from Tyack, *The One Best System*, 6.

90.    William Reese analyzed the composition of ward-based boards of education in three mid-sized nineteenth century cities between 1870 and 1890 and found board membership from business or professions to be between 71 percent and 88 percent in Rochester, New York, not less than 87 percent in Toledo, Ohio, and between 71 percent and 75 percent in Milwaukee, Wisconsin. Reese, *Power and the Promise of School Reform*, 83.

91.    These beliefs were not unique to education: as Tyack points out, the turn-of-the-century was "an age of consolidation." As an example, Tyack relates the fact that corporate capitalizations valued at $ one million or more rose from $170 million in 1897 to $5 billion in 1900 to over $20 billion in 1904. Tyack, *The One Best System*, 141. See also Robert H. Wiebe, *The Search for Order 1877–1920* (New York: Hill and Wang, 1967).

92.    See, for example, Tyack, *The One Best System*; Raymond E. Callahan, *Education and the Cult of Efficiency* (Chicago: University of Chicago Press, 1962); Katz, Class, *Bureaucracy and Schools*; Joel H. Spring, *Education and the Rise of the Corporate State* (Cuernavaca, Mexico: Center for Intercultural Documentation, 1971); David Nasaw, *Schooled to Order: A Social History of Public Schooling in the United States* (New York: Oxford University Press, 1979).

93.    Quoted in Tyack, *The One Best System*, 39.

94.    A description of this attack on the ward system can be found in Nasaw, *Schooled to Order*, 106–113.

95.    Tyack, *The One Best System*, 127.

96.    Reese, *Power and the Promise of School Reform*, 99.

97.    Educational Commission of the City of Chicago, *Report of the Educational Commission of the City of Chicago Appointed by the Mayor, Hon. Carter H. Harrison, William R. Harper, Chairman* (Chicago: R. R. Donnelly, 1899), vii-viii.

98.    Writing of the university's interest in the high schools in an 1895 letter, Harper claimed: "We have just succeeded in carrying through a plan which gives us close control of the High Schools of the City of Chicago." William Rainey Harper to Frederick T. Gates, June 24, 1895, cited in Bachin, *Building the South Side*, 70.

99.    Ibid., xiii.

100. Julia Wrigley, *Class Politics and Public Schools: Chicago 1900–1950* (New Brunswick, NJ: Rutgers University Press, 1982), 92–94; David John Hogan, *Class and Reform: School and Society in Chicago, 1880–1930* (Philadelphia: University of Pennsylvania Press, 1985), 194–214.

101.   Steven J. Diner, *A City and its Universities: Public Policy in Chicago, 1892–1919* (Chapel Hill, NC: University of North Carolina Press, 1980), 83–84.

102.   Wrigley, *Class Politics and Public Schools*, 137–141; Hogan, *Class and Reform*, 210–211. Despite the promise of a more efficient system, centralization and bureaucratization were not a panacea for the Chicago Public Schools. See Dorothy Shipps, *School Reform, Corporate Style* (Lawrence KS: University Press of Kansas, 2006).

103.   Krug, *The Shaping of the American High School*, 46.

104.   *Report of the Committee of Ten on Secondary Schools* (1893), in ibid., 64.

105.   National Education Association, *Report of the Committee of Ten on Secondary Schools* (Washington, DC: U.S. Government Printing Office, 1893), in George W. Willis, William H. Schubert, Robert V. Bullough, Jr., Craig Kridel, and John T. Holton, eds., *The American Curriculum: A Documentary History* (Westport, CT: Greenwood Press, 1993), 92.

106.   *Thirty-Seventh Annual Report of the Board of Education* (1890–91) (Chicago: Public Schools of the City of Chicago, 1892): 39.

107.   *Proceedings of the Board of Education of the City of Chicago* (1910–11), 448–449.

108.   The four-year courses were: General, Science, Normal preparatory, Commercial, Office preparatory, Technical, General trades, Household arts, Arts, Architectural, and Pharmacy. The two-year courses were: Accounting, Shorthand, Mechanical drawing, Designing, Carpentry, Pattern making, Machine shop, Electricity, Household arts, Printing, and Horticulture. John T. McManis, *Ella Flagg Young and a Half-Century of the Chicago Public Schools* (Chicago: A. C. McClurg, 1916), 232.

109.   George Van Dyke, "Trends in the Development of the High School Offering," *School Review* 39 (November 1931): 657–664 and (December 1931): 737–747.

110.   Department of the Interior, Bureau of Education, *Cardinal Principles of Secondary Education: A Report of the Commission on the Reorganization of Secondary Education*, Appointed by the National Education Association (Bulletin, 1918, No. 35) (Washington, DC: U.S. Government Printing Office, 1918). On social efficiency, see Franklin, *Building the American Community*; Ross, *Social Control*. For a critique of the role of social efficiency in the development of the comprehensive high school, see William G. Wraga, *Democracy's High School: The Comprehensive High School and Educational Reform in the United States* (Lanham, New York, London: University Press of America, 1994).

111.   Quoted in Willis, et. al., eds., *The American Curriculum: A Documentary History*, 158.

112.  Ellwood P. Cubberley, *Changing Conceptions in Education* (Boston: Houghton Mifflin, 1909), 56.

113.  Kliebard, *Schooled to Work*, 43

114.  Herbert M. Kliebard, *Changing Course: American Curriculum Reform in the 20th Century* (New York and London: Teachers College Press, 2002), 33.

115.  Margaret Haley, "Why Teachers Should Organize" (1904), in Nancy Hoffman, ed., *Woman's "True" Profession: Voices From the History of Teaching*, 2nd ed. (Cambridge, MA: Harvard Education Publishing Group, 2003).

116.  Kliebard, *Schooled to Work*, 8.

117.  Edmund M. Wheelwright, "The American Schoolhouse IX," *The Brickbuilder* 7 (July 1898): 135–138; Wheelwright, "The American Schoolhouse X," *The Brickbuilder* 7 (August 1898): 155–156.

118.  Wheelwright, "The American Schoolhouse IX," 135.

119.  See Walter A. Tenney, "The Industrial Arts Department," in Donovan, et. al., *School Architecture*.

120.  Kliebard, *The Struggle for the American Curriculum*, 87.

121.  For more on the Douglas Commission, see Kliebard, *Schooled to Work*, Chapter 2; Krug, *The Shaping of the American High School*, 217–23.

122.  Hogan, *Class and Reform*, 152–155. A 1912 survey of 300 Chicago employers, for example, found that 86 percent of them were not satisfied with potential job applicants' abilities. Ibid., 163.

123.  *Fortieth Annual Report of the Board of Education* (1893–94) (Chicago: The J. M. W. Jones Stationary and Printing Co., 1894): 43. For a detailed investigation of the relationship between Chicago's business community and the school board, see Shipps, *School Reform, Corporate Style*.

124.  An excellent study of the nuances of girls' vocational education during this period is Jane Bernard Powers, *The "Girl Question" in Education: Vocational Education for Young Women in the Progressive Era* (London and Washington, DC: The Falmer Press, 1992). See also Karen Graves, *Girls' Schooling During the Progressive Era: From Female Scholar to Domesticated Citizen* (New York and London: Garland Publishing, Inc., 1998).

125.  Krug, *The Shaping of the American High School*, 11, 171; Graves, *Girls' Schooling During the Progressive Era*, 170.

126.  *Fifty-Fourth Annual Report of the Board of Education* (1898–99) (Chicago: Public Schools of the City of Chicago, 1900), 203.

127.  Graves, *Girls' Schooling During the Progressive Era*, 170.

128.  Quoted in ibid., 262.

129.  The number of women employed in manufacturing, mechanical and clerical jobs between 1890 and 1910 increased by almost 200 percent. Powers, *The "Girl Question" in Education*, 10.

130.  Ibid., 128.

## Chicago's Progressive Era High Schools

1.    Leonard V. Koos, "Space-Provisions in the Floor-Plans of Modern High-School Buildings," *School Review* 27 (October 1919): 573–99.

2.    Ibid., 593–94.

3.    Henry F. Withey and Elsie Rathburn Withey, *Biographical Dictionary of American Architects (Deceased)* (Los Angeles: Hennessey & Ingalls, Inc., 1970), 434.

4.    "Chicago School Architecture," *American School Board Journal* 28 (February 1904): 8.

5.    First and second floor plans for Mundie's Waller, published in *The Inland Architect and News Record* 37 (June 1901): plates following page 40 are identical to those published for Patton's North Division (*American School Board Journal* 17 (July 1898): 12) except for the entry.

6.    *The Inland Architect and News Record* 37 (June 1901): plates following page 40.

7.    *Forty-Fifth Annual Report of the Board of Education of the City of Chicago* (1898–99) (Chicago: Public Schools of the City of Chicago, 1900), 115, 116.

8.    There is an extensive literature on the World's Columbian Exposition. See e. g., Norman Bolotin and Christine Laing, *The World's Columbian Exposition: The Chicago World's Fair of 1893* (Urbana, IL: University of Illinois Press, 2002); Stanley Appelbaum, *The Chicago World's Fair of 1893: A Photographic Record* (New York: Dover Publications, Inc., 1980).

9.    On Ecole des Beaux-Arts architecture, see Donald Drew Egbert, *The Beaux-Arts Tradition in French Architecture* (Princeton, NJ: Princeton University Press, 1980); Arthur Drexler, ed., *The Architecture of the Ecole des Beaux-Arts* (Cambridge, MA: The MIT Press, 1977).

10.   "Don't Like the Plan," *Chicago Tribune*, September 16, 1894.

11.   Abigail A. Van Slyck, *Free to All: Carnegie Libraries & American Culture 1890–1920* (Chicago and London: University of Chicago Press, 1995), 148. On societal change in the Progressive Era, see Robert H Wiebe, *The Search for Order 1877–1920*

(New York: Hill and Wang, 1967). Interestingly, the Columbian Exposition's grand classical architecture had appeared just as a group of Chicago architects were beginning to take urban commercial architecture in an unprecedented new direction. Major commercial firms like Jenney and Mundie, Daniel Burnham and John Wellborn Root, Dankmar Adler and Louis Sullivan, and William Holabird and Martin Roche began utilizing such technological advances as steel-frame construction and hydraulic elevators to make taller and more efficient office buildings in Chicago in the 1880s. Their work, later generalized as "the Chicago School," would be lauded by mid-twentieth century modernists as a formative influence on the development of a highly functionalist modern architecture. Their buildings' reduced historical ornamentation and the emphasis on creating a form to match the building's structural system was taken—erroneously—as a rejection of the burgeoning academic eclecticism represented by the Columbian Exposition. The modernists anointed Louis Henry Sullivan the hero of the Chicago School, and two of his most famous quotes were thought to sum up the architectural state of the nation. The first—"form ever follows function"—summarized the Chicago School approach to design. The second, his bitter tirade that "The [architectural] damage wrought by the World's Fair will last for half a century from its date, if not longer"—written thirty years after the Fair—was used to both solidify his status as a valiant pre-modernist and to describe the perceived denigration of architecture that occurred in the early century at the hands of the eclectics. But William Mundie's work challenges the Chicago School stereotype. His educational architecture demonstrates how a salient member of the so-called Chicago School was *not* an anti-historicist who sought a brave new architecture for the future. Rather, Mundie's schools showed how the new was simply incorporated into the old; steel framing, for example, became commonplace in city school buildings even when covered by a thick wall of brick and classical decoration. See Louis H. Sullivan, "The Tall Office Building Artistically Considered," in *Kindergarten Chats and Other Writings* (New York: Dover Publications, Inc., 1979), and *The Autobiography of an Idea* (New York: Dover Publications, Inc., 1956). On the heroic pre-modernist view of the Chicago School, see Sigfried Giedion, *Space, Time and Architecture: The Growth of a New Tradition*, 5th ed. (Cambridge: Harvard University Press, 1967); for a revisionist view, see Daniel Bluestone, *Constructing Chicago* (New Haven: Yale University Press, 1991).

12.    Alice Sinkovitch, ed., *AIA Guide to Chicago* (New York: Harcourt Brace, 1993), 381.

13.    Koos, "Space-Provisions in the Floor-Plans of Modern High-School Buildings," 580.

14.  John Wesley Bell, *The Development of the Public High School in Chicago* (Chicago: University of Chicago Libraries, 1939), 187–88.

15.  *Forty-Seventh Annual Report of the Board of Education of the City of Chicago* (1900–01) (Chicago: Public Schools of the City of Chicago, 1902), 64.

16.  Phillip T. K. Daniel, "A History of Discrimination Against Black Students In Chicago Secondary Schools," *History of Education Quarterly* 20 (Summer 1980): 151.

17.  Judy Jolley Mohraz, *The Separate Problem: Case Studies of Black Education in the North, 1900–1930*, Contributions in Afro-American and African Studies, No. 42 (Westport, CT: Greenwood Press, 1979), 103; The Chicago Commission on Race Relations, *The Negro in Chicago: A Study of Race Relations and a Race Riot* (Chicago: The University of Chicago Press, 1922), 245.

18.  "Gets New Hungry List," *Chicago Record-Herald*, October 14, 1908.

19.  Allan H. Spear, *Black Chicago: The Making of a Negro Ghetto, 1890–1920* (Chicago and London: University of Chicago Press, 1967), 44.

20.  On the riots, see Chicago Commission on Race Relations, *The Negro in Chicago*.

21.  U.S. Census figures quoted in Mohraz, *The Separate Problem*, 18; Arnold P. Hirsch, *Making the Second Ghetto: Race and Housing in Chicago 1940–1960*, 2nd ed. (Chicago and London: University of Chicago Press, 1998), 3.

22.  "High School Architecture," *American School Board Journal* 34 (July 1907): 8.

23.  "A Retrospect," *American School Board Journal* 42 (April 1911): 12.

24.  "Our School Architecture," *Architecture* 42 (November 1920): 325; William B. Ittner, "The School Plant in Present-Day Education," *Architectural Forum* 37 (August 1922): 45.

25.  "High School Architecture," 8.

26.  Edmund M. Wheelwright, "The American Schoolhouse VI," *The Brickbuilder* 7 (April 1898): 77.

27.  Ibid., 76.

28.  The Boston Schoolhouse Commissioners first *Annual Report* stated that "the new schoolhouses about to be erected should be plain, substantial structures, built in the most substantial manner, devoid of unnecessary or extravagant ornamentation, but attractive and tasteful from an architectural standpoint, the exterior walls to be in general of plain brick with a reasonable amount of trimmings. . . ." Cited in Walter H. Kilham, "The Work of the Boston Schoolhouse Commission, 1901–1905, I," *The Brickbuilder* 14 (October 1905): 222. For examples of the work that was subsequently built according to these guidelines, see the continuation of the series in *The Brick-*

*builder*, 14 (November 1905): 248–254; 14 (December 1905): 270–275; 15 (January 1906): 8–12; 15 (February 1906): 30–36.

29.    Quoted in "St. Louis School Architecture," *American School Board Journal* 28 (April 1904): 8. Eight years later, Ittner elaborated on his design process in a speech at the NEA convention without commenting on specific styles: "As the design of a building should be the natural outgrowth and should express truthfully the function of the plan, we will now give it attention. We find that the projection and added height of the library furnish a natural motif for a dignified treatment of the main entrance; the fenestration of the large study-room units enables us to give them proper expression on the main facade; the side entrances and smaller class units furnish the natural spacing for a less ambitious treatment of the wing facades; and the high openings in the gymnasium enable us to give its location outward evidence. Thus, without any straining for effect or warping of its parts, we find our building capable of harmonious expression in every way consistent with its uses." William B. Ittner, "School Architecture," *Journal of Proceedings and Address of the 50th Annual Meeting of the National Educational Association* (1912): 1219.

30.    "St. Louis School Architecture," 8.

31.    Ernest Sibley, "Why I Prefer the Colonial Style," *American School Board Journal* 66 (January 1923): 66.

32.    Ibid.

33.    On early aspects of nationalism and the Colonial Revival, see William B. Rhoads, "The Colonial Revival and American Nationalism," *Journal of the Society of Architectural Historians* 35 (December 1976): 239–54. Little has been done to explore the fascinating question of the link between Colonial Revival styles and white racial identity; the best example is Harvey Green, "Popular Science and Political Thought Converge: Colonial Survival Becomes Colonial Revival," *Journal of American Culture* 6 (Winter 1983): 3–24. For background on Americans' changing attitudes toward the racial identity of eastern and southern Europeans, see Matthew Frye Jacobson, *Whiteness of a Different Color: European Immigrants and the Alchemy of Race* (Cambridge: Harvard University Press, 1999).

34.    Alfred Busselle, "Domestic Quality in School Design," *Architecture* 43 (April 1921): 121. Busselle's point raises an interesting question—if schools were considered the true melting pot where "the urban realities of class disparity and ethnic heterogeneity" were to be overcome, why was there no overwhelming drive to "Americanize" the *appearance* of the school, even in Boston? The quote is from Carrie Tirado Bramen,

"The Urban Picturesque and the Spectacle of Americanization," *American Quarterly* 52 (September 2000): 444. There were a few voices hinting at such an approach: "We look to the teaching in public schools to help in the great problem of Americanizing our mixed people; why not make the buildings themselves a part of the teaching of the appreciation of architecture?" "Our School Architecture," 325.

35.    Walter H. Kilham, "The Modern Schoolhouse IV. Exposure and Plan," *The Brickbuilder* 24 (April 1915): 98.

36.    "Patton Plan a Gem," *Chicago Tribune*, June 27, 1897.

37.    George S. Counts, *School and Society in Chicago* (New York: Harcourt, Brace and Co., 1928), 36.

38.    *Proceedings of the Board of Education of the City of Chicago* (1880–81) (Chicago: publisher unknown), 83.

39.    Ibid., 90. The contents of Bauer's letter are unknown.

40.    *Twenty-Ninth Annual Report of the Board of Education of the City of Chicago* (1882–83) (Chicago: Jameson & Morse, Printers, 1884), 71.

41.    *Thirtieth Annual Report of the Board of Education of the City of Chicago* (1883–84) (Chicago: George K. Hazlitt & Co., 1885), 84.

42. "Wanted—An Architect," *Chicago Tribune*, January 22, 1888. During Flanders' second term as board architect, the *Inland Architect and News Record* defended him against an attack in the *Chicago Post*. The main issue this time was not competence but greed. The *Post* was outraged that Flanders received $42,000 for his work; the *Inland Architect* pointed out that this was for $2 million of construction and that the board architect's contract was for a percentage rather than a salary. However, the 21 percent commission reported by the *Post* does not agree with the official terms of Flanders' employment as they were reported in the *Proceedings of the Board of Education of the City of Chicago*—1 1/4 percent for preparing drawings for new buildings, 1 1/4 percent for superintending and preparing working plans, 5 percent for repairs greater than $15,000 and 4 percent for lesser repairs. "The Chicago School Board and Its Architect," *Inland Architect and News Record* 20 (December 1892): 48.

43.    *Thirty-Ninth Annual Report of the Board of Education of the City of Chicago* (1892–93) (Chicago: Public Schools of the City of Chicago, 1894): 22.

44.    Ibid., 193. The creation of the new position was not without its detractors. An anonymous writer in the *American Architect and Building News* criticized the plan: "The Board of Education in this city has this month decided on a plan which, if carried out with the success usual in such bodies, will be fruitful of most grave results.

The idea is no less than to establish a Building Bureau. Lately, work on school-buildings has been done unusually well, and at a very reasonable rate. The Board, however, did not seem to feel it was getting the most for its money, and has, consequently, created this Building Bureau," ("Chicago," *American Architect and Building News* 39 (February 4, 1893): 72). A month later the doubts continued: "All may—will—undoubtedly go right at first, but even should the head of the bureau continue to be an honest man, superior to temptation, there will doubtless be beneath him men more powerful than himself, as being the tools of prominent politicians. Such a state of things could hardly fail to bring about undesirable results, and an architectural bureau, with its contact with contractors and men of different trades, must ever be a dangerous place into which to introduce the conscience of the average politician, ever prone as it is to constitutional weakness," ("Chicago," *American Architect and Building News* 39 (March 4, 1893): 135).

45.    "Fiedler is on the Fire," *Chicago Tribune*, May 22, 1896.

46.    See "Find Fiedler a Tartar," *Chicago Tribune*, June 6, 1896; "School Arch. Defies Rules," *Chicago Tribune*, September 12, 1896.

47.    *Proceedings of the Board of Education of the City of Chicago* (1898–99) (Chicago: publisher unknown), 291.

48.    "Downey Makes Sharp Retort," *Chicago Tribune*, October 1, 1898.

49.    "Want Architect Patton Tried," *Chicago Tribune*, October 4, 1898; *Proceedings of the Board of Education of the City of Chicago* (1898–99), 291.

50.    "Hot Fight on Supt. Andrews," *Chicago Tribune*, November 17, 1898.

51.    "Mundie Taken to Task," *Chicago Tribune*, March 29, 1902; "School Desks Cause Row," *Chicago Tribune*, February 21, 1903.

52.    "Swing Ax in Schools," *Chicago Tribune*, November 4, 1903.

53.    "Head of Department Out," *Chicago Tribune*, November 15, 1903.

54.    "In Rage at Trustees," *Chicago Tribune*, November 28, 1903.

55.    "Wins Out Over Charges," *Chicago Tribune*, December 19, 1903.

56.    *Proceedings of the Board of Education of the City of Chicago* (1903–04) (Chicago: publisher unknown), 611.

57.    The author further noted: "Patton tried [to stand up to the board], and his ethical training as well as his honesty received such a shock and was so unyielding in its mental attitude, that both mentality and health were affected when his uncompromising resistance toward trickery and chicane [sic] caused him to be discharged." "Charges Against Architect Perkins by the Chicago School Board," *Western Architect* 15 (March 1910): 25.

58.   "The Architect and the Chicago Schools," *Western Architect* 4 (July 1905): 6. Later writers offered similar observations without citing their sources; see, for example, "Dwight H. Perkins—father of today's 'new school ideas,'" *Architectural Forum* 97 (October 1952): 123; Perry R. Duis and Glen E. Holt, "The Politics of Architecture," *Chicago Magazine* 10 (October 1981): 134 ("[Perkins'] two predecessors, William B. Mundie and Norman [sic] S. Patton, had been competent if not highly creative architects, and both had been hounded out of office by a school board more interested in rewarding cronies than in good architecture.")

59.   See, for example, Frank Estabrook Chancellor, "Schoolhouse Accommodations," *American School Board Journal* 38 (April 1909): 20; A. D. F. Hamlin, "Consideration in Schoolhouse Design," in *Modern School Houses* (New York: The Swetland Publishing Co., 1910), 4; John J. Donovan, et. al., *School Architecture: Principles and Practices* (New York: The Macmillan Company, 1921), 18; Thomas E. Tallmadge, *The Story of Architecture in America* (New York: W. W. Norton & Co., 1927), 273. The literature on Perkins is extensive but repetitious. The best sources are Peter B. Wight, "Public School Architecture at Chicago: The Work of Dwight H. Perkins," *Architectural Record* 27 (January-June 1910): 494–512; "Dwight H. Perkins—father of today's 'new school ideas,' *Architectural Forum* 97 (October 1952): 119–25; Eric Emmett Davis, "Dwight Heald Perkins 1894–1904: From the Chicago School to the Prairie School to Chicago's Schools," *Threshold* 5–6 (Fall 1991): 24–33. Eleanor Ellis Perkins, "Perkins of Chicago" (1966) (unpublished manuscript, Burnham Library, Art Institute of Chicago), a sentimental biography by Perkins's daughter, provides the basic facts of his life. The best compilation of Perkins's later school designs is in Dwight H. Perkins, W. K. Fellows and J. L. Hamilton, *Educational Buildings* (Chicago: Perkins, Fellows and Hamilton, 1925).

60.   Eric Emmett Davis, *Dwight Heald Perkins: Social Consciousness and Prairie School Architecture* (Chicago: Gallery 400 at the University of Illinois at Chicago, 1989). For his later work, see Perkins, Fellows and Hamilton, *Educational Buildings*.

61.   Paul M. Green and Melvin G. Holli, *The Mayors: The Chicago Political Tradition* (Carbondale and Edwardsville: Southern Illinois University Press, 1987), 42.

62.   *Fifty-Second Annual Report of the Board of Education of the City of Chicago* (1905–06) (Chicago: Public Schools of the City of Chicago, 1907), 13–28.

63.   Lane Tech was not, however, Perkins's first Chicago high school. His Englewood High School (1909) was an English Tudor building with no visual relation to any of his other Chicago schools; it may have been a project inherited from Robert B.

Williamson, who served as interim board architect for ten months between Mundie's resignation and Perkins's hiring. See Table 2.

64.    Solon S. Beman designed the city's initial Manual Training High School—which was funded by private sources and not part of the public school system—in 1884. Three public manual training high schools opened in the early 1900s.

65.    "Dedicate Lane School," *Chicago Record-Herald*, February 23, 1909. For a more elaborate description and discussion of the costs, see "$800,000 School Work of Others?," *Chicago Tribune*, February 8, 1910.

66.    William B. Ittner, "Forty Years in American School Architecture," *American School Board Journal* 82 (March 1931): 49.

67.    Ittner, "School Architecture," 1212.

68.    E. R. Robson, *School Architecture* (London: John Murray, 1874; reprint, New York: Humanities Press, 1972).

69.    Ittner, "School Architecture," 1217. The *American School Board Journal* had reached the same conclusion five years earlier in an editorial on "High School Architecture:" "The next change which has come about consists in placing the assembly hall or auditorium on the ground floor. It has been learned by experience that it is unwise to place an assembly hall on the third or even the second floor. Whenever a large body of people is assembled under one roof the means of affording safe exits must be supplied. In case of a calamity by fire no second or third floor hall can deliver its occupants as safely to the open air as can a ground floor hall. The constantly growing use of school halls for lecture and entertainment purposes, has also made it eminently practical to have these placed on the first floor. They afford easy entrance and safe exit. If so planned that the assembly hall will form the center wing of an E-shaped building, the lighting is certain to be excellent." "High School Architecture," 8. That editorial also addressed the safety of first floor auditoriums, arguing that upper-story rooms could not be evacuated as quickly as those on the first floor. Some authorities recognized this fact and attempted to mandate greater safety measures. After the highly-publicized Collinwood, Ohio, fire disaster (1908), in which 172 children and two teachers were killed, Ohio took a step in this direction when it passed legislation stating that no auditorium seating more than 100 persons could be built above the first story in a non-fireproof building, and every school room, no matter what type of building, must have two fireproof exits to the ground. See Wilbur T. Mills, "Innovations in School Architecture," *Journal of the Proceedings and Addresses of the National Education Association* (Winona, MN: National Education Association, 1908): 1075. The Chicago Public Schools mandated first floor auditoriums and assembly halls in 1904.

70.    National Education Association Committee on School House Planning and Construction, *Report of Committee on School House Planning, Frank Irving Cooper, Chairman* (Washington: National Education Association, 1925).

71.    Ibid., 39. A similar taxonomy was enumerated by William Estabrook Chancellor in 1909; Chancellor's plan types were the square, rectangle, interior court, "T," "E," "H," "L," "U," "V," "Y," and "Wide-Angle," which was a "V" extended to a larger angle. Chancellor, "Schoolhouse Accommodations," 4.

72.    "Chicago's New Manual Training School," *American School Board Journal* 34 (February 1907): 12.

73.    Wight, "Public School Architecture at Chicago," 502.

74.    A thoughtful review of the state of architectural sculpture in civic architecture can be found in Michele H. Bogart, *Public Sculpture and the Civic Ideal in New York City, 1890–1930* (Washington, DC: Smithsonian Institution Press, 1997).

75.    Lane Tech and a handful of other Chicago high schools (Phillips, McKinley, Lakeview, and Harrison), as well as a number of primary schools, featured such elaborate mural paintings. See Heather Becker, *Art for the People: The Rediscovery and Preservation of Progressive and WPA-Era Murals in the Chicago Public Schools, 1904–1943* (San Francisco: Chronicle Books, 2002), and Mary Lackritz Gray, *A Guide to Chicago's Murals* (Chicago and London: University of Chicago Press, 2001).

76.    The Iroquois Theater fire was a terrible disaster, killing over 600 people. For further reading, see Marshall Everett, *Lest We Forget: Chicago's Awful Theater Horror* (Chicago: Memorial Publishing Co., 1904); Nat Brandt, *Chicago Death Trap: The Iroquois Theatre Fire of 1903* (Carbondale, IL: Southern Illinois University Press, 2003).

77.    "School Frills to End," *Chicago Record-Herald*, October 11, 1909.

78.    "Cost of Schools Lowest Possible," *Chicago Tribune*, November 16, 1909.

79.    Dwight H. Perkins, "The Relation of Schoolhouse Architecture to the Social Center Movement," *Journal of the Proceedings and Addresses of the Fiftieth Annual Meeting of the National Education Association of the United States* (1912) (Ann Arbor, MI: National Education Association, 1912): 239.

80.    "The New Type of Public School Building," *Chicago Record-Herald*, January 7, 1911.

81.    The Bowen design had been published in the *Inland Architect and News Record* in 1906, but was significantly altered before construction began on 89th Street on the city's far south side. Features that appear in this original proposal, such as the use of strong corner piers framing a facade of windows set back from the wall surface, divided by thin vertical piers ending at a plain attic and flat roof, can be

traced back to a series of proposals by Perkins and Frank Lloyd Wright for the Abraham Lincoln Center in Chicago between 1897 and 1903. (The two architects had been jointly commissioned by Wright's uncle in 1896). There is little doubt that Wright was responsible for the facades of the Lincoln Center projects. And there is great visual similarity among the various Lincoln Center drawings, some of Perkins's grammar schools, and the first Bowen project. It is logical to conclude that Perkins was encouraged to adopt certain stylistic tendencies that he saw in Frank Lloyd Wright's work; after all, the two men worked together for years on this project, were friends, shared office space in Steinway Hall early in their careers, and attended the same church. Variations of these architectural elements can be seen in Perkins's built work, including Schurz High School. For the early Bowen design, see the *Inland Architect and News Record* 48 (November 1906): plates after page 48; *American School Board Journal* 34 (February 1907): 11. On Lincoln Center, see Joseph Siry, "The Abraham Lincoln Center in Chicago," *Journal of the Society of Architectural Historians* 50 (September 1991): 235–265.

82.    H. Allen Brooks, *The Prairie School: Frank Lloyd Wright and His Midwest Contemporaries* (New York: W. W. Norton, 1972), 113. Brooks is actually describing Perkins's Grover Cleveland School in Chicago, but the phrase applies equally to Schurz and Bowen.

83.    See e. g., Carl W. Condit, *The Chicago School of Architecture* (Chicago and London: University of Chicago Press, 1964); Mark L. Peisch, *The Chicago School of Architecture* (New York: Random House, Inc., 1964); Brooks, *The Prairie School*. In sharp contrast to the late twentieth century acclaim for Schurz High School, contemporary critics and writers ignored it—there were no articles on Schurz in any of the architectural or educational journals, and it was excluded from popular compilation books. A. F. Hussander's high school buildings received significantly more publicity in such sources, although his reputation never matched that of Perkins.

84.    In addition to his built high schools, Perkins was also involved in an unusual project to unite the educational and commercial worlds in the form of a skyscraper high school—much like the city government had attempted to create a skyscraper courthouse back in 1894, which drew Dwight Taylor-Kennard's wrath. The board wanted a commercial high school, and Perkins gave them a proposal for a fourteen-story building that combined a vertical high school on ten floors with administrative offices for the board on the upper four floors. Published drawings show a rectangular, flat-roofed slab dominated by windows and framed with thick borders (much like an elongated version of the original Bowen design). The project somewhat awkwardly

merged the lightness of contemporary skyscraper technology with the heaviness of nineteenth-century school buildings. The plan proved controversial, drawing criticism from James Downey, chairman of the Chicago Board of Education's Committee on Buildings and Grounds, and powerful businessman Montgomery Ward, who objected to a scheme to put the tower in Grant Park. In the end, Perkins's skyscraper high school project died, only to be resurrected in a different form in the 1960s by his son, Lawrence Perkins, as the William Jones Commercial High School (Perkins & Will, 1967). See *Fiftieth Annual Report* (1908–09) for a rendering.

85.    For Perkins's post-1910 work see Perkins, Fellows and Hamilton, *Educational Buildings.*

86.    On the  arts and crafts movement, see Elizabeth Cumming and Wendy Kaplan, *The Arts and Crafts Movement* (London: Thames & Hudson, 1991) or Wendy Kaplan, *"The Art that is Life": The Arts & Crafts Movement in America, 1875–1920* (Boston: Museum of Fine Arts, 1987). For Wright and the Prairie houses, see Brooks, *The Prairie School*; Robert C. Twombly, "Saving the Family: Middle Class Attraction to Wright's Prairie House, 1901–1909," *American Quarterly* 27 (1975): 57–72; Robert V. Sharp, ed., "The Prairie School: Design Vision for the Midwest," *The Art Institute of Chicago Museum Studies* 21, No. 2 (1995).

87.    "Schools to Cost Less; Hatchet Now Buried," *Chicago Record-Herald*, November 19, 1909.

88.    "Urion Bombards School Designer," *Chicago Tribune*, November 27, 1909.

89.    "'Ajax Perkins Struck By Bolt," *Chicago Tribune*, February 4, 1910.

90.    "Architects Seek to Aid Perkins," *Chicago Tribune*, February 5, 1910.

91.    There is extensive coverage of the trial in both the *Chicago Tribune* and the *Chicago Record-Herald* between March 7 and April 1, 1910. Today we do not know what the true nature of the dispute was, but certain political incidents between 1905 and 1910 can be reasonably assumed to have instigated problems. The most important seems to have been the personal animosity generated between Perkins and Urion during the cost-cutting negotiations of 1909. According to various late-twentieth century sources, however, Perkins had angered the board numerous times by such actions as refusing to use cut stone ornamentation (thus upsetting the cut stone lobby), firing a politically connected building superintendent, hiring five English draftsmen, and rejecting flooring materials manufactured by a company in which Urion had a major interest. See e. g., Davis, *Dwight Heald Perkins*, 12; "Dwight H. Perkins—father of today's "new school ideas," 123–24; Duis and Holt, "The Politics of Architecture," 136.

92.    "Plan to Abolish Perkins' Old Job," *Chicago Tribune*, April 4, 1910.

93.    *Fifty-Sixth Annual Report of the Board of Education of the City of Chicago* (1909–1910) (Chicago: Public Schools of the City of Chicago, n. d. ), 13.

94.    Quoted in "Dwight H. Perkins—father of today's "new school ideas," 119.

95.    "Sound Knell for Ornate Schools," *Chicago Tribune*, December 11, 1909.

96.    There is evidence, however, that Hussander was unable to escape the board's politics in the long run. In a 1923 corruption trial against school personnel, a witness testified that Hussander had been forced out to make room for John Christensen. ("[Albert H. ] Severinghaus," he said, "showed me a stack of papers and said he had enough evidence to fire the architect [Hussander]. I asked him why he was proceeding secretly, without the authority of the board, and he said it was on orders from [Fred] Lundin, that Lundin wanted Christiansen [sic] appointed architect. Later the architect resigned and Christiansen was appointed." "Hanson Grilled on Cross-Quiz; Bares His Deals," *Chicago Tribune*, June 12, 1923.

97.    Mary J. Herrick, *The Chicago Schools: A Social and Political History* (Beverly Hills and London: Sage Publications, Inc., 1971), 403.

98.    William C. Bruce, "Some New Schoolhouses in Chicago," *American School Board Journal* 43 (November 1911): 24.

99.    Ibid., 27.

100.    A. F. Hussander, "Recent Chicago Schoolhouses," *American School Board Journal* 60 (October 1920): 46.

101.    "Our School Architecture," 325.

## Roaring Twenties, Depression, and War

1.    Mary J. Herrick, *The Chicago Schools: A Social and Political History* (Beverly Hills and London: Sage Publications, Inc., 1971), 403.

2.    David L. Angus and Jeffrey E. Mirel, *The Failed Promise of the American High School, 1890–1995* (New York: Teachers College Press, 1999), 203.

3.    Angus and Mirel, *The Failed Promise of the American High School*, 203.

4.    Don C. Rogers, "The High School Marches On!" *Chicago Schools Journal* 16 (September-February, 1934–35): 56.

5.    George S. Counts, *The Selective Character of American Secondary Education* (Chicago: University of Chicago Press, 1922): 155.

6.    A. F. Hussander, "Recent Chicago Schoolhouses," *American School Board Journal* 60 (October 1920): 45.

7.    For more on this issue see Julia Wrigley, *Class Politics and Public Schools: Chicago 1900–1950* (New Brunswick, NJ: Rutgers University Press, 1982), and David John Hogan, *Class and Reform: School and Society in Chicago, 1880–1930* (Philadelphia: University of Pennsylvania Press, 1985).

8.    Ibid., page 7.

9.    Edward A. Krug, *The Shaping of the American High School, 1920–1941* (Madison, WI: University of Wisconsin Press, 1972), 37.

10.    According to Mary Herrick, junior high school enrollment was far from universal; she claims that at the time of their demise in 1933, only 20 percent of the city's seventh and eighth grade students attended junior highs. Herrick, *The Chicago Schools*, 148.

11.    Ralph W. Yardley, "The Development of the Junior High School in Chicago," *Architectural Record* 69 (May 1931): 442.

12.    Ibid.

13.    John C. Christensen appeared to have the best relationship with the school board of any board architect. He assumed the post in March 1922. There was evidence that A. F. Hussander may have been forced out to make way for Christensen (see Chapter 4, note 96). Christensen remained in the position until September 1928, whereupon he unexpectedly tendered his resignation. The board accepted "with great reluctance" and expressed its "appreciation and gratitude" for Christensen's service. (*Proceedings of the Board of Education of the City of Chicago* (1928–29), 283–85). Board President H. Wallace Caldwell added that Christensen left his office and immediately entered a hospital, suggesting a medical problem. Paul Gerhardt was named as Christensen's replacement, but only as the school board's temporary architect. Gerhardt held a series of sixty-day appointments for over two years until being "separated" from his position by the board in April 1931. John C. Christensen was reinstated the following day. He remained board architect until retiring in 1959. "Schools' Chief Architect to Quit Job, Aug. 1," *Chicago Tribune*, July 21, 1959; "Christensen, City Schools Designer, Dies," *Chicago Tribune*, June 4, 1967.

14.    Department of Education, City of Chicago, *Annual Report of the Superintendent of Schools* (1924–25) (Chicago: Chicago Public Schools, 1925), 100.

15.    Don C. Rogers, "One Hundred Years of School Building," *Chicago Schools Journal* 15 (January-June 1933): 79. See also, Rogers, "School Building Report," *Chicago Schools Journal* 11 (January 1929): 175–178.

16.    The BRBS disappeared by the late 1940s; later, in the 1960s, the Department of Architecture would cease to exist, and the Bureau of Architecture would fall within the purview of the Facilities Planning Department.

17.    "Takes Care of All," *Chicago Tribune*, October 11, 1896.

18.    Herrick, *The Chicago Schools*, 179; Rogers, "School Building Report," 176.

19.    George D. Strayer and N. L. Engelhardt, *Report of the Survey of the Schools of Chicago, Illinois*, Vol. 4: "Housing The Public Schools of Chicago," by Frank W. Hart and N. L. Engelhardt (New York: Bureau of Publications, Teachers College, Columbia University, 1932), 177.

20.    Cited in Michael Homel, *Down From Equality: Black Chicagoans and the Public Schools, 1920–1941.* (Urbana, IL: University of Illinois Press, 1984), 82.

21.    Ibid., 81.

22.    Metz T. P. Lochard, "$4,000,000 DuSable High School Proves A Fiasco," *Chicago Defender*, June 11, 1938.

23.    Lochard, "$4,000,000 DuSable High School," 2.

24.    Homel, *Down From Equality*, 14, 27.

25.    Ibid., 52.

26.    "Urge $200,000 Cut in Cost of a High School," *Chicago Tribune*, November 23, 1931.

27.    For a more detailed story of the crisis, see Herrick, *The Chicago Schools*, Chapter 10.

28.    The five areas studied were (1) administrative efficiency; (2) business administration; (3) school buildings; (4) school costs; and (5) student progress.

29.    Herrick, *The Chicago Schools*, 204.

30.    The scoring system allotted points for a building's site, structure, service systems, classrooms, and service and administrative space. A maximum score was 1,000 points. The categories were 700+ points = "Thoroughly Satisfactory;" 600–700 = "Fairly Satisfactory—Needs Improvements;" 400–600 = "Needs Major Improvements, Alterations, and Additions." Any score below 400 meant that the building was unusable and should be abandoned. Buildings cited in this book and their scores were: Harrison = 640; Lindblom = 607; Hyde Park = 558; Schurz = 553; Senn = 501; Lane Tech = 444; Bowen = 442; McKinley = 420; Phillips = 420; Waller = 348 (the lowest score of all high schools). The new junior high's scored well, including Von Steuben at 806 points. Interestingly, both Lake View and Waller are still being used over seventy years after being deemed "unusable" in the Strayer report, with Waller—now Lincoln Park High School—being ranked 90th in the *U.S. News & World Report* listing of the nation's top 100 high schools in 2007.

31.    Strayer and Engelhardt, *Report of the Survey of the Schools of Chicago*, 186.

32.    Herrick, *The Chicago Schools*, 221.

33.    Chicago Public Schools, *Chicago Public Schools* (Booklet for the 27th Annual

Conference of the National Association of Public School Business Officials) (Chicago: Chicago Public Schools, 1938), 25.

34.    Thomas J. Higgins, "New Lane Technical High School, Chicago, Illinois," *American School Board Journal* 90 (January 1935): 25.

35.    Ibid.

36.    Higgins, "New Lane," 25.

37.    "Move First Dirt For New Lane Tech Building," *Chicago Tribune*, June 25, 1930.

38.    Higgins, "New Lane," 26.

39.    For more information on the murals in Lane Tech and other Chicago schools, see Heather Becker, *Art for the People: The Rediscovery and Preservation of Progressive and WPA-Era Murals in the Chicago Public Schools, 1904–1943* (San Francisco: Chronicle Books, 2002). The Lane Tech artworks were part of a nationwide public art project administered by the WPA.

40.    On the efficiency movement's effects on school architecture, see Chapter Six in Dale Allen Gyure, "The Transformation of the Schoolhouse: American Secondary School Architecture and Educational Reform, 1880–1920," (Ph. D. diss., University of Virginia, 2001).

41.    "School Design and the New Architecture," *American School Board Journal* 85 (October 1932): 45.

42.    Dwight H. Perkins, "Modern Architectural Design and Its Application to the Schools of Today," *American School Board Journal* 80 (January 1930): 83–84.

43.    Ibid., 84.

44.    The Ecole des Beaux-Arts idea of "character" was a complex conception which attempted to make sure the building's appearance matched its purpose, use, and status. For a detailed explanation of "character," see Donald Drew Egbert, *The Beaux-Arts Tradition in French Architecture* (Princeton, NJ: Princeton University Press, 1980), Chapter 6.

45.    Henry Barnard, *School Architecture* 2nd ed. (New York: A. S. Barnes & Co., 1848; reprint, ed. Jean and Robert McClintock. New York: Teachers College Press, 1970), 55.

46.    Guy Study, "Architecture for School and College Buildings—Period Styles or Contemporary? Period Styles for Character," *American School and University* 5 (1932–33): 28–30.

47.    Philip Johnson, "Architecture for School and College Buildings—Period Styles or Contemporary? Modern Architecture for Efficiency," *American School and University* 5 (1932–33): 31.

48.    Ibid., 31–33. Walter Gropius made a similar remark about college architecture in 1950: "How can we expect our students to become bold and fearless in thought and action if we encase them in sentimental shrines feigning a culture which has long since disappeared?" Walter Gropius, "Tradition and the Graduate Center," *Harvard Alumni Bulletin* (October 14, 1950): 68.

49.    John C. Christensen, "The Architecture of the Lane Tech High School," in *The Albert G. Lane Technical High School Dedication, September 17, 1934* (Chicago: Chicago Public Schools, 1934), in Chicago Public Schools Archives, "Schools," Box 10. Paul Gerhardt appears to have designed the new Lane Tech building but was replaced as board architect by Christensen before construction was completed.

50.    Ibid.

51.    In terms of numbers, the high schools lost 47,885 students.

52.    George S. Counts, *School and Society in Chicago*, (New York: Harcourt, Brace, 1928), 248.

53.    On this style of architecture see Richard Guy Wilson, "Modernized Classicism and Washington, D. C.," in Craig Zabel and Susan S. Munshower, eds., *American Public Architecture: European Roots and Native Expressions* (University Park, PA: Penn State University Press, 1989).

54.    Bureau of Education, Chicago, Illinois, *Annual Report of the Superintendent of Schools* (1940–41) (Chicago: Chicago Public Schools, 1941), 521.

55.    "Must Schools Be Ugly?" *Chicago Tribune*, December 5, 1946.

56.    Ibid.

57.    "Huge Vocational School Finished," *Chicago Tribune*, August 11, 1940.

58.    Chicago Vocational School groundbreaking pamphlet, 1938, Chicago Public Schools Archives, Box 10, "Schools."

## Modernism and Education

1.    On the design of Crow Island, see Amy S. Weisser, "Institutional Revisions: Modernism and American Public Schools From the Depression Through the Second World War," Ph. D. diss., Yale University, 1995, pp. 65–88.

2.    Winnetka Parent-Teacher Association, *Your Child and Your School* (Winnetka, IL: 1933), 4. See also Carlton W. Washburne & Sidney P. Marland, Jr., *Winnetka: The History and Significance of an Educational Experiment* (Englewood Cliffs, NJ: Prentice Hall Inc., 1963).

3.    Frances Presler to Eliel and Eero Saarinen, May 22, 1939; quoted in Weisser, "Institutional Revisions," 72.

4.    "Crow Island School," *Architectural Forum* 75 (August 1941): 79–92; Lawrence B. Perkins, "When Teachers, Janitors Build Schools," *American School Board Journal* 103 (September 1941): 33–39, 87.

5.    Walter D. Cocking, "Secondary School Design Since World War II," *American School and University* 27 (1955–56): 187.

6.    Mary J. Herrick, *The Chicago Schools: A Social and Political History* (Beverly Hills and London: Sage Publications, Inc., 1971), 403; *Chicago Public Schools Facts & Figures* 1972/73, 54.

7.    National high school enrollment grew by 140 percent in the 1910s, 100 percent in the 1920s, 50 percent in the 1930s, shrank by 13 percent in the 1940s, and rose by 44 percent in the 1950s and 58 percent in the 1960s. David L. Angus and Jeffrey E. Mirel, *The Failed Promise of the American High School, 1890–1995* (New York: Teachers College Press, 1999), 203.

8.    Ward I. Miller, "Requirements of the Modern Secondary School," *American School and University* 20 (1948–49): 79, 85.

9.    Harold E. Moore, "The Modern Secondary School Building," *American School and University* 20 (1948–49): 70.

10.    Ibid., 74–75.

11.    Ibid., 75.

12.    Lawrence B. Perkins and Walter D. Cocking, *Schools* (New York: Reinhold, 1949): 38. Cocking was an educator and the editor of *The School Executive* and *American School and University*.

13.    Ibid., 236.

14.    Ibid., 49.

15.    Ibid., 55. Compare with statements from two decades earlier: (*American School Board Journal*) "The schoolhouse is becoming each year a more specialized type of building . . . a more complicated instrument whose parts are necessarily more finely adjusted." (*American School Board Journal* 57 (August 1918): 45); (A. F. Hussander) "From whatever angle it may be considered the school building is first and last the tool or instrument of the school and its sole purpose is to provide proper housing for the school so that the latter may most efficiently and comfortably carry on the work of education." ("Recent Chicago Schoolhouses," *American School Board Journal* 60 (October 1920): 45).

16.    See Perkins, "When Teachers, Janitors Build Schools," 1–8.

17.    Walter D. Cocking, "Secondary School Design Since World War II," *American School and University* 27 (1955–56): 185.

18.    Ibid., 188–90.

19.    Cynthia A. Wnek, "Big Ben the Builder: School Construction—1953–66," Ph. D. diss., Loyola University of Chicago, 1988, 214. Wnek admits the figures may not be accurate due to "great discrepancies" in the sources. John Rury claims similar numbers: 208 elementary schools and thirteen high schools. John L. Rury, "Race, Space, and the Politics of Chicago's Public Schools: Benjamin Willis and the Tragedy of Urban Education," *History of Education Quarterly* 39 (Summer 1999): 125. The 1966 *Annual Report* cites fourteen high schools. General Superintendent of the Chicago Public Schools, *Annual Report of the General Superintendent of the Chicago Public Schools, 1966* (Chicago: Chicago Public Schools, 1966). On the building campaigns see John F. Delaney, "Chicago's Mammouth [sic] School Building Program," *American School Board Journal* 132 (February 1956): 31–35; General Superintendent of the Chicago Public Schools, *Annual Report of the General Superintendent of the Chicago Public Schools, 1958* (Chicago: Chicago Public Schools, 1958); Chicago Public Schools, *More Than Bricks and Mortar . . . 1953–1966*. Chicago: Chicago Public Schools, 1966).

20.    General Superintendent of the Chicago Public Schools, *Annual Report of the General Superintendent of the Chicago Public Schools, 1953–54* (Chicago: Chicago Public Schools, 1954): 3.

21.    Ibid., 27.

22.    Wnek, "Big Ben the Builder," 124; *Annual Report* (1958), 29. While board architect John Christensen's feelings about this change are unknown, there is evidence that not everyone accepted it. The *Chicago Tribune* reported in November 1954 that the President of the American Federation of Labor's Technical Employees Union 435 appeared before the board of education to complain about the new practice, citing statistics which inferred that the board would actually save money be letting its own architects design schools. See Robert Wiedrich, "Union, School Board Argue Design Method," *Chicago Tribune*, November 4, 1954.

23.    Clay Gowran, "Willis Program Ends Century of School Jam," *Chicago Tribune*, June 2, 1963.

24.    Gowran, "Willis Program," 2.

25.    *Annual Report* (1958); Wnek, "Big Ben the Builder," 104.

26.   *Annual Report* (1958), 9.

27.   Holabird & Root had an illustrious pedigree. It was formed in 1928 by John Holabird and John W. Root, Jr., sons of William Holabird and John W. Root, Sr., thus merging the two famous late-nineteenth century Chicago firms Holabird & Roche and Burnham & Root. Known primarily for pre-Depression skyscrapers in the Loop, like the Board of Trade Building, the firm added Joseph Z. Burgee in as a partner in 1945. For more information, see Werner Blaser, ed., *Chicago Architecture: Holabird & Root, 1880–1992* (Basel, Boston & Berlin: Birkhauser Verlag, 1992).

28.   "Dunbar Trade Opens Doors of Modern Plant," *Chicago Tribune*, July 8, 1956. Campbell had a degree in architecture from Chicago Technical College and once worked as a draftsman for the board of education.

29.   Ibid.; Delaney, "Chicago's Mammouth [sic] School Building Program," 32.

30.   Clay Gowran, "Pride in Work Main Product At Dunbar High," *Chicago Tribune*, April 14, 1957.

31.   Perkins and Cocking, *Schools*, 40.

32.   Ibid., 233.

33.   Ibid., 44.

34.   Ibid., 45.

35.   See e. g., William J. Kane, "Thoughts on the School Courtyard," *American School Board Journal* 142 (January 1961): 32–33.

36.   *Annual Report* (1958).

37.   Ruth Dunbar, "City's 2–In-1 School Experiment," *Chicago Sun Times*, August 4, 1957.

38.   On Samuels, see "School Board Names New Bureau Chief," *Chicago Tribune*, March 3, 1960.

39.   Charles E. Strickland and Andrew M. Ambrose, "The Baby Boom, Prosperity, and the Changing Worlds of Children, 1945–1963," in Joseph M. Hawes and N. Ray Hiner, eds., *American Childhood: A Research Guide and Historical Handbook* (Westport, CT and London: Greenwood Press, 1985), 538.

40.   Robert L. Hampel, *The Last Little Citadel: American High Schools Since 1940* (Boston: Houghton Mifflin Company, 1986), 56.

41.   *Annual Report* (1958), 9.

42.   Kimball Wiles, *The Changing Curriculum of the American High School* (Englewood Cliffs, NJ: Prentice-Hall, Inc., 1963), 185.

43.   William C. Bruce, "School Architecture in 1964," *American School Board Journal* 148 (January 1964): 51.

44.    *Annual Report* (1958), 8; Wiles, *Changing Curriculum*, 185.

45.    Angus and Mirel, *The Failed Promise of the American High School*, 74.

46.    Ibid., 203. The percentages reached 76. 1 in 1950, 83. 4 in 1960, and 92. 2 in 1970 before dropping to 89. 8 in 1980.

47.    Ibid., 102.

48.    Frances V. Rummel, *High School: What's In It For Me?* (Washington, DC: US Office of Education, 1950): 5.

49.    A. J. Foy Cross, "A School Building Is For Learning," *American School Board Journal* 132 (January 1956): 28.

50.    V. M. Houston, C. W. Sanford, and J. L. Trump, *Guide to the Study of the Curriculum in the Secondary Schools of Illinois* (Springfield, IL: Illinois Secondary School Curriculum Program, 1948), 23.

51.    Vernon L. Nickell, "How Can We Develop an Effective Program of Education for Life Adjustment?" *Bulletin of the National Association of Secondary-School Principals* 33 (April 1949): 154.

52.    Herbert M Kliebard,. *The Struggle for the American Curriculum, 1893–1958*, 2nd ed. (New York, London: Routledge, 1995), 215.

53.    "Get Adjusted," *Time* (December 15, 1947): 64.

54.    General Superintendent of the Chicago Public Schools, *Annual Report of the General Superintendent of the Chicago Public Schools, 1950–51* (Chicago: Chicago Public Schools, 1951): 18.

55.    *Annual Report* (1950–51), 18.

56.    Arthur E. Bestor, Jr., *Educational Wastelands: The Retreat From Learning in Our Public Schools* (Urbana, IL: University of Illinois Press, 1953), 3.

57.    Cited in Angus and Mirel, *The Failed Promise of the American High School*, 107.

58.    General Superintendent of the Chicago Public Schools, *Annual Report of the General Superintendent of the Chicago Public Schools, 1957.* (Chicago: Chicago Public Schools, 1957): 11.

59.    Strickland and Ambrose, "The Baby Boom, Prosperity, and the Changing Worlds of Children, 1945–1963," 552.

60.    James B. Conant, *The American High School Today: A First Report to Interested Citizens* (New York: McGraw-Hill, 1959), 40.

61.    Angus and Mirel, *The Failed Promise of the American High School*, 113.

62.    John L. Rury, "Schools and Education," in James R. Grossman, Ann Durkin Keating, and Janice L. Reiff, eds., *Encyclopedia of Chicago.* (Chicago and London: University of Chicago Press, 2004), 741–742.

63.   Robert J. Havighurst, *The Public Schools of Chicago: A Survey for the Board of Education of the City of Chicago.* (Chicago: Board of Education of the City of Chicago, 1964), 237.

64.   Ibid., 238.

65.   Wnek, "Big Ben the Builder," 200.

66.   Casey Banas, "Willis Offers Plan to Aid 5 High Schools," *Chicago Tribune,* June 7, 1966.

67.   "New Ideas Spur New Uses for Relocatable Facilities," *American School and University* 39 (November 1966): 31.

68.   Wnek, "Big Ben the Builder," 157.

69.   On the racial issues of the Chicago schools at this time, see Rury, "Race, Space, and the Politics of Chicago's Public Schools," and Alan B. Anderson and George W. Pickering, *Confronting the Color Line: The Broken Promise of Civil Rights in Chicago* (Athens, GA: University of George Press, 1986).

70.   By 1975 the city's schools had become even more segregated, with half of the public high schools either 95 percent white or black. Dorothy Shipps, *School Reform, Corporate Style* (Lawrence KS: University Press of Kansas, 2006), 81.

71.   "Offer 750–Million, 5–Year School Plan," *Chicago Sun-Times,* December 18, 1966.

72.   Peter Negronida, "Schools Seek 140 Million Building Fund," *Chicago Tribune,* March 28, 1969. Later the park district would begin to partially fund these bond issues in return for ownership rights. See David Gilbert, "Buying of 40 Acres Okd by Board," *Chicago Tribune,* June 23, 1971. In addition to providing needed construction funds, Paul Peterson points out that this arrangement with the CPBC also allowed the board to "sidestep voter review of capital expansion policies." Paul E. Peterson, *School Politics, Chicago Style* (Chicago and London: University of Chicago Press, 1976): 19.

73.   William C. Bruce, "School Architecture 1963," *American School Board Journal* 146 (January 1963): 48.

74.   Larry Cuban, *How Teachers Taught: Constancy and Change in American Classrooms 1890–1990.* (New York and London: Teachers College Press, 1993), 151.

75.   Educational Facilities Laboratories, Inc., *Educational Change and Architectural Consequences* (New York: EFL, 1968), 16. The EFL was founded in 1958 by the Ford Foundation to research and disseminate information on educational architecture. It grew out of the "Committee on School Buildings," an early 1950s association of the U.S. Office of Education, the American Institute of Architects, and various other educational groups. Before losing its independent status of 1976, the EFL

"spurred innovation in school architecture by sponsoring research projects and programs, holding conferences, and awarding grants to thousands of school districts, colleges, and nonprofit organizations throughout the United States and Canada. " Judy Marks, "The Educational Facilities Laboratories (EFL): A History," National Clearinghouse for Educational Facilities (2001), www.edfacilities.org.

76.    Educational Facilities Laboratories, Inc., *Educational Change*, 16.

77.    Educational Facilities Laboratories, Inc., *High Schools 1962* (New York: Educational Facilities Laboratories, Inc., 1961), 53.

78.    Bruce, "School Architecture 1963," 48.

79.    Educational Facilities Laboratories, Inc., *Educational Change*, 76.

80.    Ibid., 15.

81.    Ibid., *Educational Change*, 12. See also, "New Ideas in Education Ask New Planning Solutions for Schools," *Architectural Record* 152 (August 1972): 107–22.

82.    Although little research has been done in the area, Larry Cuban has discerned that despite the multiple innovations and experiments of this period, most high school classes were still "teacher-centered," meaning the teachers controlled the learning environment through lectures and question-answer sessions—particularly in "core" academic areas: "In high schools, pedagogy since 1900 in the five academic subjects altered very little except for the formal recitation. Raising of hands, yelling out of answers, and informal discussion techniques replaced standing at one's desk or in the front of the room to answer the teacher's questions. Whole-group instruction, teacher-controlled classroom talk, little student movement, and little variety of tasks captured the high school classroom in the 1970s." Cuban, *How Teachers Taught*, 200–01.

83.    General Superintendent of the Chicago Public Schools, *Annual Report of the General Superintendent of the Chicago Public Schools, 1952–53*. (Chicago: Chicago Public Schools, 1953): 29.

84.    "A New Kind of High School," *Architectural Forum* 103 (October 1955): 146–149.

85.    General Superintendent of the Chicago Public Schools, *Annual Report of the General Superintendent of the Chicago Public Schools, 1963–64*. (Chicago: Chicago Public Schools, 1964): 34.

86.    "Builders to Bid on So. Shore High," *Chicago Tribune*, April 10, 1966. Fridstein and Fitch had previously experimented with the hexagonal school in the Blackhawk School (1958) in Hoffman Estates

87.    William C. Bruce, "School Building in 1956," *American School Board Journal* 132 (January 1956): 68.

88.    Bruce, "School Building, 1961," *American School Board Journal* 142 (January 1961): 44.

89.    Bruce, "School Architecture in 1964," *American School Board Journal* 148 (January 1964): 51.

90.    Bruce, "School Design in 1966," *American School Board Journal* 152 (January 1966): 28.

91.    Jones stood out from other schools in two ways: it sat in the Loop, on Plymouth Court just south of Harrison, and it looked like a high-rise building. Jones High School actually consisted of two buildings, a six-story classroom tower and a separate auditorium. The tower, which adopted the uniform blankness of the downtown office and commercial architecture, was designed to be expandable to fifteen stories if the need should ever arise. Jones thus fulfilled the dream of Perkins's father, Dwight, who planned a fourteen-story skyscraper high school in 1908.

92.    Chicago Public Schools, *A Report to the 78th General Assembly of the State of Illinois* (Chicago: Chicago Public Schools, 1974), 9.

93.    See *Annual Report, 1958*, 24–25; "Chicago's Program for Improvement," *Architectural Forum* 113 (Nov. 1960): 112. The idea of a Park District-Public School partnership apparently dated back to 1946. See "31st Park-School Shows Growth of 1946 Plans," *Chicago Tribune*, September 24, 1964.

94.    Bernard Judge, "Battle Rages on School-Park Controversy," *Chicago Tribune*, April 26, 1970.

95.    See Joseph McLaughlin, "Ask Ban on Park Use for Schools," *Chicago Tribune*, June 26, 1970; John Camper, "Chicago's Right to Build Schools in Parks Upheld," *Chicago Daily News*, September 29, 1970.

96.    Cyril G. Sargent, John B. Ward, and Allan R. Talbot, "The Concept of the Educational Park," in Alvin Toffler, ed., *The Schoolhouse in the City* (New York, Washington, and London: Frederick A. Praeger, Publishers, in cooperation with the Educational Facilities Laboratories, 1968), 191.

97.    Christopher Chandler, "OK $140–Million Leasing Plan for Building Schools," *Chicago Sun-Times*, April 28, 1968.

98.    Peter Negronida, "Circle Campus Site Urged for School Park," *Chicago Tribune*, March 28, 1968.

99.    Chandler, "OK $140–Million Leasing Plan for Building Schools," *Chicago Sun-Times*, April 28, 1968.

100.   Schools were not alone in this regard, as public architecture as a whole was affected. In an article describing how the modernist office building came to be accepted as the model for institutional architecture of all types in the mid-twentieth century, leading to a situation where mainstream architecture lost the ability to carry symbolic meaning, critic Matthew J. Bell observed that "institutions which formerly enjoyed a representative and symbolic architecture are now anonymous buildings immersed in the fabric of the city or even hidden in the landscape. . . . Institutional building programs. . . . which previously employed cogent symbolic urban and architectural forms, seem to have been sublimated to a subversive role of maintaining status quo and concealing authority." Matthew J. Bell, "Novus Ordo Seclorum: The County Courthouse as Object and Symbol." *Modulus 23: Towards a Civic Architecture in America* (1995): 169.

101.   Edmund M. Wheelwright, "The American Schoolhouse VI," *The Brickbuilder* 7 (April 1898): 76.

102.   Charles Zueblin, *American Municipal Progress: Chapters in Municipal Sociology* (New York: Macmillan, 1902), 240.

103.   In fact, if educational journals are indicative of school officials' attitudes, architecture as a whole seems to have been less important to administrators during this time. The *American School Board Journal* had traditionally offered considerable coverage of school architecture, but the coverage declined dramatically in the 1960s. After 1964 the *Journal* no longer included floor plans in its features on individual high school buildings, and by later in the decade those stories stopped appearing. Articles on school lighting and ventilation, or pieces written by architects, also disappeared. And the section entitled "The School Plant" dropped its "Notable New Schools" portion in 1967. By 1970, architecture had virtually vanished from the *Journal*'s pages. However, these developments may also reflect the importance of specialty organizations like the EFL.

104.   Educational Facilities Laboratories, Inc., *Educational Change*, 69.

105.   Chicago Public Schools, "Whitney M. Young Magnet High School"(Chicago: Chicago Public Schools, no date); in "Schools," Box 20, "Way-Z," Chicago Board of Education Archives.

106.   M. W. Newman, "Our city's exciting new schools," *Chicago Daily News* (September 30, 1970): 4.

107.   Angus and Mirel, *The Failed Promise of the American High School*, 139–40.

## Into the New Century

1.    Jeffrey Mirel, "School Reform, Chicago Style: Educational Innovation in a Changing Urban Context, 1976–1991," *Urban Education* 28 (July 1993): 118–119.

2.    Unfortunately, as Dorothy Shipps points out, the five businessmen who constituted the CSFA included three who headed companies that had not paid their property taxes, which alone amounted to $350,000. Dorothy Shipps, *School Reform, Corporate Style* (Lawrence KS: University Press of Kansas, 2006), 94.

3.    G. Alfred Hess, Jr., *School Restructuring, Chicago Style* (Newbury Park, CA: Crown Press, Inc., 1991), 2.

4.    Ibid., 3.

5.    Mirel, "School Reform, Chicago Style," 132.

6.    Dirk Johnson, "Illinois Legislature Moves to Give Parents Control of the Chicago Schools," *New York Times*, July 13, 1988.

7.    National Commission on Excellence in Education, *A Nation at Risk: The Imperative for Educational Reform*. (Washington, DC: U.S. Government Printing Office, 1983), 18.

8.    Ibid., 173.

9.    G. Alfred Hess, "The Effort to Redesign Chicago High Schools: Effects on Schools and Achievement," in *School Reform in Chicago: Lessons and Opportunities, A Report for the Chicago Community Trust, August 2001* (Chicago: Chicago Community Trust, 2001), 44. For a critique of these new developments on a national scale, see e. g., Larry Cuban, "1980–2000: The Bottom Line," in Sarah Mondale and Sarah B. Parker, eds., *School: The Story of American Public Education* (Boston: Beacon Press, 2001).

10.    Mirel, "School Reform, Chicago Style," 139.

11.    Chicago Public Schools, *Fiscal Year 2005 Final Budget* (Chicago: Chicago Public Schools, 2005).

12.    "New high school helps Chicago Public Schools relieve overcrowding," *Public Building Commission Press Release* (September 8, 2004) Archives, Chicago Board of Education.

13.    A serious overcrowding problem still plagued Chicago's high schools. In the 2001–02 school year, for example, almost 20 percent of the city's public high schools were filled beyond capacity, with some rates as high as 174 percent (Kelly High School) and 148 percent (Hancock High School). Neighborhood Capital Budget Group web page, www.ncbg.org/schools/hs_crowding.htm.

14.    U.S. General Accounting Office, *School Facilities: Construction Expenditures Have Grown Significantly in Recent Years*, GAO/HEHS-00–41, March (Washington, DC: U.S. General Accounting Office, 2000), 3.

15.    The cost to rectify this situation was estimated at $112 billion over three years. U.S. General Accounting Office, *School Facilities: Condition of America's Schools*, GAO/HEHS-95–61, February (Washington, DC: U.S. General Accounting Office, 1995), 2. See also the follow-up report, *School Facilities America's Schools Report Differing Conditions*, GAO/HEHS-96–106, June (Washington, DC: U.S. General Accounting Office, 1996).

16.    U.S. General Accounting Office, *School Facilities: Construction Expenditures Have Grown Significantly in Recent Years*, 4.

17.    School architect Earl Flansburgh told *Architectural Record*, "In the 60's [sic] we saw straightforward massing, usually with flat roofs. Now we see more complex forms, greater use of color, and historical recall. " "Back to bells and cells?" *Architectural Record* 176 (September 1988): 104.

18.    Ibid., 102, 104.

19.    Little Village High School incorporated the Greater Lawndale/Little Village School for Social Justice, the Infinity School (for math, science, and technology), the Multicultural Arts School, and the World Language High School.

20.    See Ana Beatriz Cholo, "Little Village getting school it hungered for," *Chicago Tribune*, February 27, 2005.

21.    Chicago Public Schools, *Chicago Public Schools Choice* (Chicago: Chicago Public Schools, 2005), 150.

# INDEX



Page numbers in bold refer to illustrations.

Dale Allen Gyure is an associate professor of architecture at Lawrence Technological University, where he teaches architectural history and theory. He is also adjunct assistant professor of historic preservation at Goucher College, where he teaches a course in American architectural history and serves as co-director of the master's thesis program. Gyure earned a Ph.D. in architectural history from the University of Virginia, a J.D. from Indiana University, and a B.S. from Ball State University. His research, which focuses on American architecture of the nineteenth and twentieth centuries, has been supported by the Graham Foundation for Advanced Studies in the Fine Arts, the American Philosophical Society, the Spencer Foundation, and the University of Virginia. In 2000, he received the Carter Manny Dissertation Award from the Graham Foundation, and in 2001 he was selected to participate in Columbia University's Buell Center for the Study of American Architecture Biennial Dissertation Colloquium.